Snobs

To the memory of my grandfather, a fine Snob of the old school, and of my parents, confused and inconsistent Snobs, who nevertheless aroused my interest in the Snob phenomenon. So it's all their fault.

The Canadian Book of *Snobs*

Victoria Branden

HOUNSLOW PRESS
A MEMBER OF THE DUNDURN GROUP
TORONTO · OXFORD

Hounslow Press
A Member of the Dundurn Group

Publisher: Anthony Hawke
Editor: Erich Falkenberg
Design: Scott Reid
Printer: Webcom
Cover illustrations: Ruth Stanners

Canadian Cataloguing in Publication Data

Branden, Victoria
The Canadian book of snobs

ISBN 0-88882-199-9

1. Snobs and snobbishness. I. Title

BJ1535.S7B72 179'.8 C98-931577-0

1 2 3 4 5 EF 02 01 00 99 98

We acknowledge the support of the **Canada Council for the Arts** for our publishing program. We also acknowledge the support of the **Ontario Arts Council** and the **Book Publishing Industry Development Program** of the **Department of Canadian Heritage.**

Care has been taken to trace the ownership of copyright material used in this book. The author and the publisher welcome any information enabling them to rectify any references or credit in subsequent editions.

Printed and bound in Canada.

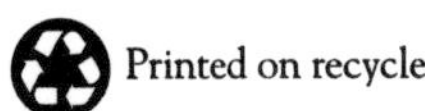

Hounslow Press
8 Market Street
Suite 200
Toronto, Ontario, Canada
M5E 1M6

Hounslow Press
73 Lime Walk
Headington, Oxford
England
OX3 7AD

Hounslow Press
2250 Military Road
Tonawanda, NY
U.S.A. 14150

CONTENTS

Ridentem dicere verum
Horace, First Satire.

To speak the truth with a smile.

PART 1

A Brief History of Snobbery, its Origins and Development; A Tentative Theory of Snobbery. (Specifically Canadian applications in Part 2)

Introduction, or Apology

The urgent, the most burning need in Canada today is for an exhaustive study of the Snobphenomenon.

It is much more difficult to be a Snob of any distinction in Canada than, for example, in Britain or the eastern seaboard of the U.S., where snobbery has flourished for centuries. There has of course always been some small scale snobbery here, but it has been undistinguished until recent times, when it has begun to show signs of flourishing, particularly sexual snobbery.

I became aware of this when, searching my bookshelves for something else, I came across Thackeray's *The Book of Snobs*, published in 1847; original title, *The Snobs of England*. An hour later I was still sitting there, mesmerized, my original project forgotten. Its coruscating brilliance is undimmed, but there's no denying that it's a trifle out of date. Some of Thackeray's snobs are characterized by such behaviour as picking their teeth with a fork, or eating peas with a knife. Why a knife, for pity's sake? Surely hopelessly ill-adapted for eating peas? Because in Thackeray's day, two-pronged forks were still in general use in England, and "it was only by living on the Continent where the usage of the four-prong is general" that one was able to eat peas gracefully with a fork: the four-pronged much more efficient than a knife. This in itself is distinguished Snob stuff, as it combines etiquette snobbery with a display of cosmopolitan one-upmanship — i.e. familiarity with continental manners, still a good method of establishing superiority. While historically interesting, fork-abuse is no longer a significant Snobindicator.

I recognized my mission at once. I must take up the torch laid down a century and a half ago by my great predecessor, whose obsession I have inherited. He says,

> I have long gone about with a conviction on my mind that I had a work to do — a Work, if you like, with a great W.; a purpose to fulfil; a chasm to leap into; a Great Social Evil to Discover and to Remedy. It has Dogged me in the Busy Street; Seated Itself By Me in the Lonely Study; Jogged my Elbow as it Lifted The Wine-cup at the Festive Board; Pursued me through the Maze of Rotten Row; Followed me in Far Lands ... it Nestles in my Nightcap, and It Whispers, "Wake, Slumberer, thy Work Is Not Yet Done." Last Year, By Moonlight, in the Colosseum, the Little Sedulous Voice Came To Me and Said, "... this is all very well, but you ought to be at home writing your great work on SNOBS."

That same little sedulous voice now speaks constantly in *my* ear, though its idiom has perhaps lost a little of its elegance and most of its capital letters, and acquired a Canadian accent.

"Hey," says the little sedulous voice, "get with it, eh? Plenty of people have written about British and American snobbery. Someone should take a swing at Canadian snobs." Since then it has been my Vocation, my Rope and my Scaffold, my Bread and my Board, my Wound and the Salt in it. (The foregoing list is stolen from another neglected masterpiece. A very valuable but inexpensive prize will be awarded to anyone successfully identifying the source.)

A small troubling item: Thackeray's title page reads,

The Book of Snobs
(By One of Themselves)

This led to an agonizing self-examination. Can I possibly be a snob? The answer, as it so often seems to be, is "We-e-e-ll, yes and no." Obviously, it depends on one's definition of a snob. Thackeray ducks it, to some extent, though at one point he says, "*He who meanly admires mean things is a snob.*" Still, although a self-designated Snob, he clearly doesn't meanly admire mean things, and neither do I. You won't catch *me* meanly admiring mean things, boy.

The reference to forks indicates that the word (Snob, not forks) has changed its meaning over the years; the fork-mishandlers were clearly lower orders, probably trying to crash a higher level and making themselves ridiculous in so doing. Dictionaries usually start with the obsolete definition of a snob as "a cobbler or shoemaker," and go on to identify it as Cambridge slang, meaning a townsman (hence, in a later idiom, non-U) rather than a gownsman (U), adding grudgingly, "A person belonging to the lower classes of society; one having no pretensions to rank or gentility; a vulgar or ostentatious person." These are unhelpful designations, because everyone has pretensions to rank or gentility. Scratch the most unprepossessing of unwashed drunks, and blue blood will flow: absolutely *everyone* is descended from exalted aristocrats, who have (to borrow the vernacular, I am a Wordsnob) got done out of their rights.

Nevertheless, the word is frequently used quite differently, to suggest connoisseurship, sensitivity to beauty, expertise in a difficult art, see Wordsnob reference, *supra*. This is usually what is implied when someone prefaces a remark in tones of laughing self-deprecation, "I'm afraid you'll think me a terrible snob, but ... " So, though I can't define a snob yet, I have tentatively identified at least one purpose of snobbery: *It is to prove that you are superior to your associates, and if possible to force them to admit it.* I will end this introduction by another condensed quotation, which I have chosen as the text of my sermon, for I believe I have the same talent.

> I have (and for this gift I congratulate myself with a Deep and Abiding Thankfulness) an eye for a Snob. If the Truthful is the beautiful, it is beautiful to study even the Snobbish; to track Snobs through history, as certain little dogs in Hampshire hunt out truffles; to sink shafts in society and come upon rich veins of Snob-ore ... It is a great mistake to judge of Snobs lightly ... An immense percentage of Snobs is to be found in every rank of this mortal life. You must not judge hastily or vulgarly of Snobs: to do so shows *that you are yourself a snob. I myself have been taken for one.* [italics mine]

After much thought I've decided to write the book first, and define snobs definitively when it's finished. No skipping to the last chapter to find out who done it, now: that's cheating. Actually, the butler done it. Butlers are the worst snobs in the world.

Revonons à nos moutons. (Note high-class Snobquotation.) But first, one more thing, which has little to do with snobbery, perhaps just a whisper of Wordsnob. I'm sick of saying he/she, his/hers. I'm going to say its or theirs or whatever comes into my head. Just don't write me letters telling me I've made a mistake in grammar.

Vocabulary

There are a few technical terms that should be mastered by the ambitious snob, which are necessary for understanding scientific Snobtalk. The short ones should be memorized, to be used glibly in conversation.

GENTEEL — A term of abuse used by U-people of *nouveaux riches* who are trying to sound U (q.v., *infra*). Do not confuse with Gentility, Transmissibility of (for which see appropriate chapter), or with Gentry, Landed, both of which are associated with PLU and OOU (q.v., *infra*). See also REFAINED.

MASSIVE(NESS) — Thorstein Veblen term for big, hefty, powerful, muscly. One of the qualities needed to gain wealth and power in the early history of the human race. (See chapters on Archaism, Transmissibility of Gentility, Ancestors.) Now used only of proles (q.v.), and weight-lifters, usually pejoratively.

OOU — One of Us. Used by possessors of inherited titles, and (with some reservations) by Oxbridge grads, to indicate an essential class distinction. OOO is also sometimes found — One of Ours. Same thing. NOOU or NOOO – Not one of Us/Ours. Most frequently used in references to graduates of uncanonized universities, not simply Redbrick, but any other than Oxbridge. (Some exceptions for a few

European universities.) Graduates of colonial or American universities are advised not to attempt adaptations or imitations. This is very Top Class Snob stuff, strewn with traps for the uninitiated.

PROLE — Short for proletariat. Used (cautiously) by all higher classes, of tough working class slobs. Caution is necessary because proles are often both massive and touchy. It is better, Snobwise, to be Prole than to be Genteel, though the Class-conscious (see Paul Fussell) rank them lower. It must be remembered that Proles are also brutal snobs, in their specialized way.

PLU — People Like Us, i.e. desirable acquaintances, who have inherited property and probably attended Oxbridge, though not as Rhodes Scholars, as these may have prole antecedents and got to the ancient seats of learning simply by being good at passing exams. They have been cruelly mocked by English authors, notably by Max Beerbohm in *Zuleika Dobson*, and less successfully by Michael Innis, who believed that all Americans of whatever class begin every sentence with "Say" or "I guess." Harvard PhD holders may be recognized as PLU, as long as they are careful not to be Genteel. They can never, even then, be recognized as *quite* OOU or OOO, but this should not distress them as PLU is an honourable appellation.

Please note: When we say "inherited property," we do NOT mean a semi-detached in Don Mills, with perhaps a cottage in Muskoka. Even a large stone house in Rosedale does not rate as well as a handsome establishment in the country, with at least twenty acres of land. Of course this would not rate as property among English snobs, but Canada is a democracy, isn't it?

Q.V., *INFRA*, *SUPRA*, *VIDE* — bibliographical snob terms, thrown in just for the hell of it. You can look them up in the dictionary if you want. Otherwise, pay no attention. No one uses them nowadays but a few Wordsnobs who do it to be annoying. Oh, all right then. They all refer to the situation of passages in the book. Q.V. — *quod vide*, which see, or look it up. *INFRA* — below, further on in the book. *SUPRA* — above; before this. *VIDE* — see, consult.

REFAINED — See Genteel.

TR. — Obviously, translation. I wasn't going to translate foreign phrases, as it is much higher Snobpractice to assume that your readership is sophisticated and polyglot. But one of my guinea pig readers complained about it, saying that he at least needed translation of French, Latin, Old English, and so on, and that it was a nuisance to have to keep looking them up in a dictionary. Of course this makes him a Failedsnob, but he pointed out that while he doesn't speak these languages, he is fluent in English, Canadian, American, and can communicate adequately in Australian. He speaks several varieties of Canadian, including academic, Classy (q.v. Wordsnob), demotic and four-letter.

U and NON-U — Upper Class and Non-Upper Class. Coined by Nancy Mitford (q.v.) in *Noblesse Oblige* (q.v.). Read the book before attempting to assimilate it into your Snobvocab. Please don't try short cuts, or your Snob career will shipwreck.

WARNING: The inexperienced snob may find the quotations from the classics in this chapter rather boring and exhausting. It is permissible (but inadvisable) to skip them. An easy acquaintance with okay literature has always been high level snob stuff. Even the lowest orders recognize the advantages accruing if you "brush up your Shakespeare." The mere mention of *Beowulf* can establish you as an intellectual in some circles (but choose your circles carefully, avoiding Old English specialists like the plague; they are usually better avoided in any circumstances). It is not necessary to have read *Beowulf* yourself. There's a man in Toronto who has achieved a reputation for scholarship and erudition simply by naming his dog Grendel.

1

Snobbery: Origins in the Mists of Time; Evolution

Let us now begin to track Snobs through history, like those little dogs hunting truffles in Hampshire. (Any reference to truffles is good Gourmetsnob stuff.) I used to have a vague idea that snobbery was a fairly recent phenomenon, which burst into full flower some time in the 19th century, but after painstaking research, I realized that snobbery is very old indeed.

Older than the human race. Birds have a pecking order, which means the top bird can peck all the others, until you come down to a wretched little bottom bird whom everyone can peck with impunity. This is snobbery in action, currently unacceptable in human social circles. We have become pusillanimous about overtly displaying our snobbery.

Horses are vicious snobs. They have a kicking order, in which the biggest and meanest horse gets to kick everybody else, and the bottom horse can't kick anyone. We once owned a top horse, but he was a benevolent tyrant, only kicking when there was a serious discipline problem. He was not the biggest horse, but he was the fastest and smartest. Alas, he caught an infection which damaged his lungs; he no longer won the morning gallop (a ritual fitness exercise) and he went clear to the bottom of the totem-pole. A mean horse named Charlie became Top Horse; he kicked out of pure viciousness, and the whole tone of the herd changed for the worse.

The true beginnings of human snobbery are discoverable in cultures dependent on the habitual pursuit of large game, for which (Thorstein Veblen says, *Theory of the Leisure Class*) "the manly qualities of massiveness, agility and ferocity" are required. That is, you have to be big and tough enough to impose your will on the rest of the tribe: you have to have "a propensity for overbearing violence and an irresistible devastating force."

So the big tough guys got to be leaders and bosses and kings and emperors, and the less big and tough were followers, until you got down to scared little fellows with no muscles, who had to stay home and help the women, who of course (since they were by nature smaller and weaker) were the lowest of the hierarchy. This is the root, source and origin of human snobbery.

Massiveness, especially if combined with agility and ferocity, could set you up as Top Person, and you could then make the rules. So naturally you made rules to suit you. The only things worth doing were those in which massiveness paid off: hunting and fighting. All other occupations were beneath the notice of the Hunter-Warrior, who (as soon as literature was invented) became the Hero, totally preoccupied with his honour. Hunter-Warrior was the only tolerable occupation for upper-class males, or to put it in reverse, the upper classes were made up of Hunter-Warriors, and these were as a class morbidly concerned with what they called "honour."

There's a bit in Book Three of *The Iliad* where they decide that, instead of suffering through a horrible war, Paris and Menelaus will fight it out in single combat, winner to take Helen and all her wealth, and everyone could go home and cultivate their gardens, like sensible people, though both sides feared their honour would be impugned. Then the gods started interfering. Aphrodite whisked Paris out of danger and into Helen's bed. A dim-bulb Trojan called Pandarus was tricked by Athene into taking a shot at Menelaus.

That did it. Back to chopping each other into pieces and more lipsmacking descriptions of blood and guts. Jean Giradoux used this bit for his play (*La Guerre de Troie n'aura pas lieu*, Englished as *Tiger at the Gates*) to demonstrate the stupidity of martial Honour, but Homer clearly believed that chopping and hacking in the name of honour was the duty and privilege of the hunter-warrior.

Here's a nice juicy bit from Homer:

> Meriones ... caught [Adamas] with his lance half-way between the navel and the privy parts, the most

> painful spot ... Adamas collapsing writhed round it, as a bull twists about when the herdsmen have roped him in the hills ... Thus the stricken warrior writhed, but not for long — only till the lord Meriones pulled the spear out of his flesh. Then night descended on his eyes ... [Meriones shot Harpalion] with a bronze arrow and hit him on the right buttock. The arrow went clean through his bladder and came out under the bone. Harpalion gasped out his life ... and lay stretched on the ground like a worm, while the dark blood poured out of him and soaked the earth.

Critics have argued that Homer really didn't approve of the promiscuous killing, but I submit that you don't write an epic poem unless you find something admirable about its subject — "The wrath of Achilles is my theme," sang the Blind Bard, and proceeded for twenty-four books to celebrate the world's most famous temper tantrum.

Sixteen hundred years or so later, in *Beowulf*, the warrior heroes were still at it. At a party to honour Beowulf, a poet described a long-lasting feud which came close to being settled through a marriage. Slightly telescoped, here's what happened.

> ... Finn
> Swore he and the brave Hengest would live
> Like brothers. When gifts were given
> Finn would give Hengest and his soldiers half —
> Share shining rings, silver and gold
> With the Danes, both sides equal,
> All of them richer, all of their purses heavy,
> Every man's heart warm with the comfort of gold.
> Both sides accepted peace, and agreed to keep it.

But Hengest's honour had not been satisfied, and after a year or so of peace, a Danish warrior dropped a sword in his lap.

> ... Hengest rose,
> And drove his new sword into Finn's belly,
> Butchering that king under his own roof ... The hall
> Ran red with enemy blood, and bodies
> Rolled on the floor beside Finn.

Sacred honour avenged. Just about everybody was dead, but that was a minor matter. This was still going on, in its way, in the U.S. in the 19th century (see the feud episode in *Huckleberry Finn)*, and in vendettas in Sicily, happily continued among the Mafia and its competitors. Rotten tempers were (and still are, in certain cultures) indicators of honour among ruling-class males. Since practically all literature was produced by males for a couple of millennia, all its heroes were hunter-warriors. Rocky, Rambo, James Bond, etc. carry on the tradition today.

Luckily for the survival of the race, women were less hung up on honour than their mates, though because of their deficiency in massiveness, their influence was negligible. As mentioned, upper class males' work was killing only, whether of animals in the hunt, or each other in battle.

Women's is productive labour, men's is "acquisition of substance by seizure." The warrior and the hunter reap where they have not sown. Prowess comes to be defined as force or fraud.

> When the predatory habit of life has been settled upon the group by long habituation, it becomes the able-bodied man's accredited office in the social economy to kill, to destroy such competitors as attempt to resist or elude him ... So tenaciously and with such nicety is this theoretical distinction between exploit and drudgery adhered to that in many hunting tribes the man must not bring home the game which he has killed, but must send his woman to perform that baser office.
> (Veblen, 14)

A certain degree of massiveness in women must have been desirable at this stage of things, or they wouldn't have had the muscle to haul home the carcass. Already in these antique times, we see the development of a hierarchy in the nature of work: that which was considered prowess, and reflected credit, and that which was subtly or overtly degrading, its performance *per se* an admission of inferiority. This latter was the province of women and weak men, and these were regarded as property.

"From the ownership of women, the concept of ownership extends itself to include the products of their industry," says Thorstein Veblen. "And so there arises the ownership of things as well as of persons."

Women were from the beginning possessions, chattels, and remained so for most of human history. Their long struggle to stake a claim of being independent, persons in their own right, is in a sense the history of snobbery. Not the whole history, but a great big part of it.

As civilization advanced, women's position improved slightly, at least among the upper classes. Female muscle was still needed by the labouring classes, but fragility became a desirable quality among the aristocracy. In spite of her inadequate mass, a lady could reflect credit on her lord by being useless except as a fur- and jewellery-display device. Soon it became a sure sign of male success, if he could afford a wife who had no practical function at all except for producing male heirs. We'll discuss this further under Sexsnobbery, and in fact right through the book.

Apart from having babies (which men couldn't do for all their muscles, so nyaah) and for their symbolic value as clothes-horses, women had little importance in top society, although they could be valuable as negotiating pawns in arranged marriages to promote tribal interests.

The real class indicator, Veblen tells us, was "the pervading sense of the indignity of manual labour." Paradoxically, the big-muscled heroes who were best adapted to manual labour declined absolutely to perform it, because of said indignity. Lower-class women and small weak men thus had to do the hard degrading work.

Snobbery, at a very early stage of human social development, has established its two most significant characteristics: the inferiority of women, and the baseness of physical labour. Never let us delude ourselves into thinking that we've outgrown either of them.

2

Passages and Transitions: The Decline of Massive Power, and Emergence of Newsnobs

The superiority of Massiveness was gradually eroded among males, since good hunter-warriors sometimes inexplicably sired thin pale sons who wanted to write poetry or play the harp instead of charging out to kill animals and enemies as an aristocrat should. Quite early on, Snobpractice made exceptions for artists (if they came from a good family) and the social standing of the priesthood, though its members were often deficient in mass, was next in importance to that of the hunter-warrior. Priests in the early days had to have some knowledge of medicine and magic, along with paranormal abilities to foretell the future, or at least to fake it convincingly. It could be a dangerous occupation in times of bad weather, crop failure, and other natural disasters, which an official with a special line to Providence should be able to control, or at least foretell.

Fairly early in social evolution, it must have become obvious that simply being big wasn't the only thing that counted, especially if you were also stupid. There were agile little guys who had special advantages. You didn't have to be huge to be a dead shot with the spear or bow, to be a fast runner, to invent tools and weapons, or to develop strategies for improving hunting techniques.

Consider Odysseus who — while girls fell all over him in the *Odyssey* — gained prestige by being intelligent. His triumph over Polyphemus splendidly illustrates the superiority of brain over brawn. Another (roughly contemporary) smaller hero was David, who handily defeated Goliath, though in a rather sneaky way, I've always felt.

Throughout history we keep encountering these sharp little guys — Julius Caesar, William the Conqueror, Napoleon. Not necessarily nice people, but they all contrived to get to the top without being massive. In fact, once long distance weapons were invented, massiveness could be a positive disadvantage: it just made you a better target. At the Battle of Hastings, the Normans got rid of massive Viking-type King Harold of England when an archer shot him in the eye. Such a target was easily spotted, while sneaky little William the Conqueror was easily concealed.

Nevertheless, there is still great prestige attached to being large: short people got no reason to live, they got nasty little hands and nasty little feet, and so on.

We have seen that as civilization progressed, upper-class women no longer were required to haul carcasses. However, they were for a long time expected to do the cooking. This was when they turned into ladies. The word comes from Old English, *hlaefdige*, loaf-kneader, so a lady was literally the breadmaker. She was also expected to be able to milk the cow, churn the butter, tend the poultry, and do the sewing, spinning, and weaving. It was knead that loaf, bake that bread, when the work's all done, serve the boss in bed. In time, as their massive husbands got richer and could provide more household help, the loaf-kneading etc. was relegated to slaves or servants. The wife had her duties as clothes-horse and heir-producer, but she had slaves to help her get dressed and do her hair. A serf in the kitchen kneaded the loaf, but couldn't fool herself that she was a lady.

Men's work was exploit, women's was drudgery. Men proudly begat babies, women brought them forth in pain and sorrow, as decreed by a benevolent (male) deity. Proud fathers still show off their male babies, but shove them at the mothers when they need changing.

Even when massiveness was losing predominance, women's lot was (Snobwise) not much cop. Men could easily demonstrate their superiority by beating their wives, since most men still are bigger and stronger than most women. Rebellious females were reminded of their proper role with a good clout on the ear. The rule of thumb decreed that a man might legally beat his wife as long as he used a stick no wider than his thumb. Wife-beating was not only a man's right, but sometimes his duty, and this has continued until modern times.

With leisure, however, wife-beating became rather *infra dig* in privileged circles, though among the lower orders it continued to flourish and be socially acceptable. Actually it still goes on in all social circles, but with diminished social approval. It's not wicked so much as lower class.

Women were also kept in their subservient position by poverty. As late as the 19th century in England, the church still decreed that they had no property rights. A husband could collect his wife's earnings, whether she was an actress or musician, or if she did sewing, charring, or took in washing. The husband could blow every penny on booze or gambling, while the wife and kids starved; even if she left her husband and moved out, her employer might still hand over her wages to her persecutor. If she tried to sneak some away to feed the kids, the husband could sue. This wasn't really cleared up until the passage of the Married Women's Property Act in 1883. I never realized how bad it all was until I read a terrifying book by Fay Weldon, called *Letters to Alice*. Highly recommended as a cure for girlish dreams about the romantic past.

Another convenient way of keeping women in their place was denying them an education. Of course for millennia no one, male or female, had any leisure for education. It's only possible when one is emancipated from continual labour, simply to keep alive, that there's any leisure for reading, writing, or the arts. This is why priests contrived to be founts of wisdom and literacy: the community supported them. They had leisure when no one else did.

A few of our ancestors were able to enjoy leisure by living in a benign climate, with slave labour. In the Mediterranean area this produced an early burst of creativity, mostly but not exclusively by men. Sappho (c. 600 BC) was the first woman poet who managed to leave an impression for posterity. Most of her work is lost, but the Sapphic metre was imitated by men!

Horace and Swinburne, for example. This makes Sappho high-class, not just a girlish amateur.

Generally, education for women languished for about two thousand years after it became socially desirable among males. Any trend to educate girls, as the gents clearly saw, would produce undesirable consequences, so that it was simple common sense to keep the creatures ignorant. When men were literate and women weren't, it was easily demonstrated that women had inferior minds. The stupid things couldn't read or write! It wasn't their fault, the guys explained tolerantly, it was just their natures, a fact of life.

"A woman without ability is normal," sagely advised a Chinese sage, and Hindus claimed that "infidelity, violence, deceit, envy, extreme avarice, a total want of good qualities, with impurity" were the natural characteristics of females. Aristotle laid down the law that women were weaker, more impulsive, less complete, and less courageous than men, though they could acquire virtue by being obedient.

Christianity did not hold with educating women, except for nuns. St. Paul's strictures on the deplorable influence of women are well known. He would have liked to get rid of them altogether, but this was impracticable, if the race were to continue: "It is good for a man not to touch a woman. Nevertheless, to avoid fornication, let every man have his own wife." He tells Timothy that women should "adorn themselves with modest apparel, with shamefacedness and sobriety; not with broided hair, or gold, or pearls, or costly array." They could do good works, he allowed, but should learn in silence with all subjection: "I suffer not a woman to teach, nor to usurp authority over a man, but to be in silence."

An unnamed abbot, in the 16th century, argued that "books destroy women's brains," and that it wasn't safe for women to know Latin. How about Roman women, who spoke it all the time?

Probably the reason for Rome's decline and fall.

In the Renaissance, upper-class girls were given a good education, and Shakespeare's delightful heroines (Portia, Rosalind, Beatrice, Imogen, et al.) were also delightfully literate. Queen Elizabeth I wrote a little poetry but was too busy governing England to work at it, though she made some brilliant speeches. She spoke French, Italian, and Spanish, and thanked God for her good education. "Were I turned out of my Realm in my petticoat, I were able to live in any place in Christome."

Nonetheless, it was a false spring, and most of the work was still to be done in the 19th century. Napoleon urged that women who *believed* were preferable to women who reasoned. Philosopher Jules Simon considered education for women futile: they simply hadn't the right kind of brains to profit by it. In the U.S., it was "improper and inconsistent" for girls to be educated other than in dame schools, which didn't teach much beyond the three Rs and needlework. Easily in living memory are parental pronouncements that a university education is wasted on girls, because they're only going to get married.

And who needs an education for that?

Snobstandards are shifting, brains have become as important as brawn, and while inherited wealth is still the only respectable standard, you may yet ascend the social ladder if you're sharp, and manage to acquire some degree of literacy!

3

Archaism and the Transmissibility of Gentility

God bless the Squire, and his relations
And keep us in our proper stations.

We saw in the last chapter how Snobstandards were no longer confined to the Massive, and as a result, how the Hunter-Warrior class might be in danger of demotion. We will now study the backlash effect by the established Snob classes.

This is a very tough chapter, based on theories advanced by Thorstein Veblen in *The Theory of the Leisure Class*, which should be studied exhaustively by all ambitious Snobs. It is absolutely indispensable to a true understanding of how Snobbery works.

However, even his most devoted admirers have to admit that Thorstein does go on and on, so (as a latter-day Snobtheorist) it's my duty to give you a simplified, boiled-down explanation. You'll keep running into this stuff throughout the book, so it's much better to understand it at the beginning. Don't complain about repetitiousness, as it can't be avoided. If you think this is repetitious, just you read T. Veblen in the original. Taken straight, he is for fairly scholarly Snobs only; naïve amateurs will be quickly discouraged, chiefly because he never uses a monosyllable where he can find a polysyllable. This is not because Thorstein was a foolish Wordsnob. He didn't use hard words because he thought it made him sound big time. He just didn't know any easy words.

So, on to Archaism and the Transmissibility of Gentility.

You'll remember that in our Vocabulary page at the beginning of the book, we warned you against trying to sound Genteel, a.k.a. Refained, which also involves using fancy language instead of plain, and never calling a spade a spade. We warned against this because of a contemporary irony, or joke by the Upper Classes about Lower Classes who *try* to sound genteel, so that the word has come to mean something like *affectedly nice*, or as Roget helpfully suggests, *mincing, simpering, namby-pamby, prudish, priggish*, and several others. We will deal with this at greater length in our chapter on Wordsnobbery, under "Talking Classy." However, when Thorstein talks about *Gentility, Transmissibility of*, he is getting into something much more complex, though related.

It has the same root as gentry and gentle (Fr. *gentil*), as in "of gentle birth" — noble, aristocratic. (It also means the larva of the bluebottle, as used for bait by anglers, but that may be irrelevant here.)

What it's really about takes us back to the rude forefathers of our race who, as you'll remember, got to the top by being massive, violent, aggressive, etc. But once arrived at the top, they scorned the base degrees by which they rose, and pretended they got to the top because they were literally made of better stuff than the average slob: of finer clay, nobler raw material, *because they were descended from gods*. Kings were God's deputies on earth, and so had divine rights.

Some resourceful monarch invented, long ago, the theory of The Divine Right of Kings. They rule not because they are massive and unscrupulous, but by divine ordination. It was very useful as a weapon against the Papacy, its chief rival for power, and one which also had divine rights. Then during the wars of religion, Protestants vs. Catholics, the Divine Right of Kings gained a lot of strength. James I wrote a book to defend the divine right, *The True Law of Free Monarchies*, which explained that monarchy based on primogeniture was divinely ordained, and unquestioning obedience could therefore be demanded from subjects. The monarchs themselves were responsible to God alone; their model was the patriarchal rule recorded in the Old Testament.

Another pleasing little perk of the monarchy was *Jus Primae noctis* or *droit de seigneur*: the right of the king or lord to spend the wedding night with the bride of any of his vassals, something which aroused a good deal of hostility in the vassal set. Most reference books tell you soothingly that the right was seldom exercised, but you'll remember in *The Marriage of Figaro*, the Count decided to claim his *droit* with Figaro's bride (giving occasion to a furious aria by the vassal) but was outsmarted by a conspiracy among Figaro, the Countess, and the bride.

Monarchs also had divine gifts, including the Healing Touch. Scrofulous little Sam Johnson was taken to London to be "touched" by Queen Anne, retaining a "confused but solemn memory" of a lady in black, with diamonds. Unfortunately he also retained the scrofula, and lost the sight of one eye.

As well as this unreliable healing gift, kings and their relatives (gentlefolk) inherited the characteristics of gentility: they were cultivated, exquisite, discriminating, righteous, and in every way a good example to the lower classes. This was ingrained, inborn, genetic, to be handed down (as in "transmissibility of") from one generation to the next. Belief in such transmissibility is fundamental to the class system, the concept of aristocracy, of royalty, the whole schmeer.

In real life, the gentility was often camouflaged to the point of invisibility. Consider the first four English Georges, for example. Not the sort to whom you'd entrust your daughter's virtue. Consider Henry VIII, that inveterate chopper-off of spousal heads. Or pious King Claudius of Denmark, who said, having treasonously bumped off his inadequately hedged brother, "There's such divinity doth hedge a king, that treason can but peep at what it would."

Of course, the Divinity theory won't stand up to any kind of critical examination. Royals are in no way superior to us vassals, or commoners, or serfs, or slaves. In fact, they are frequently worse. No better looking, certainly no smarter, and in many cases almost embarrassingly less pleasant or virtuous. The idea that you are superior, whether by divine right or by some other means, is almost invariably bad for the character. The very rich, who are today's royalty in practice if not in theory, are generally an uncharming set. As Scott Fitzgerald is too often quoted as saying, they are different from the rest of us. I agree they're different. With a few exceptions, they're nastier.

If you bought the Divinity of Kings theory, and if you yourself weren't born into the top class, you couldn't possibly work your way up; you were stuck at the level in which you were born. No such thing as upward mobility. That's why the *nouveaux riches*, the bourgeois gentlemen, were so despised, mocked on stage and off. If you didn't keep them in their place, they might well shove in and grab yours. As Thorstein so well says,

> So soon as a given proclivity or a given point of view has won acceptance as an authoritative standard or norm of life it will react upon the character of the members of the society which has accepted it as a norm. It will to some extent shape their habits of thought and will exercise a selective surveillance over the development of men's aptitudes and inclinations … by a coercive, educational adaptation of all individuals … The principles of pecuniary emulation and of industrial exemption have in this way been erected into canons of life, and have become coercive factors … [The] two broad principles of conspicuous waste and industrial exemption affect the cultural development both by guiding men's habits of thought, and so controlling the growth of institutions, and by selectively conserving certain traits of human nature that conduce to facility of life under the leisure-class scheme, and so controlling the effective temper of the community.
> (Veblen, 212)

Or, as Marilyn French puts it, "The institutions of any society function almost automatically to maintain that society as it is; and the ideology of any society functions to justify that status quo as being both necessary and beneficial." Or as the poet Pope said, "Whatever is, is right."

Any tampering with the hierarchy was fatal. Ulysses' famous speech in *Troilus and Cressida* explains how the whole world falls into chaos if the divine order is altered. (In passing, Shakespeare's awful Old snob is really no relation to Homer's genial odyssean.)

> … O! When degree is shak'd,
> Which is the ladder to all high designs,
> The enterprise is sick. How could communities,
> Degrees in schools, and brotherhoods in cities,
> Peaceful commerce from dividable shores,
> The primogenitive and due of birth,
> Prerogative of age, crowns, sceptres, laurels,
> But by degree, stand in authentic place?
> Take but degree away, untune that string,
> And hark! what discord follows …

This was exalted into a serious philosophical position (usefully studied in Arthur Lovejoy's *The Great Chain of Being*) according to which everything in the universe is hierarchically arranged. No damn nonsense about "equality" and similar Godwinian or pinko-Commie stuff. Not only society, but races, species, inanimate objects, and even such insubstantial entities as mermaids and angels were arranged in tidy hierarchical orders, and stuck there. But why?

The original Massive crowd, by being rough, tough, and unscrupulous fighters, got more to eat than the less Massive, and so were feared and catered to, thus acquiring wealth and power. Soon they could afford their own armies. Then they resourcefully invented caesars, czars, kings, emperors, aristocrats, etc., most of whom were also military generals. Sometimes they were also priests, so that they had the gods on their side, as well as a monopoly on the art of communicating with the gods.

Once having accumulated the wealth and power, it was extremely frustrating that you couldn't take it with you, but at least you could reserve it for your kids by hoking up a theory of transmissibility of gentility, and the convenient Divinity of Kings dodge.

Even today we hear some dyed-in-the-wool royalists expounding the theory. And how the Royals do scurry about looking for heirs with definite bloodline connections, acting on the principle that the family connection would create a bond! Yet a glance at any history book shows the fallibility of the theory, with brother zestfully bumping off brother, and uncles qualmlessly disposing of Little Princes and other rival relatives.

The belief that blue blood was special and indispensable led to a lot of inbreeding, and it should have become clear that kingly qualities do not bequeath themselves reliably. Heroic warrior Henry V begat mentally challenged (i.e. batty) Henry VI and turned the country into a battleground between Yorkists and Lancastrians. Frugal and cautious Henry VII was followed by reckless and extravagant Henry VIII. Formidable Oliver Cromwell was succeeded by poor Richard, who abdicated as Protector, probably because of the joke-making industry which had grown up at his expense. Sun King Louis XIV left France stuck with a run of uninspiring monarchs, interrupted only when Louis XVI had his head chopped off.

Most countries sensibly decided to junk their Royals, but the British have stubbornly hung onto theirs (with a short hiatus after poor Charles I), still insisting that some magic is handed on in the blood. Support for the theory is chiefly negative: Queens Victoria and

Liz II are alike in being short, grumpy, dowdy, boring ladies with a marked incapacity for a cheerful smile. Are these qualities worth the trouble of handing down from generation to generation?

Liz II (the dear Queen) in spite of a lifetime's training, still can't make a spontaneous speech, and has for forty years been reading her lines in the same flat uninspired voice. The offspring of both these great monarchs have been noted for their extraordinarily messy private lives, which in the Age of Media Hype cannot be kept secret.

The only persistent talent in the House of Windsor seems to be for riding horses, but they have from infancy the best horses, top instructors, and lots of leisure time. I'll bet you and I could be pretty fair horsepeople if we'd had a chance like that. The only other queenly talent seems to be to live, and to monopolize the throne to their offsprings' detriment, for inordinate lengths of time.

Nevertheless, Royalsnobs continue to pretend that their undistinguished idols are really made of some special stuff that is violated by contact with coarse commoners. All hell broke loose when the Australian PM actually touched the royal shoulder-blades in 1992: "Utter buffoon" and "idiot," huffed the House of Lords.

There's no doubt that physical characteristics can be inherited. There are families in which the same faces, hair colour, body build, and so on recur generation after generation. "Easy seen she's a Potts, look at that nose." How about leadership qualities? Nobility of character? Artistic genius? Brains? Are they in the genes, to be handed down, so that the family rightly remains in command of inferior wretches? Or is this one of the ongoing delusions of the human race?

Occasionally it seems to work. The Huxley family has for over a century been turning out distinguished scientists, men and women of letters, thinkers generally. No doubt it has also had its share of dolts and incapables and ordinary bods — we just never hear about them. How much of their success is due to the fact that they could afford expensive educations? I knew a prole Huxley once, and when I asked him if he were connected to Aldous, he didn't know what an aldous was.

Certain musical families sometimes produce several generations of undoubted talent, as witness the Bach, Mozart, Scarlatti, and Strauss families. Where are they today? The supply of genius genes seems to dwindle and disappear.

Among writing families, Evelyn Waugh's sons both set up as novelists, and very bad novelists they are, too, whereas their papa's early works like *Decline and Fall*, *The Loved One* and *Scoop* are still splendidly funny.

There are medical families, mathematics and anthropology families, even acting and skiing families, but on the whole genetic inheritance of ability is pretty dicey. The best we can usually manage is an inclination or an interest, though some of that may be culturally influenced, and nowhere do we find a reliable supply of genius-level ability, from generation to generation.

This makes all the more interesting the human obsession with blood-lines, and by derivation, snobbery. It's often been observed that successful parents (massive, agile, fierce, unscrupulous) produce as heirs pallid aesthetes, who want to be painters or interior decorators, and who fear and loathe their vulgar rumbustious papas; offspring of miserly hoarders are reckless gamblers and irresponsible spenders. The British aristocracy often degenerated into Bertie Woosters and twits, while great minds like Jeeves and Crichton wasted their gifts on serving tea and pressing trousers. We have adverted to this in our chapter on Servants.

Why must we bother with all this tough and boring stuff, I hear you plaintively ask, if the theory which is the basis of snobbery is all wrong? The theory *is* all wrong, but it's still going strong in practice. People still believe that Royals are made of some kind of superior material which makes them inexhaustibly important and interesting. Why else would the media excitedly report to the world every time Princess Anne falls off her horse? People fall off horses by the dozen, but only a Royal tumble is news, and that's because Royal falls are better class than prole falls. If you're going to start niggling away about logic and common sense, you'll never get anywhere as a snob.

Evidence of the persistence of the theory: Have you ever encountered, in life or literature, an aristocratic old character who is outrageously rude to everyone, especially those it considers its inferiors — and it considers practically everyone its inferiors — with no apparent justification, except that it's rich? And have you at the same time noticed how everyone comes slavering around to lick its boots, illustrating the coercive factor? And how everyone pretends that this nasty old so-and-so is a grand old lady/gentleman, when in fact its only virtue is that it's rich?

Lady Catherine de Bourgh in *Pride and Prejudice* leaps immediately to mind. She is rude, ignorant, bossy, selfish, opinionated, and stupid, but her wealth allows her to impose her standards on everyone around her. Mr. Collins fawns on her gratefully, licking her boots for her condescension. Much of Jane Austen can be used for practical illustrations of Veblen theory.

The theory applies to objects as well as to people, and is the basis for the antiques industry. If it's old, it must have belonged to some Ancient Lineage types. This is where Archaism comes in. The importance of the owner, by sympathetic magic, rubs off on the furniture and makes it valuable. This also works in reverse: if you have very old valuable furniture, its importance will rub off on you, the owner, even though you bought it at a flea market.

You too must have visited those houses in which lurk Antique-obsessives, who believe that if it's old, it's gotta be good. Where there is not one chair in which you can sit comfortably? In fact, where all the furniture is of priceless antiquity and liable to fall to pieces if you sink down into it? Which sinking reduces it to kindling, and you learn that you have just destroyed thousands of dollars of priceless antiquity? Then why was it in the sitting-room, or miscalled living-room, instead of in a glass case?

Most antiques today are not really old, but have been made by contemporary craftpersons, and artificially aged, by diabolical alchemies. Often their purchasers invent a romantic provenance for them, just as hard-working Ancestorsnobs will buy hideous brown portraits of God knows who(m?), to pass off as ancestors. The supply of genuine Antiques must have been exhausted years ago, as must, in an era of population explosion, the supply of genuine Ancestors.

Gentility thus applies not only to people but to objects. Their value is purely extrinsic, some of them being hideous beyond imagining. What is the philosophy, or possibly I mean psychology, behind this? That the possession of antiques suggests that they came by inheritance, which would mean you derive from a very old family? Therefore you are aristocratic and important?

Thus we derive the equation: Old = Superior. However, Old must also = Rich. Old and Poor is n.b.g. (no bloody good). Old = Time-Hallowed = Superior + Deserving of Praise + Adulation + Bootlicking + Special Treatment. But when you work through the layers of delusion and sympathetic magic, it all boils down to being rich.

However, there is another Rich theory that is directly opposed to the Old-Rich concept. This may be called the Horatio Alger or Rags to Riches principle. Few people today will remember the works of Horatio A. They dated from the Victorian era, approx., when the *Nouveaux* were fighting their way to social acceptance, and wanted to refute the axiomatic assumption that Old = Everything Good.

The heroes of the Alger books were non-aristocratic boys who worked at lowly trades like bootblack or newsboy. They were poor, but they were honest, and they attracted the attention and gratitude of wealthy benefactors, because of a deed of flagrant and shameless honesty. The benefactor would pull out his handkerchief, and, unnoticed, a five-dollar bill would fall to the ground. The newsboy would desert his stand, at risk of having his papers stolen, and run after the benefactor, shouting, "Oh, Sir, you have lost a large sum of money!"

The capitalistic benefactor, who in real life would pocket the money and mutter, "Thanks, sucker," instead is favourably impressed, and next thing you know the newsboy has become William Randolph Hearst and is living in more-than-Oriental splendour with Marion Davies. No, no, scrub that. The Alger newsboys were all virtue and righteousness, and would have saved Marion's soul instead of keeping her in San Simeon.

These improbable tales turned into what we now call Urban Legends, and there was and is genuine belief (by the very simple) that the rich got that way from working hard, being honest, and saving their pennies until they were billionaires. Remember (speaking of the very simple) Ronald Reagan on Clinton's intention to raise taxes on the Rich? "Does he believe people who have worked hard and been successful should be punished?" It's okay to tax the poor, one gathers, because although they too may have worked hard, they haven't been successful.

Society evolves. As Thorstein tells us, "Simple aggression and unrestrained violence in great measure gave place to shrewd practice and chicanery, as the best approved method of accumulating wealth." These abilities, along with adequate massiveness, "have remained in our traditions as the typical 'aristocratic virtues.'"

A glance at any newspaper headlines on any given day will confirm the Veblen thesis that the best way to get rich is to be a crook. Or, as the man who used to do my income tax frequently observed, "It's impossible to get REALLY rich, unless you're a crooked, conscienceless, slippery, sonofabitching bastard."

He also told me that I would never get rich, not because of a lack of Alger-like virtues, but because of my fatal incompetence in keeping records, and getting them to him on time. Eventually he got so furious at me that I was afraid to go back, and that's why he's the man who *used to* do my income tax. He'll never get rich, either. He's efficient and competent, but fatally honest, and so totally disqualified for wealth.

One more Thorstein reference. He points out, and no one will argue, that "the collective interests of any modern community centre in industrial efficiency … This collective interest is best served by honesty, diligence, peacefulness, good-will, an absence of self-seeking, and an habitual recognition and apprehension of causal sequence, without admixture of animistic belief and without a sense of any preternatural intervention in the course of events." (Veblen, 227)

Tr.: Don't expect God to intervene to administer justice and fairness. If you find yourself financially ruined, do not decide meekly that it is God's will, and for God's sake don't try to solve it by prayer. Look for the sonofabitching bastard who has made a profit out of your loss.

He goes on to point out that unfortunately the collective interest of the community doesn't coincide with the immediate interest of the individual who "under the competitive regime is best served by shrewd training and unscrupulous management." We can see at once that in this conflict, the interest of the community is out of luck. The quick buck wins every time over the long view, and that is why, with increasing numbers of billionaires, we have increasing numbers of depleted forests, holes in the ozone layer, disappearing codfish and salmon, and so on. That they occur in concert is not coincidence, it's Veblenesque causal sequence.

A warning: although the Alger rags-to-riches dream was very popular for a while, and is still favoured by politicians (the log cabin principle), committed Snobs — while they may use it — will always do so with a faint, almost imperceptible smile. It is still far better to be an Old School, Oldmoneysnob than to be any other kind. If you can put it over.

4

The Classes and the Masses

Nancy ... was not a snob in the sense of looking up to someone solely because he had money or rank; but Nancy was never a member of the public. She saw herself as special and apart ... she believed in privilege and tradition, in old-established families in big houses surrounded by acres of land ... her idea of Utopia "consists of cottagers happy in their cottages, while I am happy in the Big House."
— Selena Hastings, *Nancy Mitford*.

Much ink and time have been expended trying to divide society into various classes: it is a pointless exercise, though often amusing. For background in this area of snobbery, read Nancy Mitford's *Noblesse Oblige*, and Paul Fussell's *Class*. Read them for entertainment, not as practical guides, or they will only confuse you. I've known people who were so intimidated by Nancy's little exercise in Snobvalues that they could barely open their mouths, for fear of betraying humble origins.

Most of her advice is completely irrelevant on this side of the Atlantic, where speech habits are unreliable indicators of social standing or background, though it is probably just as well for ambitious snobs not to have an Ottawa Valley or Newfie accent, unless they are in showbiz, where it becomes an asset. In some circles. Sometimes.

The term "middle-class" is always used pejoratively, whether by the rich or the poor. Almost everyone in western society belongs in it somewhere, except for tiny minorities at the top and bottom extremes, but no one wants to be identified with it, although some people try to shock their acquaintances by claiming to be "unabashedly middle-class." In low-income groups, it usually means rich, greedy, irresponsible; used by high-income groups, it means *Parvenus* (*tr.*: upstarts) or *Nouveaux*, short for *Nouveaux Riches* (which I think from now on I'll write in Roman to save time, if that's all right with you). Among Intellectualsnobs, middle-class = vulgar, or crassly ostentatious.

If you want to shock your friends or acquaintances by identifying with the non-moneyed orders, it is much more effective to say that you're working-class. It sounds honest and unpretentious, is intimidating to Nouveaux who are trying to live down their working-class background, and is meaningless, anyway, since practically everyone works nowadays, unless they've been sacked by Messrs. Klein and Harris.

I suppose at one time it was convenient to divide society into upper, middle and lower, but changing times and technologies have made these classifications not only obsolete but useless. For example, in what class would you put Albert Einstein, who not only was not rich, but probably never thought about class? What do you do about Honest Ed Mirvish, once the operator of a cut-rate store for slum-dwellers, now a patron of the arts and rescuer of bankrupt theatres not only in Canada but in Britain? Who can also dance the tango? What about politicians, who may come from almost any stratum of society, but are soon mixing with the rich and famous? What about the very rich who are caught embezzling: do we class them with the Uppers, or do they go into the Criminal Class? This difficulty only arises if they get caught; as long as they get away with it, they rest happily among the Uppers. How about the distinguished university professor who hasn't any money? Profs are now quite well paid, but some of the best are terrible bunglers at getting promoted, too preoccupied with their researches or ideas even to realize that they are poor and underpaid. You eventually find you have so many sub-classes and contradictions that it becomes hopeless. Our forbears brought most of our Snobqualifications with them from England and France, and they have long since lost all relevance.

Among the very top people, in the social and financial sense, you find near-illiterates and twits of various stripes: can they really be considered Upper Class? In what order would you rank John Cleese, Wayne Gretzky, Stephen Hawking, and Charles, Prince of Wales? Royal-adorers would put HRH at the top, sullen iconclasts would demote him to the bottom. How about Princess Anne, Madonna, Linda McQuaig, and Kim Campbell? I'd put Linda way out on top, with Madonna coming in second, and the others nowhere.

Paul Fussell tried to reconcile Class anomalies by inventing a new class, X. Class X people are those who don't give a damn about class, or any of its markers: "… they dress for themselves alone, which means they dress comfortably and generally 'down' … the costume, no matter what it is, conveys the message, 'I am freer and less terrified than you are,' or — in extreme circumstances — 'I am more intelligent and interesting than you are: please do not bore me.'"

However, he goes on to name acceptable manufacturers' labels, which strikes me as suspicious. Shouldn't aggressively free people wear exactly what they want, and jeer at label-watchers, if they even acknowledge their existence? He also draws class-lines about obscure matters like the number of buttons on coats, and whether or not they are actually buttoned … surely a clear indication of Snobnaïveté? Did Einstein worry about whether two or three buttons on his coat should be fastened? But I'll bet that William F. Buckley Jr. thinks of it every day, and is sure that however many buttons he does up, it is bound to be the right number.

Fussell gets into worse trouble by describing what X people eat and drink, say, sing, read, watch, and listen to. He reads class significance into ice cream flavours, suggesting that vanilla is Upper, whereas butter almond and peach betray prole affiliations. He also tells us that it is bad form to praise the cooking, whether among Top People or among the Class X crowd. Your Top hostess won't have done the cooking, since she is honour bound to employ a cook, and in any case Top food is usually very uninteresting, so that compliments must necessarily be dishonest. Class X food is always superb, and you should take it for granted that it is good, and say nothing about it.

This is a poor thin way of doing things, if you ask me. When I am served something delicious, regardless of its social provenance, I utter loud cries of pleasure. I can't help it, they burst out of me involuntarily. And when I serve something delicious to guests, I expect shouts of joy from them. Last week I made a soufflé that was so gorgeous that some of the guests wept tears of gratitude. And yet it was so easy … remember what a chore soufflés used to be? I used to be a nervous wreck. Now I simply dump everything into the blender, egg whites and all, *plus* a few teaspoons of baking powder.

Normally I would have beaten the egg whites separately, but a little bit of yolk got into them, and I knew it was hopeless to try to get them to form those nice dry peaks, which I once thought indispensable for a good soufflé. And you know what? The baking powder compensated for the beaten egg whites, although of course I gave the whole mixture a real walloping in the blender. And it came out of the oven a foot high, light as a bubble, a *chef d'oeuvre* (*tr.* a masterpiece, a work of art) so good and so beautiful that strong men burst into unashamed tears. "Oh," I said, "it's nothing really, I'll give you the recipe."

When Nancy Mitford's *Noblesse Oblige* appeared, the socially insecure tried, as remarked, to master the intricacies of U-speech and U-habits, so that they would fit the U-mold. Fussell's wicked opus transformed a whole lot of otherwise fairly sensible people into nervous X-aspirers. I know one woman who actually put away all the family photos in her living-room, because Fussel claimed they betrayed prole or lower-middle standards.

I suspect that Class X described Fussell himself, and that X drinks, food, etc., are simply Fussell preferences. If Class X has only one member, can we take it seriously? Or did he do it as an evil Snob Test, to see if he could manipulate the anxious into getting rid of their beloved family photos, and to eschew peach ice cream? Don't let him get to you. If you like peach or buttered pecan, I say, you eat them, and the hell with Class X.

A confident snob should not give a damn about what impression it's giving. If you have to worry about what other people think, you're a Failedsnob.

5

Oldsnob, Newsnob

"*C'est du dernier bourgeois.*"
— *Tr.*: "It's horribly middle-class."

The term *bourgeois* is often used as a synonym of Philistine.
Hence the French phrase, so dear to Latin Quarter geniuses,
épater les bourgeois — to shock the middle-class fogeys.
(source lost)

We traced the evolution of this trend under "Passages and Transitions." We must now consider its contemporary applications.

If you are going to be a serious snob, and which of us isn't, one way or another, you have to decide what variety of snobbery you are going to espouse. While there are enormous numbers of ways to be snobbish, there are only two really significant divisions: you can be an Antiquitysnob, or you can be a Newness-snob. The latter, not to mince words, are usually *Nouveaux Riches*, *Parvenus*, *Bourgeois*. Upstarts, in short. Roget gives as synonyms *Impudent Person*, *Newcomer, Vulgar Person.* Don't let it get to you. Nowadays it has some better synonyms, like *Upwardly Mobile.*

Snobbery always boils down ultimately to money, but before we get to that ultimate point, there's a great deal of work for the aspiring snob to master. It isn't simply money, you see. And there's money, and money. You can see from the above that new money has long been equated with low tastes. Newness-snobs are always in danger of being considered vulgar, and may be snubbed by Antiquitysnobs, who are also known as The County, whether they live in England or not.

There are now lots of American and Canadian County, although if they tried being County in England, they would be cruelly snubbed as Nouveaux. I know, it's confusing, but who ever said it was easy to be a successful snob?

Antiquitysnobs endeavour to communicate to their inferiors (which means all the rest of the world) that they are not only rich, but have been rich for a very long time. They are Old Money, which is much better than New Money because, having been rich for such a long time, they have behind them generations of rich ancestors, who could afford servants to do all their dirty work, so that they (the ancestors) had money and leisure for expensive educations, travel, sport, culture, and big-ticket toys. This makes them superior to the Nouveaux, whose ancestors are by definition uncultured slobs with nothing to recommend them but a talent for making lots of money.

On the other hand, Old Money tends not to be as plentiful as New, because generations of Ancestors have been throwing it around, often stupidly, and the talent for making it is not necessarily hereditary. There is nothing so pathetic as Antiquitysnobs who have lost all their money, but are still trying to demonstrate superiority, and command precedence over genuinely rich people.

As you will see when you read our chapter on Carsnobbery in Part II, Paul Fussell claims that really Top People (his term), a.k.a. Oldmoneysnobs, wouldn't be caught dead driving shiny expensive new cars, which are vulgar, because "easily purchasable." So they deliberately choose to drive the cheapest and most ordinary (Ford, Chevy, Plymouth, Dodge) and don't even bother washing it. "Slightly dirty is best." Oldmoneysnobs believe that all the inferior classes (The Poor) love cars more than anything else, will cheerfully deprive their children of food and send them to school barefoot in order to flaunt a big shiny vulgar new car. So the Uppers prefer the discomfort and inconvenience of driving a dirty old hunk of junk to being confused with the crass driver of a Mercedes. (See Carsnob.)

If you are a Newness-snob, and wouldn't be caught dead driving a cheap, dirty, boring old car, then you have to make a philosophical decision for newness: you like new cars, and you don't give a hoot in hell if the Antiquitysnobs turn up their noses at you. YOU LOVE NEW CARS — their comfort, their reliability, their intoxicating smell, their pristine cleanness. You lovingly wash and polish them every weekend, not giving a curse for the sneers of the Oldsnobs. If you want a Lambourghini, you are going to, by God, drive a Lambourghini, and let's see someone in a dirty 1983 Tempo make you feel inferior.

They *will* think you are inferior, of course, because anyone who tries to prove his superiority by driving a big vulgar car has (in their eyes) automatically demonstrated inferiority. It doesn't even prove you're rich, because everyone knows that cars can be, and indeed are, bought on credit. But if you like your new car enough, you must have the courage of your convictions, and feel superior to people in rusty Tempos.

You will also run the risk of encountering the Intellectualsnob, sometimes a teacher in your child's school, who will — if given a chance — explain to you that being rich is in itself pretty nasty, and will try to spoil your fun by reading you bits from Thorstein Veblen. Intellectualsnobs are almost invariably dog-poor, and jealous. They are often Antiquitysnobs as well, allegedly from ancient families who have lost all their money, as well as the capacity to earn it. The Intellectualsnob may try to tell you about his family's ancient lineage, subtly implying that your new Caddy or Lincoln proves that you are an uncouth upstart, with no lineage ancient or modern.

Don't argue. Give your gorgeous new Merc a loving polish, smile at him affectionately and say, "No kidding. Hey, how about them Blue Jays?"

Here is the sort of thing you may expect from an Intellectualsnob, who quite probably drives a dirty old Chevy, hoping that it will fool people into thinking he really could afford a big shiny Lambourghini like yours, but considers it vulgar.

The economic basis of the leisure class, the Intellectualsnob will tell you, has always been the possession of wealth, in itself contemptible. He will then quote Veblen at you, but that's all to the good, as it gives historical background, useful for understanding snobbery, if you haven't read this book. He'll tell you what we already know, that top class is not Top because it was wise and good and noble, but because of clannishness, massiveness, ferocity, unscrupulousness — all that stuff which lets you acquire and accumulate wealth.

As we know, these were the qualities by which in the good old days, the Old Rich acquired their Old Money, and hung on to it. You had to be clannish, so that you could call in your relatives to help you in your bold aggression, or in case your free resort to fraud backfired;

you had to be massive, so you could beat up the people you were aggressing, as well as your own clan members, whenever they got ideas about grabbing some of the loot.

The fundamental qualities are still necessary today, but as we know, they require camouflage. It is still essential to be ferocious, unscrupulous, tenacious, etc. (Massiveness now optional.) You must want to make money more than anything else in the world, and have a talent for making it. But in these degenerate days, you're required to maintain an appearance of legality and respectability. You can't use massiveness to beat the competition, unless you're a professional hockey player.

In the good old days, if you were sufficiently massive, you could eliminate a competitor by clomping him over the head with a club, or calling out the clan for a nice little war, but nowadays you have to defeat your opponent by chicanery, or if there's no other alternative, by hiring a gun. You never do it yourself.

> The ideal pecuniary man is like the ideal delinquent in his unscrupulous conversion of goods and persons to his own ends, and in a callous disregard of the feelings and wishes of others and of the remoter effects of his actions; but he is unlike him in possessing a keener sense of status, and in working more consistently and far-sightedly to a remoter end. (Veblen, 238)

If you can manage to have had ancestors with these qualities, you can be a happy Antiquitysnob. It's certainly the most restful and comfortable sort of snobbery there is, and if your brutish ancestors accumulated enough assets, you won't even have to work. (This is not necessarily A Good Thing today, as we know, though it clearly distinguished the Uppers from the Lowers until some time in the 19th century.) It is now almost mandatory for the serious Snob to work at something, or at least to have a profession.

Antiquitysnobs never yearn for acceptance by Nouveaux; it is much better fun to despise them, and feel superior. However, there was at one time a brisk trade in rich American daughters, to be exchanged for poverty-stricken English aristocrats, without which we might have been deprived of most of the novels of Henry James. Not necessarily a bad thing.

Newness-snobs are often preyed upon by anxieties, and ambition to be accepted by the Antiquities, but they must resist this with all their strength, ignoring or genuinely despising, if possible, the mere existence of the Antiquities. If it is impossible, a sound ploy is to find them comic, which is not difficult, and excellent fun.

Consider London, Ontario, which once had more millionaires per capita than any other town in Canada. I don't know whether it still holds the title, but life in London afforded the serious Snobstudent an invaluable microcosm of the Old Money/New Money struggle. One of the few pleasures in the lives of the poor was making mock of the millionaires, old and new.

Among Nouveaux in London, Ontario, you can still get lots of laughs with references, preferably scurrilous, to the habits of Old London. The non-affluent could evoke hilarity on social occasions simply by mentioning membership in the London Club, a most exclusive haunt of moribund millionaires.

Long ago I worked, for a while, for Old London Old Money, on the staff of a small publication, and had great success among my poverty-stricken friends with stories about my employers. Our CEO once (at the Christmas party), to demonstrate his athletic ability, stood on his head, and a cheque for $10,000 fell out of his pocket. "Oop, forgot about that," he admitted. His secretary remarked that Mr. Old shouldn't do that [headstand], as he had only one-third of a stomach.

It was my first job after graduation and I was the only staff member under the age of ninety-eight. The rest had been with the firm for thousands of years. They couldn't quit, because there was no pension plan. Our boss's wife referred to the staff as "the hands." The Christmas Party and the Summer Picnic were the only occasions on which the Olds and the Hands socialized.

The Summer Picnic was an extraordinary festivity, with arthritic ladies and gents scampering about, affecting to be sportive and gamesome. It sometimes unwisely included races and a baseball game, downright dangerous since almost everyone had high blood pressure, rheumatism, or fractionalized stomachs.

Mrs. Old improved these occasions by explaining to the Hands how taxes were a form of legalized theft, by which the rich were systematically robbed by the government to keep idle layabouts in TV sets and beer, said layabouts including pensioners, welfare recipients, and the unemployed, as well as employees who no longer earned their salaries in the Old establishment which, as remarked, had no pension plan. The Olds were irritated when the tax office kept phoning, plaintively asking them to cash their old age pension cheques, so that said office could keep its books in order. Must the Olds be kept running to the bank for such picayune sums, just to oblige a lot of jumped-up civil servants? They had applied for the pension on principle, since they had been taxed out of reason for years, and had a right to get something back.

The pension would not be needed, said Mrs. Old fiercely, if the improvident creatures had saved their pennies during their productive years, instead of fooling them away on beer and TV sets.

She was indignant that lower-class children were being educated at her expense, while the Old offspring had to attend costly private schools, lest they be contaminated by undesirable associates.

Preferably, Old Money should date back to the Crusades or thereabouts, in England, but it is no longer thought necessary to have come over with William the Conqueror. In Canada, the date of arrival on this continent is irrelevant in every respect. To rate as authentic Old Money, your family must have had it in England or — in special cases — France or the U.S. If your begetters came over from Ireland during the potato famine, you'll never rate among the Olds. Recently there have been efforts to gain Snobcredits for being fourth- or fifth-generation Canadians, but this evokes only pitying smiles from Antiquitysnobs.

If your money is sufficiently antiquated, the means of earning it, be they ever so opprobrious, are now quaint and can be boasted about. It is quite okay to have an ancestor who was hanged, if it happened several hundred years ago. More recent hangings are better left unmentioned. Fortunes made by piracy are great conversation pieces, but it is still not recommended that you boast of, or even mention, money made in the slave trade, though many great families, both European and American, got their start in that rewarding field. Once established, they quite naturally deputized the actual dealing with slaves to hired help (or hands) and fastidiously kept their own hands immaculate.

You are aware, by this time, that wealth as such is unmentionable in Snobcompetition, in the sense that you can't boast about it overtly. You must find subtle ways of demonstrating that you are richer (smarter/better all round) than the person you are one-upping. It must be done by implication, and may be difficult, especially if you are one of the Old Money set whose clothes are indistinguishable from those of bums and bag ladies, and if you drive that 1969 Rambler.

For example, if you want to impress a waitress with a generous tip, you may not flourish large bills in an attention-getting manner, but make your gesture with at least a pretence of doing it inconspicuously. Ideally, the waitress will spontaneously fling her arms around you with cries of gratitude and admiration, but this can be an annoyance to wives, etc., if you know what I mean by etc. in this context. Regrettably, modern waiters are not as grateful for generous tips as they were in the beautiful past. They think they have a right to them.

However, you must not attempt to broadcast your indifference, or superiority to wealth with crude display: if in doubt see the Woody Allen film *Broadway Danny Rose* (now on video) where guests at a crassly Nouveau wedding burn large bills to demonstrate their unconcern for money.

There is one exception to the rule about the unmentionableness of money in Snobcompetition: First generation Nouveaux can get away with being naïvely proud of their wealth, even bragging about it, and be considered rather fetching in their lack of sophistication. It was expertly practised by Charlie Carter, for whom I worked one summer when I was a student. Charlie had little respect for higher education, aristocratic forbears, Old Money, or any of the standard Snobtouchstones. He was a self-made man who boasted happily about his wealth, and people thought it was cute. We will meet him again in the chapter on education. Charlie frequently lost everything and went bankrupt: "I'm busted, dear," he said the second last time I saw him. The last time, he introduced me to the pilot of his private plane.

"I'm back in the bucks, dear. Ain't you finished at that doggone college yet? Any time you want a job with Carter, lemme know."

The Carter approach is a good Nouveau ploy, infinitely superior to laborious attempts to pass yourself off as Old, which always fails, one way or another, and which prevents you from enjoying your ill-gotten gains. Almost all gains are ill-gotten (see Veblen, *supra*), and this is one matter in which all Nouveaux should learn guile.

You (or your father, or grandfather) may have got rich by dealing in arms, or drugs, or women, or kiddy-porn, or toxic waste, and these are indeed some of the best ways of getting rich, nowadays. But it is most unwise to admit it to anyone. If you are a second-generation Nouveau, you should become a lawyer, which is a splendid cover for every variety of nefarious dealing. If you can't stand lawyer jokes, or can't pass the exams, you should acquire a legitimate business — in addition to, and as a front for, not instead of your real income source. Computer shops are nice, and sometimes even make money; however, you must be able to speak the language. Just hiring people who are good with computers won't guard you against silly questions on social occasions; if you can't perform well, you should buy a funeral home. No one will ask you about that. Or go into Import-Export, which covers a multitude of sins. If anyone asks you what you import, say grandfather clocks, or 18th-century French armoires. Of course you're really importing drugs and porn, cigarettes and rotgut booze, while exporting weapons and toxic waste, but nobody wants to hear about it, except other importers/exporters, and possibly Revenue Canada. And CSIS. And the RCMP.

Dealers in arms and toxic wastes should also become ardent activists for peace and environmental causes, if possible taking office as president or director of several groups, and making inspiring speeches on every occasion. If some meddlesome journalist points out that arms dealing is incompatible with a true passion for peace, you admit frankly that you were once indeed engaged in that field, *in the cause of defeating communism*. This still commands respect in certain quarters. If toxic waste is your caper, don't even discuss it, but say disarmingly that you're just a simple old junk dealer. If you can make it convincing, stick in something about the dust-heaps of Mr. Boffin in *Our Mutual Friend*. This will confuse and embarrass hecklers, and you can turn the conversation to your good works and charitable activities. Just to be on the safe side, it would be wise to actually read *Our Mutual Friend*, or at least part of it. You might even enjoy it.

A word of caution to aspiring Snobs: if you don't have a minimum of two generations of wealth behind you, don't pretend to be Old Money. Either be a happy Nouveau, or keep your trap shut. Just be rich. Get a good education if possible, but if not, get your kids into the right schools so that they will have U accents and speech habits and will despise you. But that's all right. All kids despise their parents one way or another.

Don't get involved in genealogy, searching for respectable ancestors. Respectable ancestors are all middle and lower class. What you want are rich, massive ancestors, if any. Preferably you should forget about them completely; this is the true Old Money pattern. In fact, genealogical research is considered rather pathetic, class-wise. I remember an exchange (in England) in which a naïve colonial visitor urged an impoverished ex-Old Moneyite to trace her family tree.

"Thank you," she replied superbly, "but Debrett has already very kindly seen to it."

Further guidance for Nouveaux will be found throughout the book, but special study should be devoted to the chapters on Cars and Houses.

6

Servants

Servants are what economists call a "positional good," something that, by their nature, not everyone can have. No matter how rich a society gets, it will never be so rich that everyone can have a maid. Someone has to *be* the maid.
— Michael Kinsley.

It's not enough to succeed. Others must fail.
— Gore Vidal.

"*Qui alors videra le pot de chambre?*" *Tr.*: Then who's going to empty the chamber-pot? Question posed by a Frenchman whose identity I've never been able to trace, of the basic problem of socialism: in a world of equals, who is to be stuck with these disagreeable and degrading jobs? Not an issue, you say, with universal indoor plumbing? Okay, who's going to empty the bed-pan and change the diaper?

Indoor plumbing is universal in the Snobworld, at least, and is I believe mandatory in building codes. You aren't allowed to economize on plumbing by provision of an outdoor privy.

This is perhaps the most critical issue of serious snobbery. As we've seen (repeatedly) for most of human history, the only socially acceptable forms of work were killing and preaching. Being a servant had to be just about as base as you could get. Perhaps not as degrading as slavery, but until recent times, it wasn't always easy to distinguish between a slave and a servant.

Among other disadvantages, being a servant made you a legitimate subject for mockery. Funny servants were the standby of much 19th- and early 20th-century humour, from Dickens and Thackeray to James Thurber on Black cooks, and T. S. Eliot's mockery of "the damp souls of housemaids/Sprouting despondently at area gates." Servants were fair game and sitting ducks.

Tolstoy describes in his autobiography how, as a callow youth, he fell in love with "a buxom lady who rode in Freitag's riding-school." He used to hang around the school, so that he could stare at her while "lurking behind the footmen and the fur wraps they were holding."

Footmen, holding fur wraps. These wealthy women employed grown men to hold their furs, while the ladies clomped around the ring. A soft job, you might say. But what a humiliating one. What a waste of manpower. (We won't get into the threatened Snobvalue of wearing furs at the moment. See Clothessnobbery.) That would have been somewhere around 1848, by coincidence very close to the date when the immortal *Book of Snobs* was published. Snobbery was flourishing.

Move forward a century. What's happening in the Snobworld now? Nancy Mitford (in *Noblesse Oblige*, 1959) reminds us that even at that date establishments existed in England "where several men-servants wait on one young woman at dinner." One's immediate non-Snob reflex, on hearing of these male servants and their employers, is to recommend a boot in the rear for all concerned, and tell the stupid woman to get her own dinner.

Very bad Snobthinking. Servants are "more useful for show than for services performed." Men-servants are preferable to women "for services that bring them obtrusively into view." The bigger and stronger the servant, the more expensive he obviously is, and the greater his Snobvalue: only a very rich, very powerful Supersnob could afford to employ a big strong guy to stand around holding a lady's fur while she takes a riding lesson, or to wait on a spoiled brat of a girl. "Men, especially lusty, personable fellows ... are better fitted for this work, as showing a larger waste of time and of human energy," says Thorstein. "Thus the busy housewife of the early patriarchal days, with her retinue of hard-working handmaidens, presently gives place to the lady and the lackey." (Veblen, 57)

Employing servants is the ideal form of snobbery since it automatically marks the employer as superior, the servant as inferior.

This is the whole object of snobbery, and in its application to servants it may be observed in its purest form. Alas, in modern times it has one cardinal flaw: servants have practically ceased to exist. Housemaids, parlourmaids, footmen, coachmen, gardeners — all are extinct, and though cooks and butlers may survive vestigially, they are obviously threatened species.

It's happened so quickly. I clearly remember my mother's friends sitting around drinking tea and deploring in genteel tones the difficulty of finding a "girl" with any training. They had all gone to work in munitions factories, and what would they do when the war was over? Quite untrained.

Mother clucked her tongue sympathetically even though we had no maid, had no servants whatsoever, except when she had another baby and a neighbour woman "came in" and got the meals until Maw was back on her feet. After a futile decade or two, a good many of the ladies made great play of the fact that they were now managing without Help, and finding it less trouble than putting up with some rough Girl who didn't even know how to answer the door properly.

Most of these ladies were decayed gentlewomen (the Genteel Poor) for whom servants were really little more than a dim memory, but the idea of having a maid was of high importance to their self-respect, and remained their favourite topic of conversation.

Thackeray is wonderful, as always, in describing the hard labour required to give the impression that one has a staff of servants. He says, in "Dinner-Giving Snobs,"

> … suppose you, in the middle rank of life, accustomed to Mutton, roast on Tuesday, cold on Wednesday, hashed on Thursday &c., with small means and a small establishment, choose to waste the former and set the latter topsy-turvey by giving entertainments unnaturally costly — you come into the Dinner-giving Snob class at once. Suppose you get in cheap-made dishes from the pastry-cook's, and hire a couple of green grocers, or carpet-beaters, to figure as footmen, dismissing honest Molly who waits on common days …

The carpet-beaters and green-grocers, as well as the dishes from the pastry-cook's, play a prominent role among Thackeray's Snobs' servants, chiefly in the dangers they present to the Dinner-giving Snob:

> The host is smiling, and hob-nobbing, and talking up and down the table, but a prey to secret terrors and anxieties, lest the wines he has brought up from the cellar should prove insufficient; lest a corked bottle should destroy his calculations; or our friend the carpet-beater, by making some *bévue [blunder]*, should disclose his real quality of green-grocer and show he is not the family butler.

A worse risk would be that one of the guests would recognize him in his real, or carpet-beater persona, not his assumed butlerian vocation. This is one danger which modern hosts can avoid, without losing credit, now that even Honest Molly is extinct, and no one waits on us on common days, as it is entirely permissible to hire caterers. No Snobaspersions there at all. You can if necessary, though not without risking public disgrace, order meat-and-cheese "trays" from the delicatessen, or even send out for Chinese or Italian.

Servants may be extinct in the real world, except among millionaires, but they still exist, plentifully and traditionally, in fiction, on which I have been obliged to lean because of the real-life dearth of material. It's useful, too, for illustrating the fantasies of which Novelist Snobbery is concocted.

The best stuff comes from the thirties, with Ngaio Marsh, Dorothy Sayers, Marjorie Allingham, and a dozen lesser lights, all of whose detectives were aristocrats, with devoted valets who loved to serve them and considered it an honour to bring their morning tea and brush their clothes. None of them had the intellectual power of Jeeves, who chose to dedicate his talents to the service of arch-twit Bertie Wooster, although Mr. Campion's man (forget his name), was an ex-burglar whose professional skills and underworld contacts were still useful to the Young Marster, though of course he used them only for righteous purposes.

Interestingly, some Brit writers are still indefatigably producing aristocratic detectives, although they're no longer amateurs. Like Ngaio's Alleyn, they have top jobs at Scotland Yard, and believe it or not, they still have devoted valets who live only to serve their adored masters. Can't give you names or titles, though, as the writing in these works tends to have a coy quality which deters me from thorough study.

Charlotte MacLeod's books are set in America, where peers are a bit thinner on the ground, but aristocratic families abound, and they are lousy with old retainers, all absolutely devoted to The Family. And believe me, The Family treats them right. No servant-abuse here. They truly love their servants, and look on them as practically human, hardly inferior at all. It's a beautiful arrangement, and because of the true affection that exists between master and servant, the lower orders almost never get out of line, or fail to know their place.

Such idyllic master-servant relations exist only in fiction. They persist because for thousands of years, we never heard the servants' point of view, chiefly because few of them could read or write very well, and even if they could, they were probably too tired to write after putting in a sixteen-hour day. The thirties' novels were all from the U-perspective, the Lord Peter Wimsey view. However, that's all changed.

For the real life version, see the supermarket tabloids on scandals among the rich and famous, as peddled by their staff. Most servants, if they tell the truth, admit to actively despising and resenting their employers, while most employers find their servants unsatisfactory, grudge them their wages, suspect them of idleness and dishonesty, and (perversely) dislike the invasion of their privacy, since few modern homes have servants' quarters. Servants and masters traditionally and almost invariably despise each other, for the very good reason that their relationship is one of superior-inferior, which is bound to generate resentment. In spite of its inconveniences, however, employers value it highly because it places them, *by definition*, in the role of the superior being. This is beyond price, Snobwise.

Servants were originally slaves, and they included most of us, since obviously it's impossible to have more bosses than underlings. In the early days of society, all women were in effect slaves, possessions of the males, as we've seen.

Thus there early developed a hierarchy, much mentioned by Thorstein V. and me, in the nature of work: that which was considered prowess, and reflected credit, and that which was subtly or overtly degrading, its performance *per se* an admission of inferiority. This latter was the province of women and weak men, and these were simply property, slaves. Other slaves were acquired by conquest, seized as trophies.

At a later stage of social evolution, women took on a new value: daughters could be profitably married off to strengthen alliances, and to guarantee the retention of the patriarch's wealth within his family. This habit of thought still persists among our comic modern royalty, as discussed in the chapter on the Principle of Archaism and Transmissibility of Gentility, *q.v.*

This principle is also manifested in belief in the "unmistakeable stamp of aristocracy" so beloved of romantic novelists, still occasionally cropping up today. I haven't had a whole lot of experience with the aristocracy (how can one, handicapped by colonial nativity?) but I've met a few of its representatives. One was Lady Somebody, encountered at an affair given by some weird British cousins. The unmistakeable Stamp was difficult to discern in this aristocrat, possibly obliterated behind the heavy accumulation of flab she was toting around. Further, she lacked the fictional aristocrat's instinctively flawless taste in dress; she was wearing a really ghastly tweed in a shade of purple that anyone could have told her was the gravest of errors. Another peer of the realm whom I encountered (at a conference on disarmament) also failed to display any detectable Stamp. He was only about five feet tall, with very thick glasses and very thin hair. They both were earnest and well-meaning but neither well-informed nor quick-witted. The transmissibility of gentility continues to be unconfirmed, and the unmistakeable stamp of aristocracy to be mistakeable.

Evolving from the hierarchical nature of work comes the concept that labour and drudgery are degrading. "Abstention from labour," says Thorstein, "is not only an honorific or meritorious act, but it presently comes to be a requisite of decency."

Work was degrading, and it was necessary to demonstrate emancipation from it. (Foot-binding, corset-wearing.) Small white hands and long fingernails are still regarded as beautiful. It was impossible for a busy man to keep up with his fighting and hunting and still produce such evidences of aristocratic freedom, so women became instruments for its display. As civilization advanced, men too were able to enjoy leisure, and then were able to dress up as gorgeously as their women, *vide* Elizabethan court costume. Conspicuous leisure became the symbol of success, as did conspicuous waste in such formalized displays as potlatches, balls, and formal dinner parties.

The industrial revolution gave the poor and deprived at least a choice of drudgery: they could get factory jobs. These were little better than slavery, but one could in theory quit and walk away. When it came to having control of their lives, there was very little difference between the domestic servant, the factory worker, and the slave. Slaves might even be slightly better off, with a roof over their heads and regular meals, however unappetizing, but the state of being a chattel, simply another man's property, was death to the soul. Whereas the soul got a big bang out of owning slaves, a right which was given up with much reluctance, and only in very recent times.

The fun was spoiled by a lot of bleeding-heart reformers. In 1772 it was decided that as soon as a slave set foot on the soil of the British Isles he became free. Slavery was abolished in the Empire in 1833; in 1863 it was prohibited throughout the U.S. In 1861 serfdom was abolished in Russia. Snobbery has never been the same.

It didn't give in without a struggle. In my youth I was incarcerated in St. Hilda's College (University of Toronto) which offered so many and such esoteric forms of snobbery that one could write a book about that alone. Although we were able-bodied and hungry, we were waited on at table by maids. The food was abominable, and we several times sent deputations to the principal saying that we would gladly serve ourselves if they would spend a little more on provender. This was indignantly refused.

"Some of these gels," said our principal, with an air of exposing a shocking scandal, "come from homes where they have *no servants*. It's essential that they learn to deal with servants, because they may marry into families where they will have to direct servants. They would then be under a great disadvantage, with no experience in handling them."

She once told me of a girl from a poor farm family who by hard work and determination got herself to university and in residence at St. Hilda's, working at a job to support herself the whole time. I said it must have been very exhausting.

"Nonsense," she snapped. "People like that don't feel exhaustion. She's been accustomed from childhood to doing hard work. You or I might find it exhausting, but she wouldn't even notice it." I'd worked my way through university myself, doing such jobs as running payrolls and lifeguarding, and found it exhausting. Luckily I had (for once) not been dumb enough to tell the principal of my laborious past, or I would have been relegated to the nonexhaustible labouring class at once.

This is a very old ploy for appeasing the conscience — the comfortable assumption that servants and slaves have no feelings. They are really only machines. They're not like Us, all delicate sensibilities. Note the treatment of servants in Jane Austen: they barely exist as human creatures. Their function is to serve and to remain inconspicuous, not to be a nuisance to their employers. There was one lovely case — I thought it was in Jane Austen, but I can't find it, so perhaps it was some near-contemporary — in which the young ladies were preparing for a ball, and a crisis occurred: there were no shoe-roses. Panic. Anguish. Then a possibility arose that a certain neighbour might be able to help out in the contretemps. One need only walk over to her place to inquire. Unfortunately a storm was raging outside. It was downright dangerous for anyone to go out in such weather.

So they sent one of the servants.

Sometimes one's closest friends, whom one thinks one knows well, shock one with their callousness toward servants. A woman who had always displayed a fine social conscience in other directions was downright inhuman when it came to her cleaning woman, who "came in" twice a week. I once discovered her sitting halfway up the long flight of stone steps leading to the house, gasping for breath, and looking extremely ill. I rushed up and got a glass of water (I didn't know what the right treatment might be) and warned my hostess, her employer, who refused to take it seriously.

"She's just looking for attention. She's a great big strong woman, nothing hurts her."

A year or so later the great big strong woman died of a heart attack, with complications from asthma and diabetes. A very disloyal act, leaving her employer with no Help.

Why do we need servants at all, now that we have so many handy-dandy machines to take care of the drudgery? Now there's a silly question. All these gadgets don't make up for the pleasure of having a Girl (even if quite untrained) to answer your bell, to bully and snub.

Leisure, dear old St. Hilda comfortably assured me, was not valued by servants. You and I value it, but they wouldn't know what to do with it. "They" included not only domestic servants but all labourers and coarse mechanicals. Give them leisure time, and they'll spend it in the pub. Give them more money, and they'll only drink it. Give them bath-tubs and they'll store coal in them.

Mod cons had to be invented because servants were threatening extinction, even though for the "upper" ones, it could be a comparatively easy life. Nevertheless, they all hated their lot, as we know. Many of their jobs existed, not because they filled any useful function, but because their employment pointed up the superiority of their employer, as with Tolstoy's fur-bearers.

For this rather bizarre reason, some ladies made a point of choosing exceptionally pretty girls for their personal maids, hazardous though it might be to expose husbands to such temptations. The fact that you could command the services of a very attractive girl demonstrated your power and confidence. Note the descriptions of the ladies' maids in Barrie's *The Admirable Crichton*, a priceless documentary on master-servant relations in the Victorian age.

So although domestic service may now be, in some cases, quite profitable, the would-be employer still finds it difficult to get and keep servants. Same old reason — the job-labelling as inferior. In the past, poor people "went into service" when they had no choice. With no education and no marketable skills, they were stuck with it. When the Industrial Revolution and world wars offered factory jobs, domestic servants disappeared like snow in April. Factory jobs are not fun, but when the day's work is finished, you're your own boss. Domestic service knows no time-clock. Servants could be kept up for hours if His Lordship was throwing a dinner-party. And since he and Her Ladyship never had to do the cleaning-up, they saw no point in wasting money on labour-saving devices: why did one pay servants? Most domestic servants had one afternoon off a week, and there were all sorts of prohibitions on their activities: the housemaid's "followers" were not allowed on the premises in many establishments, and there was little opportunity for social life. No wonder they seized any chance to abandon The Family, and leave their Lord- and Ladyships to do the washing-up themselves.

Today good cooks and butlers can demand outrageous salaries, and are being constantly lured away from their employers by offers so tempting as to be downright irresistible. These include pensions and sick benefits, luxurious apartments, holidays with pay, use of the pool and tennis court, and privileges their own bosses might covet. Even with all this, the employers are never safe — not only from cook-and-butler raiding, often by their best friends, but from treason by the servants. Some of them may have a profitable sideline in collaboration with thieves and kidnappers. Selling scandal to the public prints has long been a fringe benefit, as witness the tribulations of the British Royals. Indeed, there are cases of unscrupulous journalists who become servants for no other purpose than to eavesdrop on their miserable masters, tap telephones, plant bugs, etc.

There's probably not a valet, maid, or butler on the face of the globe who isn't currently collecting material for, or actually hard at work on, its book, whether non-fictional exposé or novel based on real life characters. Once the book has been published, and the author has made its pile and wants to settle down to a life of luxury and privilege, the old hubris-and-nemesis syndrome takes over: the poor wretch can't hire a decent servant for love or money, and if he does manage to get someone at last, it turns out the miserable snitch is spying on him and selling sensational articles about him to the *National Enquirer*.

Although my acquaintanceship with millionaires is not large, I know of a lady (relative of some friends) who has a butler. He bullies her unmercifully, blackmailing her with threats of leaving if she has the temerity to disagree with him. Her family suspects that in the past her duties included sleeping with him but of late, as she grows older, they believe she's been excused from this task. He insisted that she hire a pretty maid who (it is popularly suspected) has taken over this side of the job. The lady is an indecently rich widow, but it hasn't done her too much good, as she has become a slave to her servant. She lives in fear of him writing his Book. She used to hear him typing away at night, and lived in a state of agonized apprehension for several weeks, when the ominous noise ceased. Alas. As she learned later, the typing had stopped but not the book. He'd bought a computer.

When tobacco heiress Doris Duke died, a good chunk of her $1.6 billion fortune went to charitable foundations. However, according to *Maclean's* (May 27, 1996), $6.2 million went to her butler and companion, Bernard Lafferty. What a difficult relationship it must have been: would he be Bernie in bed, and Lafferty when they had guests? Would one pay a salary, or would he have a discreetly provided allowance? We're told he was "high-spending."

Even more disconcerting is the bodyguard problem, as manifested in Monegasque royalty. It is one more instance of the curious turnabout in social behaviour we have witnessed this century: in the old days the wicked Master seduced the servant girl. In Monaco recently the tables were turned, with Princess Stephanie being impregnated by her own bodyguard, who had less than a year before begat an unsponsored infant on another girl, and who could easily be recognized from his picture in *Time* as a bad bet, both husband-wise and bodyguard-wise. Nevertheless, the silly princess first married and then divorced him, and few hearts have bled unduly for her.

Millionaires still have servants, though they pay through the nose for them nowadays. A good many maids and gardeners are university students, who take the jobs because they can save their entire salary — meals supplied, no rent to pay. They are unsatisfactory, however. It is much more difficult to condescend to an embryo physicist or astronomer, or even a teacher, than it is to an ignorant village girl, or one with whom domestic service is a longstanding family tradition. Students acting as servants are not inferior by definition. They *are* by definition temporary, and have no interest in establishing a reputation for good service. As soon as the new term starts they're gone. They also have a nasty tendency to require contracts precisely stating the terms of their employment, and to threaten litigation if the terms are not observed. Latter-day housemaids cannot be commandeered into the Marster's bed, as old-time housemaids frequently were, and have a tiresome inclination to yell rape if he tries it. In fact, most of the fun has gone out of having a staff of servants at one's beck and call.

Gardeners have ceased to exist, as such. They have all formed landscaping services, come around weekly with their mowers and Killex sprayers, turn your grass brown and leave residues of pesticides to kill off the songbirds and contaminate your well, for which they charge you an arm and a leg. Not like dear old McPherson who pottered around the glass house being picturesque and making quotable comic remarks. However, it's questionable whether McPherson ever really existed, outside the pages of P. G. Wodehouse, Michael Innis, and the like.

You could condescend a little to McPherson (though he was very independent and might defy you, colourfully) but it's really difficult to condescend to thousands of dollars worth of machinery and an immense truck with Landscaping, Inc. written on it. See Lawnsnobbery.

The other mentionable survivors (there are various unmentionables) of the domestic service tradition are the Nanny and the *Au Pair*. The latter are well-educated foreign girls from nice families, who are willing to do some housework while experiencing travel and improving their English.

Today's nanny must not be confused with the ones in English novels. She has taken special courses to qualify her for her job, and does not do housework. The *au pair* does it very badly or so sulkily that it's easier for the employer to do it herself. There are all sorts of social difficulties, too — are they to be allowed to entertain young men in the living-room? Would one be guilty of corrupting youth if one allowed them to entertain gents in their bedrooms? And must one include them when one entertains one's own friends, even though they have nothing to say to each other? Or when they can be relied on to flirt with every man who comes into the house?

It's often a dismally touchy situation, no fun for anyone. But if a woman has children, and wants to continue with her career, it's employ a nanny, or ferry the kids to and from day care. Otherwise, God forbid, she may have to stay home and bring up the little horrors herself.

The final category of servant is a survival of slavery or serfdom. This is the illiterate or semi-literate Third-World citizen who has entered the country illegally and is willing to do anything, but anything, rather than go back to Mexico or Brazil or the Philippines. She can be kept in the house with no time off and made to do absolutely all the work of the household, blackmailed with the threat of deportation. (She's too ignorant to know that her employer would also be in trouble.) She's useful for doing all the dreary dirty jobs, and she can be paid practically nothing: in effect, with an unscrupulous employer, she's a slave, but she can cause you great embarrassment and even lose you a good job, as Zöe Baird could testify. The minute she gets enough cash together she will leave you in the lurch, get a job as a waitress if her English is good enough, or go out cleaning, and take a one-bedroom apartment into which she will import thousands of relatives.

She has no Snobvalue whatever. You daren't admit she exists, because you're breaking the law in employing and exploiting her, and because she's simple and ignorant, and frequently pregnant, sometimes by members of your own family, she reflects no credit on you.

The demise of the servant class caused great indignation among the servant-employing class. Linda McQuaig tells the diverting tale (McQuaig, 173–174) of how Harry Jackman, papa of Ontario's ex-Lieutenant-Governor Hal, believed that general affluence was bad for the lower orders of society. One of its evil effects was that domestic servants were almost impossible to find, a situation about which he was understandably disturbed. What's the use of having millions if you can't get decent help?

The only solution to such dilemmas is a good thorough economic depression, to force the Inferior Classes to do their duty as housemaids and cleaners for the deserving rich. Mr. Jackman was also sound on estate taxes, but we'll come to that later. It is comforting to think that Hal drew a stipend of $90,000 a year for his toil as Lt.-Gov., to supplement his meagre savings of $400 odd million. He also got a chauffeured car, license Ontario 1.

Someone has to be the maid, to provide the "positional good." But no one is willing to be the maid, with the badge of inferiority stuck on her like Hester Prynne's scarlet letter. Servantsnobbery is doomed, and there seems to be no replacement on the horizon. Labour-saving gadgets are worthy of mention only as long as they are too expensive for your inferiors to afford them … and even at that, the beastly creatures will buy them on the instalment, so that one can't establish superiority by mentioning them: "Yeah, me and Ern got one a them things, too."

Real ingenuity is going to be required to find an adequate Snobreplacement for the butler, the valet, and even honest Molly who waits on common days. The actual question of housework is such a vexed one that we have decided to give it a (short) chapter of its own. Later.

Snobnote: Snobbery flourished behind the green baize door as well as in the rest of the house. Servants maintained rigid hierarchies, and were themselves cruel snobs. But this subject has been abundantly dealt with in literature. See "Upstairs, Downstairs"; see hundreds of novels of the 19th and first half of the 20th centuries.

Another Snobnote: Nannies Then and Now. The Nanny phenomenon had little application on this side of the Atlantic until quite recently. The British Nanny was a formidable lower-middle female who dominated the lives of British Uppers for at least a century, if you believe the literature. Servants have always been a favourite source of comedy among the British, and the Nanny figured prominently in the work of such distinguished figures as Evelyn Waugh (*Scoop, A Handful of Dust*) and of course Nancy Mitford (n.b. *The Blessing*). She was a curious mixture: a sort of substitute parent, who became powerless when the real parent was on the premises, omnipotent when the parent was absent. She was loved and despised by the children, who baited and disobeyed her on all possible occasions. In a sense she was part of the family, though never dining with them or joining in social occasions: she was confined to the nursery, but was sometimes waited on by the other servants, who mocked and resented her.

The distinguishing mark of the Nanny was not a mark but its cry: a kind of incessant low-key bitching, complaining and fault-finding, to which no one paid any attention. Once the children had gone to school, Nanny had no significant occupation, but she nonetheless often stayed on as part of the household, though not of the family, possibly to effect economies: if she were booted out, she might have to be paid a pension, whereas if she stayed in the house, she could be paid most of her (derisory) salary in free room and board. Mummies affected to believe that Nanny was indispensable, Daddies hated the sight of her. British juveniles, once grown up, remember Nanny with sentimental condescension: "the dear old tyrant," as T. H. White called her in *The Sword in the Stone*.

The Nanny was popularly believed to be a purely fictional

character on this side of the Atlantic, except for the Southern States, where she was supplanted by Mammy. For the archetypal Mammy, see of course *Gone With the Wind*. Mammies were even more indispensable than Nannies, because they were slaves, and didn't have to be paid. Nevertheless, a good one was highly valued and esteemed, perhaps even more than the standard (white) British model; she was more easily kept in her place because of her unfortunate skin colour.

Nannies do not thrive in the Canadian climate. Transplanted Brits nevertheless continued to believe for some time that children could not be brought up by their own parents, and had to be civilized by the hand of a Nanny, who also relieved Mummy of disagreeable tasks like diaper-changing and nose-wiping. There is a known case of a Brit husband bringing home, without warning to his Canadian wife, an old-fashioned standard British Nanny. They had had an idyllic marriage until the baby was born, when the father started Nanny-agitation. The wife responded that she was as capable of bringing up her child as any damn Nanny. The father wrung his hands, said it should be "damned" Nanny, for grammatical reasons, and confronted her with a *fait accompli* Nanny.

The Nanny proceeded to deny the mother access to her child, and to keep her busy with demeaning tasks like cleaning the house and doing the dishes. She was allowed to cook, but her cooking was subject to constant criticism. Her self-esteem sank to zero. She began to believe that she was incapable of bathing her own baby. Then her husband had to go out of town for a week, and she summarily fired Nanny, who refused to go: "I was engaged by Dr. X, not by you." So the wife, who was in much better shape, fitness-wise, than the Nanny, threatened to beat her up. The Nanny bleated about calling the police, but thought better of it, and packed her things. When the husband came home (he wasn't a medical doctor, merely a PhD) and discovered Nanny was gone, he again wrung his hands, but when he learned of the physical threat to the dear old tyrant, he decided that perhaps his wife might be allowed a chance at bringing up her own child, after all.

The contemporary Nanny is quite different. She has had college training (community college, that is) and although I have never had any personal experience with her, I gather that she is aggressive about her rights, about the number of hours worked and time off. She asserts social equality with her employers, demanding inclusion at parties, etc., which is sometimes tiresome for her employers, especially if she is young and pretty: what hostess needs that? However, Nannies are endlessly useful for bragging about and for one-upping friends who have to take their kids to day-care or Grandma's.

Since I am happily beyond the age where I need Nannies, my information on this comes solely from Nanny-employers. If I were to interview a Nanny, I might get a different account of things.

Yet Another Snobnote: The following is from a book by Angela Thirkell, title lost, but luckily I copied this bit on my PC. It is a valuable sociological document, although some left-wing pinko-Commies may feel inclined to throw up. That print-dressed housemaid who hauled all those jugs and pitchers and footbaths of water upstairs when Angela went up to dress for dinner must occasionally have been severely tempted at times to empty the china slop pail all over Angela, dinner dress and all.

> ... When there are no servants, you are grateful for central heating and perpetual hot water and fixed basins. But some of us are still unregenerate enough to think wistfully of bedrooms with a fire crackling when you went up to dress for dinner and the same fire being relaid and relighted by a print-dressed housemaid when she drew the curtains in the morning, of capacious washing stands with a large jug and basin and a small jug and basin ... and below its frilled chintz front a china slop pail and a large footbath, of a hip bath before the fire, with thick bath towels warming beside it, for no lady would have used the one bathroom which was tacitly appropriated by the hunting men, of roaring fires in hall and dining room and living rooms with footmen replenishing the huge baskets of wood and the massive coal scuttles, of valets and ladies' maids waiting until their masters and mistresses chose to go to bed ... of church on Sunday morning with a positively irreligious display of hats and toilettes, and the regulation visit to the stables or the conservatories ...

Wouldn't it be fun if darling Angela found herself for a change stuck in the role of that print-dressed housemaid, lighting fires first thing in the morning and hauling up gallons of water which have to be hauled down again when the lazy slob of a guest has finished her toilet, with the assistance of her own maid, who had to stay up all hours the previous night waiting for Angela to decide she was ready for bed?

That was the golden age of domestic service. Will it ever return? We can but hope.

And Still Another Snobnote: Return of the Golden Age? Okay, just suppose ... the rich get richer and the poor get poorer. And poorer still, until they're so desperate they'll take *any* job, just to keep body and soul together. (Un)employment insurance and welfare have ceased to exist, for any practical purpose. But the Jackmans and all that crowd are still crying out for domestic help. You see your children fading away from malnutrition. So you put them in care and take the live-in housemaid's or footman's job, and try to smuggle out a few bits of pheasant to the kids after the big dinner parties, while saving the money you would otherwise have to spend on rent. Then Angela Thirkell comes to visit, unless she's dead, in which case perhaps Fergie will drop in, and she wants a print-dressed housemaid lighting a fire in the bedroom fireplace, and bringing thin bread-and-butter and tea, and jugs and pitchers and footbaths and hipbaths full of hot water, with thick towels heated before the fireplace ... No, no, that's impossible. Among the lesser breeds without the law, of course, but not here in our home and native land. After all, Canada is a democracy, huh? Eh?

7

Sexsnobbery

When pain and anguish wrack the brow,
A ministering angel thou.
— Sir Walter Scott.

... But a good cigar is a smoke.
— Rudyard Kipling.

Damon Runyon, hallowed be his name otherwise, famously divided the sexes into guys and dolls. A doll might sometimes be a babe, a pretty thing or a beautiful; some dolls might also be classified as tamales, tomatoes, or waffles, which may have meant they were tempting but did not necessarily command respect. A doll was occasionally given the neutral status of a female party, a Judy, or more pejoratively, a bim or a broad. When she grew old she became, at best, an old doll; more frequently she was an old komoppo, a blowzala, an old sack, an old bundle, an old phlug, an old crow, or a rutabaga. But guys were always guys, *in saeculo saeculorum*. Women were only tolerable if they were young and ornamental.

Agnes McPhail, the first woman member of the Canadian House of Commons, was elected in 1921. She prevailed upon the Privy Council to declare women to be legally persons. Prior to that date, presumably, we were *not* persons. So what were we in our pre-personhood? Chattels, baby.

As any serious snob and careful reader must understand by now, women have from the beginning been inferior to men, snobwise, and practically every other wise, though the gentry had an advantage here as elsewhere. We also know that the dear old principle of transmissible gentility placed the wife or daughter of an aristocrat above the common slave — this because she could be used for breeding heirs, and daughters to marry off to other aristocrats. But "... she was still her husband's chattel, as she had been her father's chattel." (Veblen.)

Women thus started with several strikes against them, and have been axiomatically inferior to men for the greater part of social evolution. As the rich grew richer, wealth was concentrated in relatively fewer hands, the working classes increased in number and in desperation to make a living, and the rich man's wife acquired "some measure of that leisure which is the chief mark of gentility."

Remember from our chapter on Servants the transition from the housewife with her handmaidens to the lady with the lackey? This was the beginning of the emancipation of upper-class women, and the blurring of the male-female roles. Some women could order around some men, a great advance. Occasionally the theory of Transmissibility of Gentility produced other startling results: in the absence of a male heir, a woman could occupy the throne.

In the early days queens didn't have much of a life, unless they were tough cases like Boadicea, who could drive a sabre-toothed chariot with the best of them. Even by the time of Elizabeth I the job of queen was anything but a sinecure. However, when women like Elizabeth and the two Russian Catherines got the chance, they demonstrated beyond argument that they could run a country just as well as any man, and better than most.

Catherine I of Russia did another great job in demonstrating the non-transmissibility of non-gentility: she was the daughter of a peasant, and orphaned as a child. She became a servant, was sold as a sex-slave to Prince Menshikov, in whose household she met Peter the Great, who fell in love with her. They had a child, got married, and when he died, she became the Empress Regnant. She and Peter adored each other, and he gave credit for winning the campaign of Pruth in 1711 "to her courage and sang-froid." She was illiterate but clearly a smart cookie, who succeeded in winning the respect of the court, and ruled until her death.

However, the old transmissibility theory took over again, and her children did not inherit. A Prussian princess, Sophia, was married to the grand duke Peter, to strengthen the relations between Prussia and Russia. The gentility which had been transmitted to poor Peter was subnormality "in physique and in mind" (in Politically Correctspeak, both mentally and physically challenged), and Sophia, after changing her name to Catherine, staged a coup d'état with the help of one of her many lovers. She was acclaimed empress, and ruled for thirty-four years, to become known to posterity as Catherine the Great.

So there was occasionally room at the top, but generally the inferiority of women remained self-evident. Less than twenty years ago, wife-beating was still a good joke, and the occasion of much applausive laughter among males of the British Columbia legislature.

In England, the Sex Disqualification Act barred women from sitting in the House of Lords, and wasn't removed until 1919. Not until 1958 were life peeresses entitled to join its august ranks.

The only place women had the vote before the 20th century was in New Zealand, and that only happened in 1893. Most of the English-speaking world grudgingly gave (sometimes limited) suffrage to females around 1918.

Women have always been out of luck in other ways. God obviously had a spite against females, for he stuck them with the role of child-bearers. Okay, okay, it has its compensations, but the capacity to become pregnant also makes you vulnerable in a way no man ever has to worry about. Every month you have your menstrual period; we used to call it the curse, and so it is. I can't understand why that appropriate appellation has lost currency. With the curse come the discomforts and embarrassment of bloating, cramps, depression, messiness, and smelliness, as well as TV commercials about tampons.

Then you enter the menopause, with hot flashes and all sorts of accompanying miseries, and you spend most of your leisure time crying and feeling helpless and victimized. When at last it begins to let up, you find you've got fat, sometimes you've grown a beard, and no man will look at you sideways; you have ceased to be a sex object, and they treat you as if you were subhuman. The only role you can becomingly accept is that of grandmother. If you haven't any grandchildren, you have no useful function left, and everyone starts thinking in terms of involuntary euthanasia.

For most of human history, men outlived women, who were often exhausted by child-bearing before they were thirty-five. My great-grandfather, who was probably fairly typical for his generation, wore out three wives, by whom he produced approximately thirty children; the family-tree tracers had trouble keeping count.

In the 20th century, with the advent of better hygiene, there were fewer deaths in childbirth. With practicable contraceptives, and consequently smaller families, women began to outlive men, because they usually followed a less violent lifestyle. However, lately they've been losing ground, as more of them take to heavy smoking, drinking, drugs, reckless driving, and so on.

It is now popular to pretend that men also have a menopause, but they don't have the same symptoms; theirs usually take the form of an affair with their secretary or a student, or one of their daughter's girlfriends. Or they start taking a feverish interest in the boy scout movement, or in coaching Little League baseball.

All this has brought to mind a solemn discussion among my classmates when I was in university. We were sitting in the cafeteria, talking (as usual) about sex, a subject on which we were much less expert than subsequent generations would be; we were still in the dark pre-pill age, which was also still the era of the difficult divorce.

The males in our group were deeply concerned about the question of marriage. They wanted to marry early, to channel their sexual needs without the risk and expense of casual sex. The trouble was, if they married a woman their own age, they would find themselves around the age of forty or forty-five chained to a menopausal woman with flabby arms.

The females inquired about channelling *their* sexual urges, and learned they didn't have any — or not as men did. At least, nice girls didn't. Nymphomaniacs, pushovers, and cheap creatures who became prostitutes might, but girls like us didn't want sex. We were happy with affection and tenderness, a little necking.

"Oh," we said. "Isn't that convenient? Aren't we lucky?"

It's always been a cherished male belief that nice girls don't want sex, except with them, of course. As that revolting old goat Lord Chesterfield said, "A lady doesn't move." If she shows signs of enthusiasm, a husband might worry about her libidinous nature, and wonder if her virtue could be depended on. Such views of women must once have made for a brisk trade in chastity belts, and in later times, employment for detectives.

It couldn't have made for great fun on the matrimonial couch, where sex was approved only for procreation. Geeze, as a friend of mine used to groan, what a system.

We learned further that while we were going to turn into fat old women with flabby arms, *they* were going to stay young, virile, and sexually irresistible forever. Women couldn't have children after forty or so, but men could go on siring them in their nineties.

Their best plan was to marry young (one of us, possibly) and divorce her when her arms got flabby. Then they would marry a little blossom of seventeen, who would have twenty-odd good years before the flab set in.

"You'll be about seventy when she's still in her thirties," we reminded them nastily. "What's going to happen to her when you die?"

"She can marry again," they said defensively, and we laughed jeeringly. What man would look at her at that age, second-hand goods as she would be, and just on the edge of flabby arms and droopy breasts? They told us that we should not be hostile about this situation, it was simply a fact of life that men remained young much longer than women, and there was nothing personal in it, what were we so sore about?

We reported this outrage to all our women friends, urging that no one accept dates with these male chauvinist pigs (though the term had not yet been invented) but needless to say it didn't work. Girls were going into the professions by that time, and we all figured on working for a living, but we still regarded marriage as the true and only meaningful end of life. One girl who was going into graduate school, and a good-looking girl, too, was so frantic to get married that she swore she would marry anyone and anything, rather than go home and admit that she still hadn't hooked a husband. Men are hooked, women are hookers. In various senses.

"She had been brainwashed, like the rest of us, into believing that a girl with no husband was a total failure. Better be married to a psychotic syphilitic dwarf than not be married at all." (Valuable prize offered for identification of quotation.)

Intelligence and higher education failed to liberate us. Generations of social pressure still made us believe that a woman who had not managed to attract and keep a man was a failure. A friend who had married late in life, and was widowed after a very short time, told me through her tears that her one consolation was that after all, she HAD been married.

"Everyone treats you differently if you've been married. They respect you," she explained. "It proves a man wanted you."

A bachelor who evaded the toils of would-be wives was admired by other males, and sought after by single women and hostesses in need of an extra man. He didn't have to worry about proving that women would want him. Recently he has had to be more careful, because men are always suspected of gay tendencies if they stay single too long. The proud old male bragging song "A bachelor gay am I" now has ironic overtones. However single males can always win admiration from their peers with the classic line, "Why buy a cow when milk's so cheap?" I thought that would have lost currency, but I heard it only a few weeks ago, and it was greeted with applause, as if it were witty. It should be noted in passing that hostesses are never in need of an extra woman.

This is a favourite discussion topic among antique females. A bunch of us were chewing it over recently, sneering at the male delusion that they stayed young and desirable forever, while we grew old and flabby, when one participant made an unforgiveable remark.

"I get lots of proposals of marriage," she said. We all turned and glared at her, but in spite of her insufferable claim, she wasn't looking at all smug or triumphant.

"The world," she explained, "is full of old goats hunting for housekeepers and nurses. They take a look at me and say, 'There's a good healthy one, she can push me in my wheelchair.' They can't believe it when I turn them down. They still think they're irresistible, they still think women have only one interest in life, and that's to get married. Huh! I should give up my freedom and lose my pension for the privilege of washing some old goat's socks? I spent the best years of my life having babies and ironing my husband's shirts, it's no damn fun. But they think I should feel honoured. One of them said he'd paid me the greatest compliment a man could pay a woman, I should feel flattered."

She didn't ask, out of pure human kindness, whether he'd looked in a mirror lately, to assess the value of the compliment.

For the last thirty years, the Pill and its successors have freed most women in the West from unwanted pregnancies. Attitudes toward divorce and abortion have changed. With less punitive views of premarital sex and pregnancy, these factors at least theoretically have given women more freedom.

Unfortunately a great many of them have used it badly. Teenage single parents have become one of the major social problems of our time; the provision of welfare and mothers' allowances has made mass production of unsponsored infants a career choice, a procedure which sets back by many years the hard-won emancipation of women.

In the dear dead days, the villains would have been forced into marriage at shotgun point, but the single-parent syndrome tends to be self-perpetuating, so that the girls probably had no father on the premises to wield the shotgun. The pattern looks like continuing forever until girls are cured of thinking that if they get pregnant, the man in the case will want to (or have to) marry them. Somehow girls must also be cured of thinking of marriage as the answer to everything, a delusion which persists in spite of all evidence to the contrary, including legions of battered and deserted wives and mothers.

Males and females alike must be cured of the delusion that having a baby is the answer to all women's problems, especially in times of exploding population. You know what's happened in China, or if you don't, you damn well better find out.

Women know that in many ways we're superior to men, who are far less responsible and disciplined; they're ten times as likely as women to commit violent crimes and spend years in jail. As Thorstein pointed out, they originally arrived at their ascendancy over us by being "massive," i.e., bigger and stronger. Can we ever compensate for our lesser mass?

We can keep in shape and learn some martial arts techniques. If they show any inclination to use their superior mass to abuse us, we never give them another chance, but walk out immediately because they *won't change*, no matter how earnest their promises.

We can stay in school and qualify ourselves for a profession, or at least a good job, so that we're not dependent. Then we can hold out until we find a good marriage prospect, and not take that psychopathic syphilitic dwarf just for the sake of being married.

Consider, for instance, Hillary Clinton. Lots of men dislike her, chiefly because she makes them feel insecure about their natural superiority to women. Bright, well-educated, independent, recognized by her husband and everyone else as the intellectual equal of top-level males, she illustrates what a woman can achieve by intelligence, ambition, and self-discipline. Of course it did her no harm to be good-looking as well, but she didn't depend on her looks alone. She was thus able to confidently accept the role of First Lady. This is not an unqualified privilege, of course. I used to think Bill was the world's best chance for sanity; he made his recent predecessors look like Fred Flintstone. But at this writing he's acting like your standard presidential klutz. I don't believe in— or give a damn about — his sexual carryings-on, but his handling of international problems can start World War III. He seems to be reverting atavistically to the mind-set of our Massive ancestors: solve all problems with a club, or in this case, bombs. No better than

George Bush. But let us not give up hope. By the time this is in print, he may have smartened up. Or we may all be smoking in a heap of radioactive ruins.

Hillary still, in a man's world, commands admiration and respect, without sacrificing an ounce of femininity. She makes film stars look like Barbie dolls, the Queen like a dowdy housewife, the Monaco girls like petulant spoiled brats. She has a great sense of style, but declines the role of half-wit clothes-horse. There's your role model for rising above the one-down position of women.

I still think it's a good idea to have a well-educated male with a smart wife at the head of the most powerful country in the world. So they're not perfect, show me someone who is.

There ARE nice men in the world, good husbands, Nonsexsnobs who don't want women to be inferior. If you find one, treat him well, and don't let your eye stray to the macho slob with a lot of sex appeal.

Remember: get an education, don't get pregnant, and don't kid yourself that either marriage or motherhood will solve life's difficulties. That's male propaganda, to keep women in the kitchen, barefoot and pregnant.

There is also a huge Snob organization against gays, who are one-down all round, for they can't have babies and they are often less massive than the macho boys. However, the sufferings and snobberies of gays and lesbians have been thoroughly documented, and indeed are the currently favoured topic in film and literature, so I'll not attempt them here.

Is there a reverse side of this most repressive of snobberies? Of course. Probably from time immemorial, women have struggled for freedom. But because of their lesser massiveness, they didn't have much luck with reprisals against their oppressors.

The first documented case of organized rebellion (which was also the first successful peace organization) is recorded jocularly in Aristophanes' *Lysistrata*. After the Peloponnesian War had been going on for twenty-one years, the wives of Athens, led by Lysistrata, decided to deny the guys access to the matrimonial sheets until they made peace. The girls hid in the Acropolis. Affected in their most vulnerable maleness, the heroes surrendered, and Lysistrata dictated the terms of the peace.

It's a nice story, but I don't think the ploy would work. Surely the guys would have found a way to use their massiveness to put the wives in their place (bed, kitchen), i.e., by slugging them over the head? Or they would simply have availed themselves of prostitutes, wouldn't they?

We have few records of tough wives who achieved ascendancy over their husbands: Socrates was nagged by Xanthippe, who (Xenophon said) had a "high temper," and as a result she has come down in history with the reputation of a shrew. They had three sons, none of whom supported the transmissibility of brains theory.

But let's not fool ourselves: our emancipation from chattel status would never have come about if it weren't for the Pill. It was no accident that the permissive sixties coincided with the availability of the Pill. Many women thought it was a philosophical principle, but there's no sense in proclaiming a philosophical principle if you're going to get pregnant every time you get into bed with a man. There are still no hundred-percent fool-proof contraceptives, and the burden of prevention still falls squarely on women, but we're nevertheless making progress. The evidence is the increased number of women in the professions, politics, the arts and sciences.

All of this has made men terribly anxious, and hostility between the sexes has become more acute than ever in history, chiefly because in the past women had no way of expressing their hostility that didn't get them a sock on the nose. This is still one of the male responses to women's rejection of chattel status; wife-battering cases have increased tremendously, and not simply because in the past the offence did not rate publicity. The altered behaviour of women, particularly through the feminist movement, has baffled and infuriated men who are unable to accept women other than as chattels.

Among these are certain judges, whose powers can be not only a filthy nuisance but a positive threat to women. Consider Justice Jean Bienvenue of Quebec Superior Court, who believes women can be much crueller than men: "... when they fall, women reach a level of baseness that the most vile man couldn't reach." The furor over his remarks "baffled" him.

Then we have Lewis Matheson, a provincial court judge in Glace Bay, Nova Scotia, who sentenced Colin Boutilier to two years' probation for forcible entry into his estranged wife's home. He wondered whether Mr. Boutilier was at fault, or if the trouble arose from "a very sensitive mate who is easily rattled." That was in 1995; the previous year, Judge Matheson sentenced a man for sexually assaulting teenage girls. This was serious, said His Honour, but "... if these were thirty-five-year-old women ... I might smile and throw this out of court."

Mr. Justice Kenneth Langdon, in Brampton, Ontario, imposed a light fine instead of a jail term for a man who punched and kicked his girlfriend, and stopped only when he was pulled away by two other men. He claimed the woman provoked the man. Family court judge Raymond Bartlett, in Dartmouth, Nova Scotia, told desperate wives looking for protection against brutal mates to go home and obey their husbands. A woman was subservient to her husband and must obey everything he demanded. It was her responsibility to do as he said. "The Bible says, God says, Christ says, that a woman is to be obedient to her husband," said Judge Bartlett, waving a Bible.

These are not isolated or unusual cases. Can these male chauvinist dinosaurs be educated into enlightenment? Unlikely, when the world is so much pleasanter for them when the Bible, God, and Christ are on their side.

I suppose I should be grateful to those young dinosaurs in the university cafeteria, so long ago. In order to refute them I started doing arm exercises with weights, and though I am now an old lady I by God still DON'T HAVE FLABBY ARMS. So nyaaaaah.

Worksnobbery 1

... the distinction among classes is very rigorously observed [at the higher stages of the barbarian culture] and the feature of most striking economic significance in these class differences is the distinction maintained between the employments proper to the several classes. The upper classes are by custom exempt or excluded from industrial occupations, and are reserved for certain employments to which any degree of honour attaches. Chief among the honourable employments in any feudal community is warfare; and priestly service is commonly second to warfare.
— Veblen, *The Theory of the Leisure Class*.

"I have no profession," said Cecil. "It is another example of my decadence. My attitude — quite an indefensible one — is that so long as I am no trouble to anyone I have a right to do as I like. I know I ought to be getting money out of people, or devoting myself to things I don't care a straw about, but somehow, I've not been able to begin."
— Forster, *A Room With a View*.

The serious and dedicated Snob should be familiar with both of the above-cited books, but he must read them warily and sceptically, like a devout Christian studying a serious work on atheism, in order to refute its heretical arguments. Such reading is like a journey in strange and dangerous country, where if one is not continually on guard, one runs the gravest risks of losing one's way, of being seduced, and of falling into the hands of the enemy. Snobbery is in this respect rather like a religion; one must accept its tenets unquestioningly, holding to them by faith, not logic.

In the contemporary world, you must, with Ronald Reagan (q.v., *infra*), believe that the rich deserve to be rich because they are hard-working, clever, and charitable, whereas the poor are poor because they are lazy, stupid and irresponsible.

William F. Buckley Jr. believes there are no poor people in the U.S.A. or, if there are, it's only because they are drunks and drug addicts, and who should know more about poverty than Bill, a Yale man with hundreds of honorary degrees? Just because Buckley Sr. was a multi-millionaire oilman doesn't mean that Jr. can't be an authority on The Poor.

One of the great paradoxes which makes snobbery so fascinating and bewildering has to do with work, at which we have glanced earlier, but which now must be studied in greater depth. Before we tackle this unappetizing subject, yet another brief historical review is indicated. Do I hear groans of protest? Don't be so lazy. Do you want to be a successful snob or don't you?

As we've seen, from the late-barbarian age forward, physical labour was degrading, and fit only for the lower orders. By the 18th century, and probably earlier, any form of gainful effort conflicted with the ideals of leisure, with belief in the baseness of productive labour, and the contempt of the aristocracy for the ambitious middle classes, who made their money *in trade*. But if it was discreditable to earn money, how could you get it? What a question. You inherited it, naturally.

If a young gentleman of good family had too many brothers and so didn't inherit enough to live well, and hadn't found a convenient heiress to marry, he could join the navy, and get rich by seizing enemy ships, as Captain Wentworth did in *Persuasion*. Such procedures were a bit difficult to distinguish from piracy, but Snobwise were beyond criticism.

In the post-barbaric, post-feudal world, it has in some quarters (notably among the clergy) been considered appropriate to praise hard physical work, claiming that it is ennobling. The harder the work, the more ennobling. That is, it was ennobling for the working class, not for the clergy themselves. This possibly came about because the clergy, or the upper ones, at least, for many generations had never lifted a hand at any kind of physical labour, or in many cases, had done nothing more strenuous than buttering up rich old ladies. The church, as we know, was second in prestige only to war as a gent's occupation. Young clergymen might play football with the villagers, or cricket, or baseball, or even croquet, depending on the local culture. If they were criticized for this unclerkly behaviour, they were apt to reply with *Mens sana in corpore sano*, which is unanswerable if you don't have any Latin. *Tr.* for linguistically challenged: A healthy mind in a healthy body.

In our present desperate times, the church has fallen on evil days. I have with my own eyes seen the local vicar mowing not only the lawn, but the considerable acreage surrounding the church, a task which in less dreadful eras should have been done by small boys, who could be bullied into believing it was their Christian duty. (Or their parents could be bullied into bullying the small boys, who are seldom deeply concerned with Christian duty.)

In passing, this vicar is exceedingly unpopular with the conservative element in the church (rich old ladies) and is suspected of closet-atheism. He has been known to refer to the Power which created the universe as "God, if you want to call it that." Such heretical pronouncements may be attributed to low (as well as Low) origins, or even agricultural ones, in view of his willingness to perform physical labour. Still, the ladies admit that closet atheism is preferable to some even more deplorable closet practices which afflict other religions.

In humanity's rude past, as we know from Veblen, hard physical work was degrading, and assigned to the lower orders: "Leisure is honourable and becomes imperative because it shows exemption from ignoble labour. The archaic differentiation into noble and ignoble classes is based on an invidious distinction between employments as honorific or debasing … " (Veblen, 92)

As we should know by now, the archaic tradition deprecates all productive labour, and necessitates slave labour to produce not for its own subsistence but for its masters. We still find, in the 18th and 19th centuries, many able-bodied males who take it for granted that they won't work at anything for their entire lives. Consider Jane Austen's Mr. Bingley, who never did anything but go riding and give or attend balls. But the rot sets in not long after: consider E. M. Forster's glorious Cecil, quoted at the head of this chapter: it can be seen from his defensive tone that he had been criticized for not working. Of course he wouldn't have been expected to do anything so depraved as *go into trade*, but even if he was wealthy enough to be an idle dilettante, by the end of the 19th century, he would be expected to have some sort of profession — preferably law or the church.

The ladies, while it was unthinkable that they do any real work, occupied their time with "accomplishments." If they had any aptitude, they would play the piano or the harp, or sing. Many of them had painting lessons, which occasionally led to dreadful scandals, since the young ladies (if we can trust the novelists) were sadly vulnerable to the attractions of their mentors; painters, as we all know, are seldom gentlemen, and could never be trusted not to take advantage of their fair pupils. Many a shockingly unsuitable romance arose from painting lessons.

The accomplishments available to less talented ladies are described by Mr. Bingley:

> It is amazing to me [said this amiable dimbulb] how young ladies can have patience to be so very accomplished as they all are ... They all paint tables, cover screens, and net purses. I scarcely know one who cannot do all this, and I am sure I never heard a young lady spoken of for the first time without being informed that she was very accomplished.
> (Austen 1957, 41)

It will be observed that all the "accomplishments" are useless and silly. Other acceptable occupations for young ladies were charitable errands: we find Emma visiting a poor sick family.

> Emma was very compassionate; and the distresses of the poor were as sure of relief from her personal attention and kindness, her counsel and her patience, as from her purse. She understood their ways, could allow for their ignorance and their temptations, had no romantic expectations of extraordinary virtue from those for whom education had done so little, entered into their troubles with ready sympathy, and always gave her assistance with as much intelligence as goodwill.
> (Austen 1957, 72)

Yeah, yeah, yeah. Emma was not quite twenty-one, and had never done a hand's turn of work in her privileged life, never known what it was to go hungry or suffer the smallest deprivation. It's difficult to believe she could be a whole hell of a lot of use to a poor sick family, apart from ordering a child from the cottage to take a pitcher and fetch broth from Hartfield.

Why didn't Emma take some broth in the first place? Are you mad? Emma carry a pitcher? Ladies and gentlemen did not carry parcels, let alone pitchers. Janeites will screech with outrage, but there's no doubt that Jane saw nothing wrong with the system.

If you're lazy enough, no doubt a life of such privileged leisure might be pleasant. However, for most of us the boredom would be close to intolerable. In Jane's time, ladies couldn't occupy themselves with sports; it was permissible to ride, if accompanied by a trustworthy groom, or they might walk in the shrubbery, but girls would have to wait another hundred-odd years to play tennis, or swim, or ride bikes. Emma therefore occupied her time with meddling in other people's lives, and very entertainingly, too.

Men were less prey to boredom: they could have a profession (law, the church) and still be socially acceptable. Medicine was suspect, not really a gentleman's occupation. Preferably, they might without losing face manage their estates, like Darcy and Mr. Knightley, and they could, in season, occupy themselves creditably by killing birds and animals: hunting was, and still is, of the highest Snobvalue. (If you hunt the right things: see Sportsnob, *infra*. No Snobcredits for shooting groundhogs or crows.)

Ladies whose incomes were unequal to their social position were in a tough spot: there was no way a Nice Girl could earn a living, other than as a governess, and this was far from a sinecure. It was also the first stage of the downward slide from the privileged class into the persecuted. No snobbery could be more deliciously satisfying than Governess Snobbery: here the *nouveaux riches* had at their mercy a young woman, possibly pretty, sometimes talented, well-educated by the standards of the time. Was she to be allowed to dine with the family, as if socially acceptable? Or did one banish her to the school room and the company of the brats? If she caught the eye of the man of the house, the opportunities for abusing her became practically limitless.

If a girl couldn't stick it as a governess, had failed to hook a husband, and had no money, she was in real trouble. She could go home and be a poor relation, treated like a servant and tolerated impatiently, or she could "find a protector," or go on the streets. There were a few intermediate occupations such as dressmaking or millinery, but they allowed for little more than keeping body and soul together.

Emma's competition, Jane Fairfax, was one such near-victim. She played the piano well, and was very pretty, but she hadn't any money.

The only way she could earn a living was as a governess, when, as she gloomily predicted, she would "retire from all the pleasures of life, of rational intercourse, equal society, peace and hope, to penance and mortification forever."

The horrors of such a life were sharply emphasized by the friendly agency of Mrs. Elton, the vicar's wife, herself only recently escaped from a family who made their fortune *in trade*.

> "... with your superior talents, you have a right to move in the first circles. Your musical knowledge alone would entitle you to name your own terms, have as many rooms as you like, and mix in the family as much as you chose; that is — I do not know — if you played the harp, you might do all that, I am very sure; but you sing as well as play; yes, I really believe you might; even without the harp, stipulate for what you chose ..."
> (Austen 1957, 239)

Wax candles in the school-room were among the glories promised to Jane, if she would just go to the superior Mrs. Smallridge, whose nursery establishment was liberal and elegant.

Nevertheless, even the most privileged, the most splendidly work-exempt, must sometimes have found things terribly tedious, and this problem was solved (for some of them) by what Veblen calls "the instinct of workmanship." Most human beings have a strong need to feel useful and creative. The most important thing *always* is to be rich, but *just* to be rich, and therefore frequently idle and useless, and as a result stupid, is galling. You have to be good at something, in order to be a successful Snob, or at least give the appearance of being good.

Gainful effort is now of course perfectly respectable, but in the late 18th and 19th centuries, it conflicted with the ideals of leisure, and with the belief in the undesirability of productive labour. People gifted in the arts might be exempt from the strictures against work, but what of the unfortunates who while not really talented, were vigorous and energetic? They must have chafed against idleness and uselessness?

The solution for such people was to engage in an interest which produced "immaterial goods." Fundamentally useless in any practical sense, these still may carry a little prestige today. Veblen lists some of them: "knowledge of dead languages and the occult sciences; of correct spelling; of syntax and prosody; of the various forms of domestic music and other household arts; of the latest proprieties of dress, furniture and equipage; of games, sports, and fancy-bred animals, such as dogs and horses."

Some of these, particularly sports, are now top-class occupations and money-makers, far more rewarding than war or the church. Unfortunately, they have been invaded by undesirable elements, snobwise, some of them with quite the wrong skin colour. (Racistsnobs may say they were far happier back on the plantation, with all the watermelon they could eat.)

Knowledge of the occult sciences is sometimes well-paid. CBC's "Tapestry," a programme which takes itself very seriously indeed, recently carried an interview with a Channeller who is paid enormous sums of money for "readings" — possibly of crystals, I should have listened more carefully. What she was doing, in fact, was fortune-telling, but in tones of such grandeur as to intimidate her customer, who was being informed about her past lives when I went out.

Before these social revolutions occurred, many young ladies with comfortable incomes and not enough to do became "artistic." They could thus be busy and important, superior to their do-nothing contemporaries, without descending to the shame of earning a living. These ladylike occupations survived, in a vestigial form, well into the 20th century. I believe I mentioned, under "Servants" a group of terrifying old ladies to whom my father referred as "the genteel poor." They were graduates of something called "Ladies' College," even in those days a comic anachronism, which purported to instruct girls of good family in the art of catching a husband, though naturally this was not blatantly advertised. As girls they had learned French, riding, music, painting, possibly tennis, and (optimistically) how to manage servants and to sweep a court curtsey. I wouldn't be surprised if they had also learned to net purses and cover screens.

Their French was awful, and their horsewomanship never included coarse matters like grooming or saddling their mount: their accomplishments were symbolic, valuable only for ladylike credits. By my time they lived alone in enormous old houses which had been built in the palmy days when a staff of servants was taken for granted. Now the big houses were cold and dirty, and each lady occupied perhaps two rooms, except when she entertained, which was seldom.

They were obviously dog poor, but the idea of working at a job (suppose a job existed for which they were qualified) was unthinkable, though some of the "gifted" ones gave classes in painting and music. It was a gallant but futile effort to live by the standards of the 19th century, while the 20th galloped remorselessly onward.

Is there a contemporary equivalent of these old girls? They were pathetic, but they were also shocking Oldsnobs. Their favourite topics of conversation were the difficulty of finding trained servants, and the annoyance of tradespeople who didn't know their place. Ah, how long ago it seems!

Perhaps I'm the contemporary equivalent, God help me. Veblen's list of "immaterial goods" gave me a bad shock. I still believe that correct spelling, syntax, and prosody have some practical value. As I once explained to a student who argued that there wasn't any point in learning to spell, suppose you want to go to a basketball game, but think gymnasium is spelled with a "J"? You could wander for hours looking for the "Jim" and miss the sign saying "Gym," and so never get to the game.

Most of the items on Thorstein's list would today be classified as hobbies, and respectable as such, Snobwise, but not as serious work. Their practitioners call themselves artists, even though they're not good enough to be professional artists. Consider all those hobby-potters, for example, who while wearing expressions of artistic austerity, turn out god-awful little pots and leaky vases, which they give you for Christmas, if you're not careful.

Grave Socsnob issues arose in the late 19th and early 20th century concerning the entertainment of university professors and members of the lower clergy. They didn't make enough money to be normally acceptable, but clearly their long years at university, their presumed wisdom and knowledge of some esoteric field, lent them a mysterious — but limited — glamour. They were always on a fairly shaky footing, snobwise.

"Because of a presumed superiority and scarcity of the gifts and attainments that characterize their life," says Veblen, "these classes are by convention subsumed under a higher social grade than their pecuniary grade should warrant ... as a consequence there is no class in the community that spends a larger proportion of its substance in conspicuous waste than these." (Veblen, 113)

We find a nice illustration of the social dilemma posed by scholarly practitioners in Nancy Mitford's *Love in a Cold Climate*. The nasty little narrator, Fanny, had just announced that she was engaged to marry an Oxford don, and Lady Montdore was shocked. Dons were unsuitable husband material.

"I daresay they're all right for dinner ... Montdore does have them over sometimes ... but that's no reason they should go marrying people."

But long before this, the old order had begun yielding place to new. The Industrial Revolution hit the Old Order like a blight. Modern weaponry made wars expensive and dangerous, even to the officers and gentlemen who hadn't previously been expendable cannon-fodder. A career in the church, while still a sinecure, became practically a guarantee of poverty. Successful businessmen grew too rich to be disregarded, in spite of Emma's contempt for people *in trade*. By the time George Eliot was writing, it was socially okay for a bright young man to make a living as a doctor.

The newly rich tradesmen in Britain gave jobs in their factories to agricultural serfs, infuriating the landed gentry because they now had difficulty in getting dirt-cheap farm labour and household servants. The factories exploited workers quite as badly as the squires had done, but they gave them a community and centre, and before you knew it, there were trade unions. With the abolition of those comfortable old familiars, serfdom and slavery, and the unknown quantity of unions to cope with, Socsnobbery was in a dreadful state of confusion. Unions created a brand-new form of Worksnobbery, as complicated as the feudal system; we will come to it shortly.

Work is respectable today, but the situation is far more complex because we have a confusing number of aristocracies, some of which cross each other in surprising ways. For example, a former weight-lifter can marry into the Kennedy tribe, if he happens to be big and good-looking and a successful, if lousy, actor. Of course a few generations back the Kennedy tribe itself was disreputable, with Old Joe involved during Prohibition in bootlegging, and a part of the mob scene. It is a symptom of the upward mobility of our age that his son could (with the help of a Harvard accent) become president of the United States. If he were a lowly and unsuccessful gangster, a mere gofer or hired gun, he would be unacceptable in any Snobcircle. But if you make enough money, no Snobcircles are closed to you.

It is a measure of the change in the last century that to have any social standing nowadays you almost have to work. Jackie Onassis, for example, worked for a publisher. She didn't need a job to make a living, obviously, but full-time leisure no longer carries much status. However, she could afford to take a pleasant job in a notoriously low-paying field, publishing, which is one of those oddities, classifiable as a scholarly pursuit, where you can be quite poorly paid and still have Snobvalue. Of course the likes of Jackie don't depend on their jobs for Snobsuccess.

Certain ethical problems arise from the new respectability of work. Wealthy women take jobs they don't need (in order to feel important?) while hundreds of bright young people are coming out of universities to join the jobless. Isn't it selfish and anti-social of the Jackie-types to hold down paying jobs in such circumstances? Why can't they do volunteer work? Alas, no kudos attach to volunteer work. You have to get paid, or it doesn't count. Snobvalue has turned inside out.

On the other hand, very little Snobcredit arises from working at a job in order to make a living. Glamour attaches to the jobs that are done by people who could easily afford to win "best-dressed" awards without ever showing up at the office. But working at home, even at something esoteric like research or writing, is subtly less apt to confer credit than having your own office in a big downtown building. This may be because if you are at home, you aren't meeting important and glamorous people with whom you have power lunches, etc., and can show off your best-dressed wardrobe.

Nothing confers less credit than staying at home, preparing meals, and looking after your kids, even if you enjoy it. You must get a job and hire a nanny (see Servantsnob).

Ideally, you should be highly paid to get real Snobjob-credit, though it's not necessary as long as you don't need the money. You can be quite poorly paid, and spend every cent of your salary on clothes, if you don't really have to work, and if the work has an aura of importance. Advertising and publishing both retain the aura, although almost all publishing jobs are abominably paid, and the lower echelons of advertising people are not highly rewarded, propaganda to the contrary, though both require university educations. People at the top make good money in both fields, but not the ones who actually do the slogging.

Generally, let's not equivocate: money is what matters. Few professors live in the jet set or the fast lane. CEOs, bank presidents, advertising execs, professional team-sports players, pop singers, and successful actors constitute the real aristocracy today. Doctors, dentists and, lawyers are now unmistakeably middle class, as are scientists and university professors, unless they have showbiz careers on the side.

There may be a few permanent social shibboleths, though I say this subject to correction. A friend of mine, an impecunious artist, grew extremely angry during a strike by garbage collectors. He was outraged that they should demand higher wages, when their work was the lowest of the low, requiring no special skills, no education, no intelligence.

"But it's essential," I argued. "If they go on strike, life is unbearable, especially in cities. Besides, they have to pay rent and buy food like the rest of us." That had nothing to do with it, according to my friend. He felt that garbage men should be forced to acknowledge their inferiority and accept a lower standard of living.

A little further discussion revealed that, if garbage men got the increase they were demanding, they would be making more money than my friend. *That's* what really bugged him: he would be valued lower than a garbage man. He worked as an illustrator for a printing company, designing calendars and so on, and painted in his free time. But illustrators, it seems, are a dime a dozen, and they can be got cheap, while people willing to do the garbage job are thin on the ground. Illustration-drawing has a low priority in our economy, whereas garbage collecting is essential to everyone's health and comfort. "Essential schmessential," he sneered.

This is another social puzzle. The arts demand respect, don't they? But there are too many artists of various stripes for many of them to make enough money to live on. *Everyone* wants to paint, or write, or act, or sing, or play an instrument, and only a tiny percentage can even get a job in the arts field, much less get rich. And the ones who do get rich, and exalted reputations, and their names constantly in the newspapers and on TV, are not necessarily the best. They're more frequently the ones who are skilled in manipulation, and have shoved their way to the top by sheer gall, or by knowing (in several senses of the word) the right people.

An interesting change in work prestige involves the ubiquity of the computer. In the dear dead days beyond recall, no self-respecting male would admit to being able to type. It might have been a useful skill, and to be a good typist was perfectly respectable for a female. But for a Real Man, it was more degrading than eating quiche. If you wanted to rate in the masculine world, you had a secretary to do your typing, and you dictated to her, in a manly and dominating way.

It is curious that no such infamy attaches itself to computer operation. Of course they wouldn't be caught dead using it simply for word processing, and most males deny having learned "keyboarding," which is in effect typing. But because the gadget is electronic, it is not only respectable but actually confers prestige. No presidential office could survive without its presidential lap-top. If you travel Business Class, observe the Notebooks which break out like a rash before the plane leaves the ground. Admission that you don't know how to use a computer puts you in the timorous-old-lady class, along with non-drivers and peppermint-eaters.

I did meet one defiant non-computer-user, this one female. She said grandly that her secretary was a skilled computer-er, so that she didn't need to know how, but she had a desperate, defiant note in her voice. She was pretending that computer-skills were beneath someone who had her own secretary. She didn't fool anyone for a minute.

"But don't you need one at home?" someone asked snidely, and she didn't actually burst into tears, but we all knew she had admitted to a fundamental inferiority. Computersnobbism is one of the most widespread and flourishing new Snobforms.

Snobbery is even more generally ubiquitous than the computer. White-collar workers may try to one-up blue-collars, but they don't find it easy, if the Blues make more money than they do. And the snobbery among the Blue-Collars is as fierce and unremitting as any among their self-constituted betters. It requires a chapter to itself.

Snobnote: Second Thoughts on Computersnob. While most people feel it essential to know everything about computers, and to be able to talk about them knowingly, there is a small but growing group of rebels who may hark back to an older, more aristocratic tradition. We want to *use* computers, of course, even if only to write letters or to get on the Internet and sneer at the lower classes, but we don't want to do all that hard work of learning how the damn things work.

We want to have a relationship with our computer like the one we have with our cars: turn the key (or press the button) and away you go. We don't want to know how the ignition system works, or how to change the carburetor. I predict that when computers have lost their novelty, that's how we'll regard them.

I don't know exactly how it will work, though. It would be a drag to have to take them into sort of computer-garage, but then it's a drag to have to take one's car into the garage, too. However, determined Snobs will find a way.

Snobnote: The Professions. The professions as we know them today hardly existed before the 19th century, in western society. (They rated pretty well in ancient Greece.) In England, doctors and apothecaries seemed to perform the same services, among Jane Austen's characters, and not long before, the leech was often associated with the barber. Dentists as we know them today were non-existent until around the 1840s since there were no practicable anaesthetics until then. Now they live in more than Oriental splendour in gated communities and drive Jags. No one dares criticize them, for an offended dentist is a fearful thought: friendly ones are terrifying enough.

Lawyers as a profession have always been generally hated (see Dick the Butcher in *Henry VI Part 2*, "The first thing we do, let's kill all the lawyers") but I know a lawyer who is an absolute angel and so won't hear a word against them, although I'll admit he is perhaps atypical.

Where do we draw the line, profession-wise? Medical practitioners would like to confine the title (of doctor) strictly to themselves. I know one who insists on addressing his dentist as "Mr. Smith." They also angrily repudiate the rights of chiropractors and veterinarians to so style themselves, forgetting that until very recently (19th century) they didn't themselves rate the honorific. What's more, some of them don't even know what it means: it comes from the Latin meaning "a learned person, a teacher." So don't get too uppity, you quacks.

Another Snobnote: Ladies and Publicity. "In the old-fashioned tradition, a lady has her name in the newspapers on only three occasions: when she is born, when she marries, and when she dies. Anything else is vulgar and ostentatious." (Babson, 114)

We append this note to the Work chapter, on the assumption that being a lady is a trade by which one makes one's living. In the early days, we kneaded loaves. Now we are careful not to be vulgar and ostentatious, while performing our duties of wearing furs and jewels to indicate how successful our husbands are, and keeping our names out of the newspapers.

9

Worksnobbery 2: Blue-Collar

Tanner: This man takes more trouble to drop his aitches than ever his father did to pick them up. It's a mark of caste to him. I have never met anybody as swollen with pride of class than Enry is... . Sherbrooke Road! Would any of us say Rugby! Harrow! Eton! in that tone of intellectual snobbery? [The Polytechnic] is his university ... You despise Oxford, Enry, don't you? ... Oh, if you could see into Enry's soul, the depth of his contempt for a gentleman, the arrogance of his pride in being an engineer ... He positively likes the car to break down because it brings out my gentlemanly helplessness and his workmanlike skill and resource.
— G. B. Shaw, *Man and Superman.*

So, he's got a PhD. He didn't know how to open the hood on his car. So I sent my eight-year-old kid over to show him.
— One of my neighbours, of another of my neighbours.

I consulted a specialist for information on snobbery in the blue-collar world, and was thrilled to learn that the antique taboo against drudgery still applies. The further you are from actual physical labour, the higher your Snobstanding. The aristocrats of the blue-collar world are the operators of heavy equipment like bulldozers and cranes, who simply sit in their mechanical monsters pushing levers and things, by which they effortlessly move mountains. Blue-collar aristocrats would never be caught picking up anything heavy, or carrying a load of anything. Then come elevator mechanics, who install elevators, and must in no circumstances be confused with elevator operators, who are lower than garbage men, of whom more later. Elevator operators may not do heavy lifting, except by proxy, but they are slaves to a buzzer, at the beck and call of anyone who can push the button, and so at the base of the totem pole. However, they're practically extinct, slain by mechanization.

Next in the blue-collar hierarchy come electricians and plumbers, who serve long apprenticeships. They make very good money but not as much as doctors and dentists and lawyers, though these trades would like to have us so believe. They are followed by sprinkler fitters, gas fitters (who do heating and air conditioning), and carpenters. Next step down we find drywallers, tilers, and carpet installers, who serve no apprenticeship and may have to actually carry things.

Each trade has its crew of labourers who do the fetching and carrying, the hard and heavy work. They are known as "Emmanuel Labour," because so many of them are Portuguese. "Don't carry that, get Emmanuel Labour to do it." Or get "a Portugoose," singular of Portuguese (usually intended facetiously). Although the despised Emmanuel Labour types can make as much money as the skilled trades, and sometimes more since they put in a lot of overtime, they have no prestige and are at the bottom of the hierarchy. It's rather like the armed services, with the distinctions between officers and enlisted men. The low men on the totem pole do not eat lunch with the élite trades.

Drivers of cement trucks are in a special category: no apprenticeship served, but they have to have a D license, which makes them special in blue-collar circles. They can eat lunch with upper tradespeople.

Here we have a paradox: while money is almost invariably the crucial issue, the taboo against drudgery continues to function, so that even today if you make your millions by lifting heavy things and getting your hands dirty, or if you have no special skills, you still are stuck at the bottom of the social totem pole. Nevertheless, Massiveness commands respect, or perhaps simply fear.

Élite trades heartily despise non-tradespeople. They distrust lawyers, and are contemptuous of academics. When teachers formed unions, they knew nothing about how to bargain or conduct negotiations. They only learned about it when the Tech streams brought in skilled tradesmen as teachers. They didn't have degrees, and the academics looked down their noses at them indulgently. But at the union meetings, the tradesmen looked down their noses at the bumbling academics, not indulgently but contemptuously. Humiliating but salutary, Snobwise. And, appropriately, educational for all concerned.

I took part in a teachers' strike once. How enthusiastically we academics joined in singing "Solidarity forever," how democratically we brandished our placards on the picket-line! And how snidely the old union types condescended to us, as we carolled our belief that "The union makes us free." The real tradesmen despised us, and didn't bother to conceal their contempt.

Certain teachers, however, boycotted the strike. Strikes, they said loftily, were for the labouring classes. *They* were professionals.

"Yah!" shouted the strikers. "Then you have no right to a pay increase!"

In this age of technology, surely our multifarious modern conveniences and labour-saving devices should emancipate us from hard labour? Not a damn bit of it. As Veblen reminds us,

> The strain is not lightened as industrial efficiency increases and makes a lighter strain possible, but the increment of output is turned to use to meet this want, which is indefinitely expansible, after the manner commonly imputed in economic theory to higher or spiritual wants.
> (Veblen, 111)

Blue-Collar Snobbery is currently suffering from dangerous pressures, with far-reaching and scary consequences. As we've seen, degrees of inferiority/superiority have in the past defined themselves primarily in two ways: that of gender, i.e., women by definition inferior, and that of work — the degradation of manual labour. Certain types of manual labour are more degrading than others, as we will see from the sociologically interesting case of garbage and sewage men.

Garbage men are well paid, since they belong to the ancient and powerful union of teamsters. So far as I can learn, their work does not require any highly sophisticated skills or long training. But as any survivor of a garbage strike will testify, *they are indispensable*. Without them, rotting masses of junk pile up in the streets, polluting the air and attracting rats. They have us over a barrel. Of course if the public was less slovenly and wasteful, it would be less at their mercy, but even though we compost and recycle like mad, there will always be *some* garbage, and we will need garbage men. What's more, it is unpleasant work and surely the people who do it should be amply compensated?

Here we come to one of the fascinating paradoxes of Worksnobbery. There is a powerful prejudice against paying people well to do unpleasant work, a feeling that we should have an Untouchable caste, as they do in India, who not only do the dirty work but are penalized for doing it. They do dirty work, and so are themselves intrinsically dirty and therefore contemptible, deserving of ostracization, *vide* the outrage of my friend, the illustrator, when the garbage men went on strike.

Of course if we were logical about this, we would equally despise doctors, particularly surgeons who have to burrow about in people's unhealthy and smelly insides. Instead we reward them generously. Well, they argue, but we save your lives! So do the garbage men, if it comes to that; if everyone refused to work at that unhealthy and smelly job, life in cities would not be worth living and we'd soon all be dead. And indeed certain medical specialists suffer from the derision of their own colleagues. I once knew a doctor whose specialization was in haemorrhoidectomies, and other afflictions of the posterior. He had to listen to many wearisome jokes by specialists in tidier parts of the anatomy.

"I have spent my life," he said poignantly one evening, after perhaps a few too many drinks, "peering up arse-holes."

There is an uptown word for this specialization: proctologist. It was popular for Snob-humorous effects in the medical fraternity, who in mixed company could make coarse "In" jokes which the laity did not understand. But then it was bandied about one night on "Seinfeld," and has since lost much of its cachet.

Apropos of this subject, and moving from garbage to sewage, there is a sharply defined hierarchy which varies directly according to the distance maintained from the — ah — raw material. The closer, the lower. A second-class stationary engineer at the Ashbridge's Bay sewage plant in Toronto had sufficient status to be safely distanced from the — er — product; he maintained a similar social distance between himself and co-workers who were obliged more nearly to approach … it.

Blue-Collar Snobbery is a life-study, but more detail would take too long for this modest project. Generally, its aristocrats are union members in skilled trades. The stronger the union clout, the higher the prestige. Great satisfaction derives from the power to frustrate Administration: we are all familiar with the sight of five men on a job which requires one to work and four to watch.

Because of technological change, many occupations which were exclusively the province of males, and frequently massive males, are now practicable for women. Some years ago there was a shortage of operators of heavy machinery in Ontario, and courses in this stern discipline were offered by the community colleges, with the promise of well-paid jobs. Disconcertingly, a lot of women turned up, demanding admission to the courses. No one had been far-sighted enough to issue a caveat against acceptance of women. Some of them forced their way into the courses, in a very unfeminine way. Some actually *passed* the courses. And then some actually got jobs, as Heavy Equipment Operators, the peerage of the Blue-collar world. It's still reeling from shock.

Technology, which was to set us all free from degrading and laborious effort, has made the superior massiveness of the male obsolete, in many occupations. It has also eliminated jobs for both males and females. And it has narrowed the gap between the White- and Blue-collar worlds: if your job consists of pushing buttons, what's the difference if they're on a crane or a computer?

Even worse, the facility of the Blue-collars with computers is quite as high as that of the Whites. In some cases higher. And higher than anyone is a generation of revolting little smart-ass kids who have been born computer-literate. Just about anyone who sets its mind to it can work a computer. *I'm* writing this on a computer, and in the technological-facility world, I rank low in the submoronic category. I hate my computer and it hates me. It is forever playing nasty little tricks on me. Let me call in an expert at $1 million per minute, and it purrs away like a dear little kitty, only to stop the minute his car pulls out of the drive. Nevertheless, at a primitive level, I too have learned to operate the bloody thing. But will never be good at it.

So. Where were we? Blue-collars.

Blue-collar work was for our first several millennia done by slaves, whose collars (if any) were probably made of iron, with no shirt attached. They hauled and heaved huge chunks of stone to build the pyramids, which Isaac Asimov called "the most useless project, without exception, ever undertaken by man." Why are we so impressed by the pyramids, which had no function except to provide tombs full of riches to guarantee that nasty selfish little pharaohs would suffer no deprivation in the next world? The pyramids were almost immediately raided and rifled by sensible thieves, who reasoned that they could make better use of the contents in this world. I suppose it could be argued that pyramids have some historical value, especially that of Tutankhamen, which escaped the raiders until AD 1922, when it was raided by archaeologists, all of whom died in agony immediately afterwards, slain by a remarkably durable curse which was put on the tomb 3,265 years previously, and serve them right, too. Don't believe it? *The National Enquirer* says there's indisputable proof! I forget now just what form the proof takes, but I know it's indisputable.

Herodotus claims it took 100,000 men thirty years to build the Great Pyramid, as a tomb for Cheops. They died like flies, but who cared? There were lots more where they came from. There is a New Age theory that building pyramids was beyond the ability of human beings in those non-technologized days, and the big lumps must therefore have been the work of technologically advanced Aliens from a yet unidentified planet. Herodotus figured that if you had enough expendable slaves, and no iron-clad closing date, you had no need to postulate Aliens. When you think of it, why would Aliens, if they were so advanced and brilliant, go to the trouble to build a tomb for Cheops, and stuff it with valuable property, shortly to be abstracted by ingenious thieves?

I mention this as an interesting, if silly, case of Specie Snobbery, arising from uncritical addiction to Star Wars and related entertainments dealing with pseudo-science.

A current pyramid theory claims the pyramids were not built by slave labour but by willing workers who cheerfully donated their time, because when the pharaoh became a god, in the next world, he would remember his dear helpers and see they too got a good deal in the next world. They just loved hauling those hunks of rock.

Yeah, sure.

The labouring class was stuck in its subservient position until well into the 19th century, as we've seen. Its recent assertiveness developed as a result of the formation of unions, which made subservience-demanding and -imposition unprecedentedly difficult. Up until that stage, the Upper Classes had had things pretty well their own way. There had been working-class movements, but they never got very far, although the French Revolution had looked rather ominous for the Aristocracy, however promising for proles and poets. (Bliss was it in that dawn to be alive.) But after all, they were a bunch of foreigners, what can you expect from Frogs? Or from poets? One of the most tiresome agitators in England was the poet Shelley, who was difficult to deal with because he came from a very U family. His biographer says,

> The first thought of the ruling oligarchy of mercantile capitalists and great landowners represented ... by the Tory party, when confronted with the new classes, was that of suppression ... Trade unionism was forbidden by the Combination Acts of 1799 and 1800; political demonstrations were broken up by the military; the punishment for food rioting or machine breaking was death or exile; a bill to limit the daily working span of children in the mines and mills to twelve and a half hours and set the beginning age at ten aroused a fury of denunciation.
> (Cameron, 181–2)

In passing, Cameron tells us, Luddite riots were not caused, as is popularly supposed, by the opposition of the workers to machinery, but were a protest against unemployment, low wages, and inflationary prices. So what else is new?

I mention this as it has become very vogue-ish, Snobwise, to call one's self a Luddite, in the belief that these were machine-breakers. According to one authority, they were called after their legendary leader, Ned Ludd, and the outbreaks were often attributed to "General Ludd." However, the *Encyclopaedia Brittanica* says they did too bust up machinery, especially stocking frames, because the quality of the stockings was so poor, and the prices so high. (How well I know the feeling, from the days when I wore stockings/tights and the damn things laddered the minute you put them on.) The Luddite demonstrations were non-violent until the government called in the military and shot them all dead. Again, it's nice to know that the workers were supported by a few enlightened Uppers, as well as poets, particularly Byron and Shelley, who were both Grade A poets and authentically U.

Contemporary self-styled Luddites are mostly people who don't want to have to learn to operate a computer.

The Uppers clearly saw the danger of unions, and they put up a splendid fight for their rights, nipping insubordination in the bud, and banning heretical literature. William Cobbett protested the use of flogging in the army, and got two years in jail. A bookseller, Daniel Eaton, was jailed and put in the pillory for publishing part of Thomas Paine's *The Age of Reason*. When things got sticky, Secretary of State Lord Sidmouth created an elaborate spy and police system, suspended *habeas corpus*, gagged the press, and made all reform agitation illegal. What do you expect when the dividends of honest aristocrats are attacked?

The proles won a few concessions, though it was a long slow process. Unions became legal, Blue-collar standards of living rose outrageously, until in some cases it was difficult to distinguish one class from the next. Everyone had cars and TV sets and indoor plumbing (where the Lowers kept their coal) and even luxuries like boats and season tickets to Leaf games, and a fur coat for the old lady. This was gall and wormwood to the Old Order; see letter in Snobexercise 1, Part 2. How were the upstart creatures to be kept in their place?

The lower orders became uppity. Hitherto there had been no disgrace like poverty, and people were deeply ashamed of their failure to be rich and respectable. Now they were claiming that it wasn't their fault if they were poor if they were paid derisory wages, if there was a depression and there were no jobs to be had. Unemployment insurance had to be invented.

Education became (sort of) free and universal, old age pensions replaced Poor Houses, welfare systems took over from The Dole and Poor Relief. In Britain, free and universal health insurance became available when the Labour Party was elected after the war; in the sixties, in spite of furious opposition, a national health scheme was introduced here in Canada, by the Liberals under Lester B. Pearson. The Liberals didn't want to get involved in anything so dangerously Leftish, but they could see that if they didn't, the New Democratic Party was going to win the election. They therefore appropriated the NDP's health program, and have been congratulating themselves on their enlightened, courageous and visionary platform ever since. These measures had a social levelling effect. In the past, medical bills often meant bankruptcy for The Poor who had the misfortune to become ill. They were so terrified of doctors' bills that they preferred to be killed by their disease rather than by the burden of debt.

Naturally, all this social spending outraged the Old Régime, who believed it was being done at their expense, and theirs only. It is now being blamed for all our financial woes, although these would never have become acute if the tax system were more rational.

"Labour has brought us to this!" was the cry of an Old Régimist living in a dusty Toronto mansion (dusty because she couldn't get Help). Her income was so eroded that she was obliged to rent some of her sixteen rooms to students. Said erosion was caused by insane spending on such foolishness as old age pensions, for the spendthrift poor who didn't save their pennies in their youth.

Well, as we shall see, the Olds & Uppers lost the battle but not the war, which is still going on, and has in fact been stepped up with subtle and crafty techniques in the last few years. We will examine this phenomenon later.

You will remember, if you are the kind of reader we admire, the quotation at the head of this chapter from Shaw's *Man and Superman*. We will close with another borrowing from the same source. John Tanner has been mocking his chauffeur, Straker, for Worksnobbery. Octavius, the idealistic poet, comes to Straker's defence: "I believe most intensely in the dignity of labour."

Straker: "That's because you never done any, Mr. Robinson."

10

The Housework Dilemma: Slavery or Squalor?

… it is questionable if all the mechanical inventions yet made have lightened the days' toil of any human being.
— J. S. Mill.

"She's a bitch and a sadist and a good housekeeper," said a character in a Peter de Vries novel: a damning indictment of an acquaintance "… who fancied herself a sensitive aesthetic type, far above distaff chores."

And yet to be a bad housekeeper was damning, too. "Who of late for cleanliness / Finds sixpence in her shoe?" carped Bishop Richard Corbet. He claimed fairies once rewarded good housewives with that big fat mythical sixpence until, in the degenerate days of the 17th century, "foul sluts in dairies" might fare as well as the most deserving, let her sweep her hearth as clean as she would. Typical male propaganda. When it comes to housework, you can't win, whether you work your fingers to the bone for a figmental sixpence, or settle for being a foul slut.

"What do you do about housework?" a travelling acquaintance once asked me. She was trying to decide whether I was worth cultivating socially. She'd already checked my husband's profession, whether I'd been to an okay university, what kind of car(s?) we drove. Housework was the crucial test: top marks for live-in help, B for a daily, C for a weekly cleaner, abject failure for do-it-yourself. So I said flippantly that I ignored it, but I was lying. You can't ignore housework, unless you adopt the method of famous "screaming queen" Quentin Crisp, in *The Naked Civil Servant*. His message of hope to a drudging world: "There is no need to do any housework at all. After the first four years, the dirt doesn't get any worse."

To obviate bedmaking, Quentin practised sleeping on his back "as still as if I were in my coffin. I slid out of bed in the morning like a letter from an envelope. Except for the thickening film of sullied cold cream ... on the pillow-slip, no one would have been able to detect that my bed had been slept in."

He had to jump in the air while putting on his trousers to avoid trailing them in the dust, but otherwise "this omission brought in its filthy wake no disadvantages whatsoever." (Before anyone jumps me, "screaming queen" was Quentin's own designation for himself.)

But there *are* disadvantages, there are, there are. After a while you can't find anything, you have nothing to wear, there are no dishes to eat off.

Classically, housework and snobbery have been indissolubly linked. Nowadays upward mobility is praiseworthy, but until the emergence of a rich middle class there was no ambiguity about social status; the big joke in Moliére's *Le Bourgeois Gentilhomme* is the rich tradesman's presumption in wanting to become a gentleman. He should have *known his place*, and stayed in it.

But the *bourgeoisie* refused to accept a humble role. If they could pay servants to do their dirty work, they were as good as the Earl of Snob. And housework *is* dirty work. What's more, it's never done.

For most of recorded history, there has been little change in the status of housework. It's always been women's work, a degradation in itself, as we know from the researches of Thorstein Veblen. (Any kind of manual work is demeaning.) The industrial revolution brought factory jobs, and for the first time since the bubonic plague epidemics, there were shortages of poor people for servants. In the great wars, munitions factories and the armed services devoured potential domestic help. However, the Industrial Revolution brought a balancing factor, with mechanization of every variety of labour; whether they actually lightened labour is arguable, but they certainly threw lots of people out of jobs.

Naturally, commercial and industrial labour-saving devices came before domestic ones. Until the invention of the vacuum cleaner, the most sophisticated cleaning device — apart from the housemaid — was the carpet sweeper.

"How did you keep the house clean, before you had a vacuum cleaner?" I once asked an elderly lady who, after a moment's reflection, said, "We didn't."

Twice a year, carpets were taken up, hung outside and beaten to get out six months' accumulation of dust. By modern standards, most houses were filthy. In general, rich employers of servants probably had relatively clean homes, while the poor had a choice: they could work themselves to death keeping the place clean, or die of infections from grunge accumulation.

All the Clean things — indoor plumbing, vacuum cleaners, clothes washers/dryers, dishwashers — came with a rush in the middle of the 20th century. The rich had had bathrooms and "Hoovers" way back when, though often one bathroom per house was considered ample, as we know from Angela Thirkell's nostalgia for the little maid with the cans of hot water.

By the 1960s, everyone had all mod cons, and went nuts on cleanliness. The advertising business practically existed on cleaning and washing products. Happiness was keeping your floors immaculate. The happiest people who have ever existed were ladies who had discovered how clean they could get their children's socks with Tide. The most miserable were those whose husbands had ring-around-the-collar.

As gadgets like vacuum cleaners and washing machines became available, there was much anxiety that housewives would get in trouble with all this new leisure time on their hands. The *Ladies Home Journal* worried that too many women were "dangerously idle." Editors of women's magazines, presumably career women, condemned career ambitions in others, preaching that housework was a full-time career in itself. So it is, if you believe a home must be as immaculate and dehumanized as an advertising photograph. No messy kids, dogs, cats, husbands, whatever, allowed to violate its flawless cleanliness.

Housework was increasingly automated. Houses were heated by comparatively clean gas and electricity, instead of coal and wood. Innumerable gadgets lightened the housewife's burden. Yet she was not content. A plethora of books like *Diary of a Mad Housewife* described the desperation of the homemaker, frantically cleaning floors and walls, while cooking a gourmet dinner to impress her husband's boss, prior to appearing — serene and exquisite — in a stunning dinner dress.

When the domestic servant was on the edge of extinction, there was a deliberate effort to glamourize housework. Women were advised, when asked what they "did," NOT to say *Oh, I'm just a housewife.*

There's nothing "just" about it, the glossies urged, and a favourite filler listed the skills of the humble Mum: psychologist, chef, chauffeur, teacher, referee, etc. Women were encouraged to take pride in their sparkling homes, even if kids dimmed the sparkle as fast as Mum created it. Advertisers chimed in, urging the purchase of expensive appliances and powerful cleaners, in the interest of germ-free hygiene.

One solution was to keep certain rooms sacrosanct. The families actually lived in the kitchen and basement, while living- and dining-rooms were permanently closed, furniture and lamps shrouded in plastic. They were opened once or twice a year — at Christmas, when important visitors called, at funerals. Everyone sat hushed and awe-stricken in the sacred chairs, trembling with fear of spilling something.

Kids in these families could never have a pet, because animals shed hair and have other slovenly habits. The fireplace, except for a ceremonial flame at Christmas, was never lighted: fires are dirty. The reward for these privations came in compliments such as "You could eat off her kitchen floor."

Anthropologist Margaret Mead documented the fifties' attitude to housework in *Male and Female*: At first it really looked as if American life was being enormously simplified. But instead of creating more leisure — time to play with the baby, to curl up with a book — the new equipment made the homemaker's life more exacting in "the impossibly clean and polished home."

The next great revolution came with the acceptance and ubiquity of the working wife, and that means working outside the home, for pay. There have always been women who worked outside the home, but in earlier times they were stuck with menial and ill-rewarded tasks (charring or washing, done by the desperately poor) or with prostitution, at which a few got rich and the majority got syphilis, or murdered. But these didn't count as "working" in its current sense. Even now, the wife who stays home and runs the house isn't *seriously* working.

With education for women, more big changes. By acquiring marketable skills, women could get decent jobs which they were reluctant to give up to stay home scrubbing floors. In response to the query "*What do you do?*" who wouldn't prefer to say, "I'm a computer operator/brain surgeon/aesthetician/nuclear physicist" rather than the dismal stock response, "Oh nothing. I'm just a housewife."

The Tide has turned. Mr. Clean is passé.

Now research shows that women in the U.S. have been eliminating half an hour of housework for every hour they work outside the home — or up to 20 hours a week; can you work that out in terms of soiled laundry, of accumulations of dust bunnies under the bed? I would rather not think about it.

So here we are today, confronted by the old choice: be a slave to the blasted house, or live in squalor. Many women have opted for squalor, settling for a clear track to the door so that they can get out and go to work. Housework as a vocation is obsolete. Even older women, after lives dedicated to the immaculate home, have stopped making beds. They eat out, order in Chinese or pizza, defrost frozen dinners, decline to stay in the kitchen bakin' cookies. Dog and cat hair accumulates under and on furniture. It's alleged that wives no longer mend their husbands' clothes, but stick them together with a glue gun; can this be true?

Husbands who yearn nostalgically for the old days of "gracious living," with the house-proud wife in her immaculate home, are told brutally to get up off their duffs, turn off the football, and do the vacuuming themselves. In double-income families, most husbands still cop out on housework, or do it with deliberate inefficiency, hoping it will be snatched from their hands with an impatient, "Here, let me." Children are conscripted: "Whose turn is it to stack the dishwasher?" Result — dirty dishes, incessant nagging, bickering and cheating among the brats.

The one bright spot on the housework horizon is the Domestic Engineer, the erstwhile cleaning woman. She is a new breed, a business woman who has elected to do disagreeable work because there is always a demand for her services, whereas jobs in other fields are almost non-existent. She sets her own rates and hours. If the customer isn't satisfied with her terms, then the customer can look elsewhere, because the Domestic Engineer always has a backlog of hopefuls waiting for her to have a free day.

An inefficient and reluctant housekeeper myself, I have a team of DEs who blast through the house like a benign hurricane, once a month, leaving it sparkling. I'd have them oftener, but I can't afford it, for they are fearsomely expensive.

My great fear is that one day Domestic Engineers will disappear. Everyone still hates housework, especially other people's, even if it's well-paid and they're free agents, not serfs. They have to go home, after working all day, and do their own housework.

If the DE does disappear, where will we be? In our old dilemma, caught between slavery and squalor, servile good housewife or foul slut. Will someone please, quickly, invent a robot intelligent enough to do the housework, and stupid enough not to hate it?

Snobnote: Quentin Crisp (né/née Denis Crisp, "as my name was before I dyed it"). Famous British "screaming queen" and queer (his preferred designation; he only uses "gay" once), born in 1908 "when one of the largest meteorites the world has ever known was hurled at the earth." According to Quentin, it was intended for him, but it missed and landed in Siberia. He came out of the closet almost immediately and "paraded the dim streets of Pimlico, blind with mascara and dumb with lipstick." His autobiography, *The Naked Civil Servant*, is one of the funniest books ever written. Thames Television based an award-winning film on it, which I've never seen, but for which I will give large sums of cash if I ever get any. The book is a Good Wordsnob's delight.

Snobnote: We append the first verse of *The Fairy's Farewell*, by Bishop Richard Corbet. This is a shameless hunk of male propaganda, designed to make women feel guilty about their housework. Fairies *never* left sixpence in any good housewife's shoe, even if she swept till she was blue in the face. But to admit it was to brand yourself a foul slut. Oh very crafty, Bishop Corbet, you old goat!

> Farewell, rewards and fairies,
> Good housewives now may say
> For foul sluts in dairies
> May fare as well as they,
> For though they sweep their hearths as clean
> As they were wont to do,
> Yet who of late for cleanliness
> Finds sixpence in her shoe?

Summary of Part 1

We have so far discussed the theory of snobbery, and presented a rough sketch of its history, from barbarian times forward. We have seen that snobbery (having established itself by massiveness, let's not get into that again) was demonstrated by: (1) the axiomatic inferiority of women and servants/slaves; (2) the degradation of productive labour and dirty work; (3) the contaminating effect of association with productive labour and dirty work; (4) the entitlement of the upper classes to the improving and refining influence of leisure, requiring armies of slaves and/or servants.

It is important to remember that dirty and laborious effort is okay Snobwise if it is NOT productive. It is admirable and prestigious to half kill yourself and get filthy playing football, but ignoble and degrading if you're working as a navvy. If navvies still exist. They've probably been extinctified by large machines. There is no such word as extinctified, but there should be.

Slavery provided the most satisfactory exercise of snobbery in history; we shall not see its like again. Of course the slaves weren't particularly enthusiastic about it, and sometimes they did make their owners rather nervous, as paradoxically they often displayed greater Massiveness than their betters. However, they're gone, and there's no use whining about it.

Servants have also gone, except in privileged households, and their presence there is a far from unqualified privilege. They are no longer grateful for a sound training in domestic service, although splendid opportunities abound on all sides. Such servants as we have are rarely satisfactory, and we cannot correct them with a damned good whipping, as we did in the golden days. Few of us actually have a whip on the premises, were it otherwise feasible.

In these degenerate days, Snobs have to make do with machines, robots, and so forth for domestic work, as noted *supra*. Some of these may be efficient, but Snobwise they are far below even honest Molly, who used to wait on common days, even though she might have been only a rough girl from the country, and quite untrained. In passing: some servant work may be quite clean (we no longer require them to empty chamber pots, unless we're Sadismsnobs) but it is still degrading, because that's what servants are *for*, to be inferior.

Women are still with us, of course, but they have been ruined for traditional Snobpurposes by education. Many are worse Snobs than men, and it is unsafe to beat them into good behaviour, even when they deliberately provoke their betters. Indeed, many women have taken advantage of their new freedom by behaving *worse* than men, particularly behind the wheel of a car. Which takes some doing.

While it has been established that leisure is indeed improving and refining for the Uppers, it is unfortunately true that its effect among the Lowers is not happy, leading as it invariably does to idleness, drunkenness, and life-long dependence on social assistance.

The traditional Snob must still demonstrate his superiority by proving that he is richer and more successful than his associates, but is obliged to suggest it in a rather unsatisfying way. As we've seen, display of wealth is now considered bad form, which takes a lot of the fun out of being rich; how is one to impress people with one's superiority, without a little potlatchery? Majestic condescension to inferiors may entail considerable risk of broken noses, black eyes, etc. Nor can ancient ancestry (even if recent and fictional) be invoked, without risking the response of the raised eyebrow. This may take a lot of the best sport out of being rich and important.

Most Snobsuperiority is, of course, based on wealth but nowadays some means must be found of demonstrating such wealth so craftily that no one can accuse you of vulgarity, and this gets trickier and trickier.

There is another form of Snobbery, which is considered in some circles superior to the familiar kind (Traditional, or "Tradsnob"; sometimes Badsnob) of purely financial superiority. This superior superiority may be achieved by the comparatively poor, and labelled *connoisseurship*, or Goodsnob. That is, it's based on values more exalted than mere wealth, if you'll forgive the expression, and if such a thing is possible. It is often involved with ecology, animal rights, mysticism, and something enormously elevated known as "spirituality." This is not to be confused with religion, than which it is much more esoteric. Its possessors decline to define it, replying with dignity when you ask for definition, "I think you know very well what I mean."

This Highersnobbery is strewn with landmines, since it has high potential for phoniness and fakery, as manifested in New Agery and pseudo-mysticism, but some of its manifestations may inspire awe and anxiety in more conventional Snobs, as you'll see under Wordsnob, Foodsnob, and so on.

Next we have provided some Snobexercises, after which it's on to Part 2, and the emergence of Post-modern Snobbery!

Snobexercise 1

Ambitious Snobs who are not quite sure of themselves may find it useful to work out on a few Snobmuscle-building exercises, so that they may avoid traps which will betray them to longer established Snobs who will look down noses at their artless efforts.

The following Letter to the Editor appeared many years ago, when some precognitive wisdom made me cut it out and keep it. I never dreamed that I might one day write a *Book of Snobs;* how splendid to run across it in my hour of necessity. Your assignment is to appraise this for Snobexpertise, endeavouring to place the writer as representative of Old Money, New Money, Jumped-Up Prole, or whatever category seems to you most probable.

Note: Certain people have accused me of inventing this letter to fit my purposes. I can only assure you, as Dave Barry so often does, *I am not making this up*. I can show you the clipping, yellowed with age though it is. I must admit, though, to shivering with ecstasy every time I re-read it: it's so unbelievably perfect.

> Those of us with large incomes are shocked whenever we visit the large shopping centres or downtown department stores. This is particularly so at this time of year. What shocks us is the sight of scores of poorly dressed people purchasing heavy goods, jewellery, silverware and the like, all of which must cost them

> two or three months of pay. The majority of these working folk surely must go deeply into debt each Christmas. It is literally impossible for the average affluent [citizen] to imagine waking up on New Year's morn thinking he was in debt up to his proverbial ears.
>
> Unfortunately the same does not hold true for members of the middle and lower classes of our society. For some odd reason (compulsiveness probably or a desire to keep up with the rich Joneses), many of these working folk do wake up on Jan. 1 with not only a headache from too much strong drink but an empty feeling in the stomach caused by facing a new year filled with debt and more debt.
>
> I feel terribly sorry for these unfortunates and wish there was someway whereby the government could curtail their foolish spendthriftness.

No name was signed to this remarkable Snobdocument. Shows how long ago it appeared, before correspondents were required to identify themselves.

How does it rate Snobwise? It betrays the worst possible Snobtechnique: the writer starts off bragging about her large income. As we know by now, *wealth is unmentionable*, and all rich people must continually claim to be poor, and to be living in a very deprived state.

"As you see, we have no staff!" is one of their cries. "You see how simply we live!" It's a kind of Rich People's Union rule, because if you admit you're rich, you're asking to be pestered by poor relations and other deadbeats, for handouts. (They may have no *resident* staff, but you can bet they've got a "daily" coming in, both indoors and outdoors.)

One suspects that Ms. Large Income is out of touch with current trends and probably lives reclusively, unaware that a mink coat no longer carries prestige. "Poorly dressed" may mean wearing jeans or some grunge garment which is currently high fashion.

There are some Old Money types who bitterly hate seeing the less privileged enjoying things like jewellery, silverware, and similar junk, which they feel should be reserved for the Superior Classes only. They want to return to the good old days when The Poor were clearly labelled as such, lived in leaky thatched cottages, went out charring, and pulled their forelocks respectfully when Lady Catherine de Bourgh drove by in her pony phaeton. Such nostalgia is sometimes expressed by the genteel poor, who live in fear of finding the Lower Classes trying to condescend to them. It is a great trial to the large income set when the ex-Poor start trampling on the preserves of the Superior Classes in areas such as European travel.

My guess is that our correspondent is either Genteel Poor or that some Anti-Snob is having us all on in a bad taste joke.

Valuable Snoblessons can be learned from this little exercise. First, as mentioned, you must never NEVER boast about your "large income." The worst possible form. Second: she is begging for Reverse Snobreactions: "None of her goddamn business if we want to buy heavy goods, jewellery, and silverware. And how does she know we can't afford it? Maybe she's just jealous." Third, condescension is an unloveable habit, and your pity for the unfortunates will not be appreciated. If you pursue your kind wish for government interference with their Christmas shopping, they may even throw rocks at your carriage as you drive by their hovels. Finally, you shouldn't put such sentiments in writing. There's always some malicious potential author of Snobbooks who is just hungering for such choice tidbits to discredit your motives, and make you a laughing-stock among better practised Snobs.

Snobexercise 2: Practice in Snobrecognition and Snobanalysis

Still insecure about your Snobskills? Let's do another exercise, just for fun and to build your confidence. Our text is Samuel Butler's poem, "O God! O Montreal!", which is peculiarly well-adapted for use by Canadians, since some of them may know where Montreal is.

> O God! O Montreal!
>
> Tucked away in a Montreal lumber room
> The Discobolus standeth and turneth his face to the wall.
> Dusty, cobweb-covered, maimed and set at naught,
> Beauty lieth in an attic, and no man regardeth:
> O God! O Montreal!
> Beautiful by night and day, beautiful in summer and winter
> Whole or maimed, always and alike beautiful —
> He preacheth gospel of grace to the skins of owls,
> And to one who seasoneth the skins of Canadian owls;
> When I saw him I was wroth and I said, "O Discobolus!
> Beautiful Discobolus, a Prince both among Gods and men,

What doest thou here, how camest though hither, Discobolus,
Preaching gospel in vain to the skins of owls?"
And I turned to the man of skins and said unto him, "O thou man of skins,
Wherefore hast thou done thus to shame the beauty of the Discobolus?"
But the Lord hardened the heart of the man of skins,
And he answered, "My brother-in-law is haberdasher to Mr. Spurgeon.

"The Discobolus is put here because he is vulgar,
He has neither vest nor pants with which to cover his limbs,
I, Sir, am a person of most respectable connections —
My brother-in-law is haberdasher to Mr. Spurgeon."
Then I said, "Oh brother-in-law of Mr. Spurgeon's haberdasher,
Who seasoneth also the skins of Canadian owls,
Thou callest trousers 'pants,' whereas I call them 'trousers,'
Therefore thou art in hell-fire and may the Lord pity thee!
Preferrest thou the gospel of Montreal to the gospel of Hellas,
The gospel of thy connection to Mr. Spurgeon's haberdashery to the gospel of the Discobolus?"
Yet nonetheless blasphemed he beauty, saying, "The Discobolus hath no gospel,
But my brother-in-law is haberdasher to Mr. Spurgeon."
O God! O Montreal!

As the perceptive reader will immediately observe, there are several varieties of snobbery displayed in this poem. There is the obvious one of Social Snobbery — the man of skins bragging about his connection with the very important Mr. Spurgeon (of the Montreal Spurgeons). Next the Wordsnobbery: "Thou callest trousers 'pants,' whereas I call them 'trousers.' Therefore thou art in hell-fire." As all good Wordsnobs know, 'pants' is stigmatized by the *Oxford* as "colloq." It has a colonial, as opposed to a Brit. flavour, along with prole associations.

There are other, more subtle snobberies. Quite apart from the simple "pants," we have generally throughout the poem classic British condescension to colonial crassness; we have righteous or puritanical (lower-class) snobbery, condemning the Discobolus for vulgarity because he has no pants [*sic*] on. We also have Artistic Snobbery, whereby the poet despises the owl-skin seasoner for his insensitivity to beauty, which is perceived by the more cultivated visitor. An excellent Snobperformance.

Did you pick up on the contribution to Snobvalues in my introduction? "Some Canadians may know where Montreal is." That "may" is Snobgenius, if I do say so myself, since by a single word it contrives by implication to sneer at: (a) the Canadian education system, which allows people to live in ignorance of the location of Montreal, or even of its existence; (b) non-Canadians and their disgraceful lack of knowledge about our important country; and (c) Canadian chauvinism, which naïvely assumes that the rest of the world gives a single damn about Canada or Montreal or our geography.

So (b) contradicts (c): so what? Goodsnobs don't waste valuable time on logic. In fact, snobbery almost by definition defies logic.

Snobexercise 3 and Case History

We first thought of the journalist Barbara Amiel's activities as another Snobexercise, like that preceding, on which to exercise your developing Snobmuscle, and you may indeed do that. Later we decided that she offered a good illustration of failed Snobtechnique. She should be carefully studied and contrasted with the Snobmodel in the next chapter.

As we know, really skillful snobbery at the highest level should not be perceptible as snobbery. It must be veiled, merely suggesting in the subtlest possible way, to all listeners and observers that they are — possibly through no fault of their own — just a trifle inferior. The expert snob may gently suggest that it (we've abandoned he/she, remember) ... does not despise its inferiors, or regard them as in any way undesirable; perhaps there are extenuating circumstances, they have suffered misfortunes. There is an implied gentle condescension in such a position, but the successful snob must carefully avoid any betrayal of belief that it is in any way superior.

Any resentment by the inferior should be attributed (with a regretful sigh for the frailty of human nature) to envy. We discovered a rich vein of envy-deploring in Barbara Amiel, as documented in her columns in *Maclean's*. Unfortunately, she fails on the gentle condescension technique, which must be done with great skill and subtlety or it doesn't work. Our Barbara's technique of slamming down with a sledge-hammer is an example of How Not To Snub Your Inferiors.

My documentation of the Amiel technique begins with the October 28, 1989, issue of *Maclean's*, which I found in the laundromat one night when my washing machine broke down, leaving me stuck with several hundred pairs of dirty socks and a lot of wet towels, since my son had recently paid me a visit. It is illegal for laundromats to stock magazines less than ten years old; 1989 was one of the most recent years, and so in high demand. When I read Barbara's article, I at once recognized the didactic value of Barbara's article at once, and so sneaked the magazine in with the bath-mats and brought it home. Yes, reader, I stole it, and the laundromat can sue me, but I did it in the interest of scholarship.(Attention! Note high-class reverse snob action: Serene acknowledgement of repairing to resorts of the underprivileged, in fact a real prole place, the laundromat. Notice also brazen admission of theft, justified by exemplary objective of scholarship. True connoisseurs of Snob will pick up on the Brontë echo: "Reader, I ... ")

Well, anyway, Barbara's article is called "In Defence of the Right to Spend," and it combines several interesting (if inelegant) forms of snobbery. See if you can identify them.

It seems that one of Barbara's colleagues, Fred Bruning, had written an article ("New Standards of Outrageous Excess") about ostentatious birthday parties thrown by Gayfryd Steinberg and Malcolm Forbes. Gayfryd, the wife of an American multi-millionaire, spent $1 million on her party. No dollar value was given for the Forbes binge, but it took place in Morocco, in an air-conditioned party tent, with costly diversions like Berber horsemen, belly-dancers, Elizabeth Taylor, and live models posing as figures in 17th-century paintings. Bruning thought that such extravagance was "profligate" and that it diminished the work of "those who for their labours, do not earn millions."

Barbara asks, "Could envy have actually reached such pathological proportions ... ?" and suggests Mr. Bruning should see a psychiatrist. The institutionalization of envy, she says, is the great thrust of our age. (For truly advanced snobs, such parties are a foretaste of hell.)

She had once sat next to Mrs. Steinberg at a literary luncheon. Gayfryd was wearing a huge necklace of what Barbara took to be "faux" jewels (faux = Snob for fake) but later discovered to be real rubies and pearls. Was Barbara envious? Not a bit! "'Isn't that nice,' I thought." (How did she learn they were real? Did Gayfryd brag? Did Barbara say, "Hey, I like your faux jewels," and Gayfryd reply, "These ain't faux, you stupid working journalist, they're Real!"?)

After lunch, Barbara went back to work, to earn a needed $2000 by staying up three nights to write a piece on Margaret Thatcher for *Chatelaine*.

How many varieties of snobbery did you spot?

First, an easy one, is the name-dropping. Barbara casually tosses out the fact that she associates familiarly with a female billionaire wearing a high tonnage of pearls and rubies — "I had been breaking bread next to a cool million or two worth of jewels."

Next, a professional Snobcoup, disguised as a confession of humble effort: working-girl Barbara stays up nights to earn a mangy $2000 writing an article for *Chatelaine*, about Margaret Thatcher. If she was sufficiently well-informed about Old Ironclad to do an article on her, can we presume that they are acquainted? Surely, two good right-wing girls like Babs and Maggie must be soul-mates. Another easy name-drop. But that ain't all.

There are thousands of journalists, would-be journalists, and starving freelancers in this country who have tried in vain for many a long year to sell an article to *Chatelaine*, a tough market, but one of the best paying in the country. Barbara tosses it off whimsically as a chore for a poor working-girl with no ruby necklaces, who uncomplainingly stays up nights to scrape together a meagre $2000. Thus she is lightly informing us that she is a top-level journalist, regarding as chicken-feed what the proles of the newspaper world can only dream of, wistfully.

Next score: Fred Bruning and his envious friends think the birthday bashes vulgar and deplorable. They forget, laughs Barbara, "that the rich often give generously to charity and are thus entitled to their private pleasures."

Actually, as Fred might have pointed out, given the chance, this isn't true: the rich are notoriously stingy about giving to charity, and the major percentage of donations come from people of modest incomes. When the rich *do* give any of their money away, it is less from generosity and public responsibility than from a desire to evade taxes. Barbara's unverbalized premise is that the rich are rich because they deserve to be rich, and their wealth a reward for virtue, intelligence, and hard work.

Beginning snobs should learn to identify and master such unverbalized premises. But learn to camouflage them with more expertise than Babs has demonstrated here. This premise is the

Horatio Alger myth at which we have glanced earlier.

Actually, as everyone knows, great fortunes are rarely made by simple hard work and honest dealing (see Veblen on massiveness, ferocity, et al.). Far more frequently the indispensable ingredients are an eye for the main chance, a hard-nosed freedom from scruples, and simple greed. Of course as Ivan Boesky pointed out, "There's nothing wrong with greed."

Ivan pushed it a little too far, and had to do time, but only in a minimum security prison. He's probably out now (I haven't been following his career with the attention it deserves) and being invited to dinner parties with the wealthy and privileged, as long as he still has some money. The rich are very forgiving of other rich, as long as they don't get poor. It's okay to be greedy and dishonest, but to be poor is in very bad taste.

This position displays one of the true essentials of snobbery. It boils down to the assertion, or the insinuation, "I am richer than you, and therefore better in every way." If one is rich enough, one can even be *morally* better, by giving (with maximum publicity) handsome donations to worthy causes. When the non-rich give to worthy causes, they don't get any publicity.

The burden of Barbara's argument is that the very rich have a right to spend as much money as they like, in whatever way they like, and damn the poor and the bleeding-hearts, who are really only envious. She lines herself up firmly on the side of the rich, where she properly belongs, and this is the real communication underlying her article: I belong with the rich, and they have a right to do whatever they like.

The implicit message for the rich, from Barbara, was that (although not really rich herself, just a top-level working journalist) she was by nature one of them. She was sublimely unenvious of the rich, with whom she is sympathetic and understanding.

As we know, since Barbara wrote that article, she has married her own multi-millionaire, and doesn't have to slave for weary nights writing *Chatelaine* articles for a sweated $2000.

After her marriage to Conrad, Barbara found herself assailed by insinuations that as the wife of a multi-millionaire she didn't need to go on working, or did so out of greed. She was referred to as "the rich-bitch." Barbara riposted: "Journalists such as [Stephen] Glover utterly disregarded the explanation of why I remain in the profession." (*Sunday Sun*, Nov. 14, 1993). She had been married to rich men before this, but was forced to go back to the job. "My husband is very rich but I am not ... reversal of fortune is this rich bitch's reality ..." She concluded that she might as well keep working, and have the Vuitton suitcases packed.

Well, but, *Barbara* ... you ain't exactly poor. I mean, Conrad lets you live in his house[s], doesn't he? Doesn't charge you room and board? Pays your passage on the Concorde? Even if he doesn't give you a dress allowance, as millionaire husbands used to do for their dependents, his papers give you a big market for your work. Couldn't you put away a little nest-egg against a Black crash (cf. the collapse of the Austro-Hungarian, British and Soviet Empires? That's Barbara's comparison, not mine).

With what passion Barbara leaps to the defence of the rich against that pathological poison-tooth of envy! In another *Maclean's* article (Jan. 22, 1996) she demands imperiously that journalists "... stop the petty sniping at philanthropists. If a person's private property and income belong to him, then the more say he has in how the government spends his money, the better."

She directs a spirited defence against an editorial in *The Globe and Mail* which suggested that big donations to universities and art galleries from millionaires are not wholly disinterested: "There are some who would question the real generosity behind such donations" — because they earn big income tax reductions, and give the philanthropists virtual control over policies of the institutions benefitting. Wouldn't real altruists donate from after-tax income? Barbara recommends that her millionaires "move to a more hospitable country where their charity is not scrutinized to make sure it is free of 'self-interest.'" (*Maclean's*, Jan. 22, 1996.)

She believes that "money or property lawfully generated and acquired belongs to the individual." We are again confronting, slightly disguised, the Horatio Alger principle — the belief that the rich get rich by hard work, honesty, and frugality. As we've seen, this is not invariably the case. In fact, it's a great recipe for ending up on the Old Age Pension, non-supplemented. Whereas profits from arms sales, child porn, toxic waste, the slave trade, exploitation of labour, dealing in drugs and booze, and just plain chicanery are among the most promising paths to vast wealth. And supposing the money *wasn't* "lawfully generated and acquired"? Suppose you inherited it, with no effort on your part, from some unprincipled old ancestor?

Barbara blazed out in fiery defence against journalistic detractors of Hilary Weston on her appointment as Lt.-Gov. of Ontario, said detractors motivated by that old poison tooth of envy, naturally.

"Taking potshots at the rich in a modern democracy is a shooting-fish-in-a-barrel sport." (*Maclean's* Jan. 13, 1997.) Somehow, I can't see the rich in such a pathetic light. They're fairly well able to take care of themselves, especially if they own their own newspapers. Far easier and safer to take potshots at envious journalists, ain't it, Barbara?

With William F. Buckley Jr. and Ronald Reagan, she believes passionately in the virtue and nobility of the rich. Like them, she has a poor opinion of The Poor. As we've seen, William F. believes there are no poor in America — just drunks and drug addicts. President Ron claimed that street people prefer sleeping on the street (it makes them feel free).

"Your laughter speaks poorly of you, ma'am!" The Reverend Clifford Elliott spoke severely in his *Toronto Star* column (March 25, 1995) of another *Maclean's* article, which we missed. She had described how, watching Judy Rebick "talking about the terrible plight of the dispossessed in Canada, specifically women, single mothers, 'minority persons' and other ill-treated groups in our land," Barbara let out whoops of laughter. "The only ill-treated groups in Canada I can see ... are hard-working Canadians of every socio-economic class who fork over a lot of their hard-earned money to the government so it can subsidize Rebick's various causes." That is, one assumes, Barbara and her set are ill-treated Canadians? Do they suffer terrible deprivations from this ill-treatment? Suffer from malnutrition? Have to sleep on the street?

Later, someone on the programme suggested that people in comfortable circumstances should help take responsibility for the poor and dependent. That sent Barbara into "stitches of laughter." She believes the "non-productive classes" are responsible for the deficit, although (Dr. Elliott reminds her) the Council of Canadians has published statistics indicating that tax breaks to corporations and wealthy individuals have caused almost half the national debt while government spending, including social programmes, has caused a mere 6 percent. What it seems to boil down to is that Barbara thinks she shouldn't have to pay taxes. But if we exempt millionaires and their spouses, how in can we run the country? The Poor don't have enough income to pay enough tax to repair the roads Barbara drives on. (Conrad prefers to be chauffeured.) How bravely they bear their ill-treatment! And the hard work they do? Writing columns in defence of the world's richest and most extravagant, who can easily defend themselves? Oh, it's tough!

Despising the poor is of course a primary essential of snobbery. But you must do it with a little less inelegance. Barbara's attitude, in my opinion, is the kind of Badsnobbery that gives all snobbery a bad name.

Snobnote: Barbara has nonetheless achieved an enviable Snobpinnacle: her name is being incorporated into the language the way Ampère's was, or Parkinson's, or Alzheimer's. In the last few days I have heard several cases of such usage: "Hey, are you doing an Amiel on me?" and "They really Amieled me on that." When *an Amiel* is accepted in a dictionary, we'll have to accept Barbara as a successful Snob, no matter how grave her weaknesses.

Snobmodel: PET

"Just watch me!"
— Pierre Elliot Trudeau

One of the most successful snobs of our time, indeed of all time, is our former Prime Minister, Pierre Elliot Trudeau. Aspiring male snobs should study him carefully, but should in no circumstances try to imitate him, because it won't work. You must develop your own unique, idiosyncratic snobstyle, if you hope for success.

Still, some analysis of the Trudeau technique might be instructive. I believe it will prove to have something in common with Peter Pan's mastery of good form: i.e., they both ignore it. However, their way of ignoring it is completely different, since Peter didn't know it existed, and Pierre clearly does; he just doesn't give a damn about it. He does what he wants to do, and if people don't like it, too bad. He has defied all the shibboleths and broken all the rules. He has done some incredibly stupid things, but the world still thinks of him as a Great Mind, a man of extraordinary gifts, of the most exalted intellect and culture.

He was still a bachelor, at a fairly advanced age, when he first came conspicuously into the public eye; there was a good deal of speculation as to his sexual orientation, and some hope on the part of Conservatives that he might be disqualified as PM by rumors of a tendency to sexual gaiety. He effectively scotched these by marrying

Margaret, who was young enough to be not merely his daughter, which is fairly commonplace, but his granddaughter.

She was not only young but extremely pretty, so pretty that the most macho anti-Trudeau faction retreated in confusion and envy. His once-suspect masculinity was eloquently vindicated. There was a feeble effort by the gay-theorists to suggest that the marriage to Margaret was only a cover-up, a front to conceal his real interests, but this was speedily refuted by Margaret, who adored media attention. Reporters never tired of asking what it was like for so young a girl to marry so mature a husband. Margaret responded with gushing descriptions of her PM's youthfulness: "He has the body of a twenty-two year old."

If further proof were needed, it was amply supplied by Pierre's siring, at extraordinary speed, three sons whom Margaret (who was proving to be a committed exhibitionist) breast-fed in public, for the benefit of photographers.

Thus, although he never worked at presenting a macho image, he outdid the most macho of the lads in a most convincing way. When the marriage broke up with sensational publicity, none of it redounded negatively on PET: Margaret was the villain, and played the role as if being coached, making an idiot of herself with maximum publicity at every opportunity. Pierre got all the sympathy.

He lost an election to Joe Clark and, unable to tolerate the officially second-gun position of leader of the opposition, he took his famous walk in the snow and resigned. Then he changed his mind and came back, was in fact drafted to come back and again lead the Liberal flock, the sheep who had got lost in that snowstorm. It is difficult to imagine any other Canadian politician being able to pull this off, instead of turning into a figure of fun. He won the next election by a landslide, somehow contriving to make Joe look silly while he, Pierre, was still considered a distinguished statesman. Poor Joe has never been able to live down the brevity of his tenure as PM, whereas Trudeau's walk in the snow has turned into a kind of romantic legend.

His great achievement was the "repatriation" of the constitution, precipitating a Quebec problem that looks like remaining unsolved perennially, but nevertheless still wins praise.

He established himself as a supporter of peace and environmental movements, and in spite of his invocation of the War Measures Act — "Just watch me!" — continued to win praise for his sane attitude when American politicians went on anti-Communist rampages. Then he let the Cruise Missile into Canada, and nobody remembered it against him, except me.

He was spectacularly rude to the press, who nonetheless treated him much more kindly than they did his successors. He was lucky in those successors: John Turner won top prizes for ineptness, political and otherwise, and Brian Mulroney was talented beyond all competition for arousing hatred. They made PET look glorious, retrospectively.

The Mulroney style offers an interesting contrast. They did painfully obvious snob things: Brian had as many shoes as Imelda Marcos, with roughly the same PR effect. Mila had a gorgeous couturière-designed wardrobe, and manifested the same sense of values as Nancy Reagan.

Trudeau could show up at a black-tie occasion wearing a turtle-neck under his dinner jacket, occasioning great media excitement. He was not criticized, but admired for his daring. In the period when it was the ultimate term of adulation, he was "With It." Hip. Cool. He wasn't afraid to defy convention and tradition, if he felt like it. On the other hand, if he chose to observe it, he contrived to make everyone else look like slobs.

Margaret's wardrobe ran chiefly to jeans, T-shirts, and swimsuits. Occasionally she appeared flamboyantly in a gorgeous gown, in which she looked like a raffish film star, but her instincts tended toward hippy styles. Margaret came in for plenty of criticism, but not the kind levelled at the Mulroneys, for their irresponsible waste of money.

The Mulroneys impressed the public by knowing rich and important people, and by being buddies with the Reagans and Bushes. They blasted around on fishing trips in the Bush power boats. The Trudeaus called on Fidel Castro. Brian, on his taxpayer-defying final tour, aroused wrath and contempt by a much-publicized photo of himself and Boris Yeltzin, posing with their guns over the corpses of several dead animals. Did the great dumb-dumb really think this would reflect credit on him?

Pierre was abundantly photographed canoeing in environmental virtue on a quiet lake. In pre-Margaret days, Pierre dated Barbra Streisand, an unconventional figure even in Hollywood; Margaret was a Stones groupie. The Trudeaus travelled, whether together or apart, without any particular ostentation, whereas the Mulroneys tried to look like royalty, surrounded by servants, bodyguards, and hangers-on, costing the furious taxpayer small fortunes every time they took a trip.

While Pierre was regarded with great ambivalence at home, he was treated with reverence abroad, especially in France and the U.S., where he was spoken of with admiration as a man of high culture, fit to associate with the greatest minds, political and otherwise, of the world.

He was annoyingly good at all sorts of things. He was expert at a variety of sports, including skiing, swimming, and diving; one day he was an image of icy correctness and decorum, the next he was clowning for a photo opportunity, upside-down on a trampoline, or sliding down a banister in a way most unbecoming to prime ministerial dignity. And got away with it. Had Joe or Brian tried it, all Canada would have winced with embarrassment.

No one in history has worked harder at bilingualism than Joe, but the poor soul has a tin ear, and Joe-Clark-French is synonymous with the worst kind of Anglo accent. Trudeau spoke both languages with almost insulting effortlessness.

He was rude in a superior, *de haut en bas* style which made his enemies grind their teeth with frustration. Poor old Joe tried once to use his own weapons against him; someone suggested he disconcert Trudeau by laughing at him. That laborious laugh was mocked by comedians for years, long after he was out of office. Trudeau's exchanges with Flora Macdonald were phrased with exquisite politeness, in tones of exquisite rudeness. He referred to her as "the lady," in a way which made his hearers equate the phrase with "the moron."

Often his rudeness was done for simple pleasure. It is said that Jean Chrétien once remarked to him that it was raining out; Trudeau inquired whether he had expected it to be raining in?

After his retirement, people went right on consulting him, soliciting his opinions; he roused the media by laying down the law on a variety of issues, always to the detriment of his bungling successors. His books are automatic bestsellers.

At an advanced age, he unapologetically sired a little Illegitimate, and was admired rather than censured for it.

He is one of the most successful snobs of all time, and he doesn't even work at it. It comes naturally. I have heard Prince Philip nominated for Greatest Snob of our Time laurels, but he is an amateur compared to Trudeau. He has to work too hard, furiously correcting people who ask about the Queen by insistently referring to her as "my wife," as if that were the higher title. Perhaps he feels perpetually one down because he married above him. Besides, he has no charm; he is merely obnoxious in his snobbery.

Trudeau is the only politician in postwar history who has excited mania, in the manner of a pop star. Beatlemania, Trudeaumania. He succeeded simultaneously as swinger and as intellectual. Before anyone considers emulating his technique, however, let them bear carefully in mind that, as well as being Prime Minister, he is a hereditary millionaire, and that makes everything a lot easier, including snobbery.

Finally: his Snobmasterpiece. He had two sons born on Christmas day, making him the only human being in history to one-up God.

Before we plunge into the heavy stuff, first a glance at

Some Briefly Noted Snobberies

Remember: an advanced Snoblevel requires great skill and hard work. The successful snob contrives to persuade the world of its superiority, and is at the same time — if not loved — generally envied, and its company sought everywhere. To expect to be superior *and* loved is asking too much altogether. But if you do the job properly, everyone will be obliged to pretend to love you, in order not to appear envious, though their devotion often has a parasitic element. Successful snobs attract parasites, as May Beetle larvae attract skunks and starlings, or the human gut tapeworms. You must always carefully conceal your belief in your own superiority to preclude envious derision.

There are certain types of snobbery to which one may in no circumstances confess. The most obvious one is *Wealth Snobbery*. We repeat: never boast about how rich you are. You have to imply it, as delicately as possible, all the while protesting that you're poor. This is also useful in discouraging collectors for charities.

We proceed with a few briefly noted but important Snob forms.

Horsesnobbery

Some of the most exquisitely tuned snobbery is found in horsey circles, where everyone is busy subtly denigrating everyone else in every possible way — their horses, their riding clothes, their riding technique, their intelligence, their morals. A proper study would run to many volumes, and much research, and I will leave it to someone young and strong.

Canada has a special brand of Horsesnobbery. It's found in the U.S. too, but it seems to be more virulent here in the true North strong and free. This is the English vs. Western Riding Snobbery. In few areas of life has mutual contempt reached such dizzying altitudes. English riders are proud of the long tradition behind their style, describing its ancestry in jousts, the cavalry, and the hunting field. They look down their noses at Western style, associated as it is with drudgery, dirty hands, and cows, rather than with exploit in the classic aristocratic manner. Western riders despise English saddles, English bridles, the English seat, posting, jumping ... it is, they sneer, sissified.

It isn't riding, they say, it's exhibitionism, intended only for the show-ring, not for the real world. Western riding is serious: working-riding, where you move with the horse, sitting down at a trot as well as at a walk or canter (nothing is so sissified as posting) and neck-reining your horse, so that you have a hand free; you can fasten your reins around the horn and gallop with both hands free to lasso a calf. And so on, often becoming very boring.

A truly accomplished (and rich) Snob can achieve distinction merely by owning horses, and need never risk life and limb by actually riding these dangerous beasts. Unless you are a competent horseperson, it is inadvisable to attempt riding, although it's useful to know how to hold a bridle in a casual way for photographs. This won't impress authentic horsey types, who will jeer at you, but it can get your picture in the papers, which still has some Snobvalue. In certain circles.

Kidsnobbery

While it is obvious that your offspring are laughably superior to the grubby little creatures begotten by your friends, relations, and (especially) neighbours, it is inadvisable to point this out to them. You can't imagine how they can be blind to it themselves: surely they should be begging for the privilege of allowing their brats merely to hang about in the vicinity of your infant genius, basking in its effulgence. But you must repress the temptation, and pretend that your marvel is just an ordinary kid like the other little horrors. Otherwise you may be stoned to death by infuriated parents, or at the very least given a fat lip.

It is impossible to be a successful kidsnob, and if you insist on trying to prove your kids' superiority, you will be hated by everyone, including your kids.

Kidsnob parents plan to give their begats Every Advantage. They expound on their methods for turning out well-rounded individuals who will distinguish themselves in every field by careful indoctrination in the arts, science, and certain approved sports. This theorizing induces severe ennui among guests, who are obliged to sit still while each brat in turn abuses the piano, reads its "compositions," performs ballet steps, etc. I will not pursue this unseemly subject further, though it deserves exposure and condemnation.

Perhaps I would have been more tolerant if my own offspring had displayed better show-offing talent. Unfortunately, when politely asked by a guest what he planned to be when he grew up, he said (instead of an architect, or a doctor, or a great musician), "A hood."

Race and Species Snobbery

Racism was once thought entirely respectable, and even

commendable. Following Kipling's instructions, one could assume the White Man's Burden as a duty to the lesser breeds without the law. Now, alas, it is apt to make you unpopular in some quarters and to invite abusive noises from fanatics in civil rights organizations. It was also correct, and even religious, to assert that all other species were put on earth for the benefit of man, to be used as he saw fit. Now a bunch of tiresome environmentalists have taken all the fun out of it, and many a jolly fox-hunt has been spoiled by their tasteless protests.

Even though you are doing the lesser breeds a favour by instructing them in White standards, by letting them work for you, learn your language, and be converted to your religion, you should keep quiet about it, as it is politically incorrect to broadcast it, and a Goodsnob is always politically correct.

While racism has been abundantly discussed, and probably needs no further investigation here, I can't resist introducing my favourite Racist, whom I'll call Leslie, a small myopic bow-legged gent who loves expounding on the superiority of the white race.

Leslie believes the abandonment of apartheid was the gravest of errors, because the non-white population of South Africa is not ready to handle the difficult job of self-government. Non-whites are too childish, and their intellect just isn't up to it. Instead of the reckless haste with which things have been precipitated, it is the duty of the superior race to institute a long, slow programme of education, which over a century or so may bring the lesser breeds into a more capable state. Leslie says he's not a racist. It is simply a fact that the white race is more evolved than any others.

He also has some biblical arguments, to do with Ham, the son of Noah, who when Noah got drunk, saw the nakedness of his father. His brothers decorously walked in backwards and covered their drunken old pa with a garment. When Noah woke up, he cursed Ham and told him that his son Canaan would be a servant of servants to his brethren. So, says Leslie, since non-white races were intended by God to serve their white superiors, they should reverently accept the divine intention and not presume to demand equality. No one has explained how Noah contrived to have one black son and two white ones.

The practical motivation for establishing a superiority/inferiority hierarchy among races is economic. If one bunch is by definition inferior, slated by God to be servants of the servants of the higher races, then they can be used as slaves with no moral culpability: it's doing God's will, as well as being charmingly convenient in the supply of free labour. This is why Racism is classed as a form of snobbery, is in fact one of the essential forms of snobbery, permitting the existence of slavery and the flourishing of tyrants.

A nice example of classic Race Snobbery is found in E. M. Forster's A *Passage to India*. The scene is the trial of Dr. Aziz, who has been accused of assaulting a rather plain English girl, Adela.

The prosecutor explained that the darker races are physically attracted by the fairer, but not *vice-versa*. Not a question of prejudice, simply scientific fact. "Even when the lady is so uglier than the gentleman?" asked a little voice from the audience.

Leslie is getting a little nervous about broadcasting his views in the present political climate, but he clings to his white supremacy (the only supremacy he has, poor dear) which allows him to condescend to inferiors like Nelson Mandela, Paul Robson, and all those seven-foot basketball players.

Speciesism carries racism another step, with the same rationalization. God gave man dominion over every living thing that moveth upon the earth, including the fish of the sea and birds of the air. Man was made in God's image, which puts him in a top category, snobwise.

It gives us superior beings the right to do anything we choose to other creatures. Since carnivorous animals eat other animals, they're in no position to pass moral judgements. However, the fanatics riposte, no animals other than man imprison other animals, or torture them, or subject them to humiliations, or inflict unnatural lifestyles upon them, as we do to our victims. Again, God's ruling is convenient for the human race, but a visitor from outer space might consider its morality a trifle dubious.

Pierre Berton believes seal hunts should be restored because some native tribes are having a tough time since the cod were wiped out. Pierre blames the cod shortage on greedy seals, though seals and fish have co-existed for millennia, maintaining a nice balance, whereas the cod wipe-out is clearly the work of creatures made in God's image. John Cabot found the Grand Banks "swarming with fish," weighing up to 200 pounds; today's average cod, if you can find one, weighs five to six pounds.

There was no shortage of seals, either; Jacques Cartier reported them in huge numbers, as well as sea lions, sea leopards, sea elephants, walrus, all of which are now either extinct or threatened, along with whales, dolphins, sea otters ... the list is endless. Some of them have simply been hunted to extinction, and some have been starved out by overfishing of their primary food source by a two-legged predator, and

I don't mean cormorants. David Suzuki says that within his lifetime many species of Pacific salmon have disappeared, as have pilchard and haddock. This is not the work of seals, but of that same two-legger, one of the few species on earth of which there is no shortage.

Pierre Berton, whose work on behalf of humans I have sometimes admired, is a disturbing case of destructive Species Snobbery. Another case is that of a publisher whose name I have forgotten, but who once told me piously, "I'd see every elephant in the world slaughtered if I had to choose between them and one human child." Elephants are intelligent and sensitive creatures, deeply devoted to their children, living in closely knit families, vegetarians who don't kill other species for food, who once roamed all over Africa, Asia and even parts of Europe, but who are now chronically in danger of extinction. Why are they so eminently sacrificeable, while human life is sacred?

The human race is very intelligent in some respects, astonishingly stupid and short-sighted in others. We've done brilliant work at reducing the human death rate, but not at controlling the birth rate. In the last 150 years, population has grown from one billion to six, while practically every other species either is already extinct, or threatened with extinction. In spite of this we refuse to acknowledge our guilt for damage to the environment, and instead of dedicating our vaunted resourcefulness to reducing our numbers, we've started having litters of seven — and bragging about them.

Most scientists agree that the human race has polluted poor old Earth almost to the point of no return, but the Fraser Institute, many economists, and various religious cults including the big R. C. still fail to recognize that the planet is finite. No one dares challenge the assumption that the happiness of the human race is the whole purpose of the universe. We had been triumphantly ridding the world of flies and mosquitoes with DDT, and who could argue with that? They made our lives a misery. Then along came spoilsport Rachel Carson with *Silent Spring*, telling us we'd also been ridding the world of songbirds and bees and pollinators and all the natural enemies of flies and mosquitoes, who were displaying a fiendish ability to outsmart us by developing immunity to our toxins.

We've been congratulating ourselves for millennia on being the highest order of beings in creation. But if an asteroid bumps us, or we wipe ourselves out in a nuclear war, or fail to clear up the pollution we've caused, it won't be a serious disaster for the planet. According to a cheerful gent on a science documentary (I believe it was J. Lovelock, the Gaia man) we won't be missed. While most of the large animals will be wiped out, no SERIOUS harm will be done, since the really important life-forms — blue-green algae, soil bacteria, some forms of plankton — will probably survive. As long as they're around, the ones made in God's image can be dispensed with, which should be the end of Species Snobbery.

Petsnobbery

Large volumes could be written on his subject, but we will be brief, simply noting that dogs are seldom snobbish enough (they indiscriminately adore the whole human race) while cats are shocking snobs, despising everybody, including other cats. Every cat is born thinking of itself as the centre of the universe; human beings are provided to cater to its every desire. However, we are really concerned with human snobbery as manifested by choice of pets.

You can usually identify Petsnobs by the breeds they buy, which are chosen to attract attention to themselves. Fashions change, as they do in other areas, but preferred breeds for years have been the Afghan, the Borzoi or Russian Wolfhound, and the Irish Wolfhound. These are amiable idiot dogs; I'd like to see the wolves they're supposed to have hunted. We used to have one each of Irish and Russian Wolfhounds nearby, and they were regularly sent home crying by a tough cocker spaniel.

Other Snob-preferred breeds are poodles, though these are now a little dated, Dobermans, Great Danes, Bouviers, Rottweilers and Dalmatians (because of the Disney picture), and a variety of small dogs which are usually chosen simply for novelty. Large dogs have more Snobvalue than small ones because they are more expensive to feed, and spend most of their lives at the vet's. Owners of Dobermans, Rottweilers and pit-bulls spend most of *their* lives in court, defending at great expense themselves and their dogs on charges of assault, murder, etc. Throwbacks to the Hunter/Warrior stage esteem such activity highly. We once had a Lab whose sole ambition was to eradicate all other dogs from the face of the earth, but I hadn't enough Hunter/Warrior genes to get any fun out of it.

Dogsnobs, as distinguished from dog-lovers, do not hesitate to mutilate their pets' ears and tails to conform to the dim-bulb standards of dog-shows. We are currently lobbying for legislation requiring dog-mutilators to first have their own ears and tails cropped.

Reverse Dogsnobs insist that mongrels are smarter and healthier than pure-breds and will tolerate nothing else. It is in fact well to avoid any fashionable dog breed until its vogue has been long past, because the poor things have all their brains and natural immunity to illness bred out of them.

Vogue dogs are frequently not dogs at all but costume accessories, and this is a degradation to the whole canine race. Even this does not satisfy low-class Petsnobs. They must have exotics — boa constrictors, orang-utans, deodorized skunks, lions and leopards, pot-bellied pigs — anything to attract attention. The miserable animals are sentenced to lonely and unnatural lives so that these most contemptible of snobs may indulge their feeble egos. There oughta be a law.

Travelsnobbery

One of the most entertaining forms of snobbery, but we will not deal with it at length because it has been well worked over by more skillful hands than mine. Particularly recommended is E. M. Forster's *A Room with a View*, in which Miss Lavish wanted all British tourists to pass an examination before entering Italy. In Rose Macaulay's *The Towers of Trebizond*, Aunt Dot, who has been everywhere on earth with her missionary husband, now (1950s) finds absolutely every place *ruined* by tourists. (She should see them today!)

Travelsnobbery can be entertainingly observed in Stratford, Ontario, where the Shakespearean Festival brings many tourists, who are amused by the quaint natives while the natives are irritated by the crass tourists, who eat picnics on their lawns and pick their flowers, in the belief that the whole town is a charming amusement park. Same situation in Niagara-on-the-Lake.

A perennial sport for North American tourists in Britain is listening to natives who, in freezing corridors and icily inadequate bathrooms, proudly explain that they don't like central heating. Britsnobs dearly love to watch North Americans' reactions to their questions about double-glazing, and vie with each other in little games to trap their guests into saying "drapes" and "backyard."

North Americans probably get their biggest kicks when they get off the beaten path a little and discover that the most primitive of plumbing still lurks in unexpected places — castles, yet — making us thank God for our superior civilization. (I will not give descriptions, the self-respecting Snob will prefer to supply its own.) But those Stone Age holes exist only for the tourists, thus preventing them from invading the indoor facilities. It is sometimes disappointing to find that the Europeans have *better* plumbing than we do: no middle-class home without its bidet.

Winesnobbery

Winesnobbery is not recommended because it must be done well. Ideally, you should know something about wines, or you will make an idiot of yourself, and even become a joke, which is the fate Snobs fear most. It is possible to learn to be an accomplished Winesnob, and it is one of the most gratifying forms of Snobbery, done successfully. But it takes much research, and you have to be rich. If you're rich enough, you can hire an expert to coach you, but you will be ridiculed if discovered, and the expert may blackmail you, forcing you to hire a hit-man to bump him off, which is expensive. Another danger is that you will bore people to death.

If you are at an early stage of your Winesnob career, be sure you do your bouquet-inhaling inconspicuously, in a quiet corner of a dark restaurant. You don't want an audience until you're sure you know your stuff. Remember, too, that wine waiters (*sommeliers*, in Snob) are the cruellest snobs in the world. The minute you've finished your performance (or sent back the bottle) your waiter will be winning plaudits from his peers for a comic imitation of your efforts.

Don't in any circumstances warn your friends laughingly that you're a dreadful Winesnob. They will either start spitting on the floor and demanding beer or cider, or they will one-up you with exotic vintages like Gobi Desert Sparkling Red or Aleutian Islands Chablis.

Warsnobbery

A special variety of snobbery flourishes in the armed services, because of their hierarchical nature. Any officer, be he ever so feeble-minded, is axiomatically and by definition superior to the lower ranks, who have to salute him and obey him without question. Obviously a thorough study of this delicious arrangement would be a life's work, but we will examine only one (but a classic) case, that of the Light Brigade who, in a battle during the Crimean War, were ordered to "charge for the guns," which they obediently did.

> "Forward, the Light Brigade!"
> Was there a man dismay'd?
> Not though the soldier knew
> Some one had blunder'd:
> Theirs not to make reply,
> Theirs not to reason why,
> Theirs but to do and die ...
> — Tennyson, *The Charge of the Light Brigade*

One is tempted to protest that these noble fat-heads, before riding boldly and well into the jaws of death, should have pointed out that absolutely nothing would be achieved by the charge, while they and a bunch of expensive horses would all be shot to pieces. But war is based on an exquisitely ordered Snobsystem by which the lower ranks never question an order by their superiors: theirs not to reason why.

Why not? Because their officers were (again, axiomatically) their superiors. They may have been feeble-minded twits, but they came from Top Families, they had been to the right schools, they wore much handsomer uniforms than the simple soldiers. Besides, if one of the noble six hundred had questioned the order — "Now hang on a minute there, Colonel, we're all going to be filled full of lead and won't have achieved a thing" — he would have been court-martialled and shot immediately, for treason or insubordination or whatever.

It doesn't make sense, you say? Who's talking about sense? We're discussing Snobvalues, which would go out the window if you start blithering around about sense. It is only fair to say that after the golden days of the Crimea, such noble squandering of men and valuable horses was rather frowned upon, even though it produced some whizz-bang poetry.

PART 2

Post-modern Snobbery

11

Agesnob

Agesnobbery changes from generation to generation. In the Victorian era, the vogue was for sophisticated older women, knowledgeable and experienced. In a rather ill-advised poem called "My Rival," Kipling has a young girl lamenting the hopelessness of her love, since she is only seventeen, and her competition is an irresistible siren of forty-nine. She describes her misery at parties, when no one asks her to dance, and all the young men grovel at the feet of the middle-aged man-killer.

> The incense that is mine by right
> They burn before her shrine,
> And that's because I'm seventeen
> And she is forty-nine.

Difficult to credit in today's climate, when youth is the first requirement for desirability. Fashion models peak at about sixteen, and after that it's downhill all the way, until they are withered crones of twenty.

In Jane Austen's time, one was tottering on the edge of the grave at forty, if we believe the John Dashwoods, in *Sense and Sensibility*. They were debating whether John's stepmother should be given an annuity from her husband's fortune. Fanny objects:

> "But then if Mrs. Dashwood should live fifteen years, we shall be completely taken in."
> "Fifteen years! My dear Fanny, her life cannot be worth half that purchase."
> "Certainly not; but ... people always live forever if there is an annuity to be paid them; and she is very stout and healthy and hardly forty."
> (Austen 1961, 11)

In the late 19th and early 20th century, the vogue was all for sophisticated ladies like Kipling's senior siren, "of a certain age." This mysterious phrase, according to Roget, means slightly over-ripe, or over the hill. Why would men prefer menopausal women to fresh young things of seventeen? Several possible reasons: the lady of a certain age was often her own boss, and could make her own decisions; in the pre-pill days, if she wanted to have a love affair, she wasn't in nearly as much danger of getting pregnant as was Sweet Seventeen. She was probably already married, and possibly widowed; she was far less likely to be husband-hunting than her juniors, especially if she had money of her own. She was often inclined to gather rosebuds while she still might. Altogether, probably more fun, if less toothsome, than her juvenile rival, who (in those benighted days) had to worry about whether she would get a reputation for promiscuity, as well as about pregnancy.

Concomitant with the vogue for riper ladies was a conscious effort to keep the young very young indeed, for as long as possible. If they were officially uninteresting sexually, they could be kept out of competition. On the other hand, they could also postpone middle-age practically forever. Thus we have Nancy Mitford telling us over and over how fabulously YOUNG she was. "I was very young ..." And she went on being young, indefinitely. According to her, at least.

Michael Innis's detective, Top Cop John Appleby, also a member of the class and generation which believed in keeping The Young infantile to quite advanced years, had a son, Bobby. Still called Bobby after graduating from Oxford, learning to drink and drive, acquiring the stigmata of maturity. However, he continued to call his father Daddy, and his mother referred to Sir John as "Your Daddy." The senior Applebys could not resist exchanging humorous glances when the cunning little fellow would do something precociously adult like wanting coffee instead of milk for breakfast — and he was only twenty-three!

Just to keep us confused, in Nancy's *Love in a Cold Climate*, Cedric Hampton's father married "an elderly Canadian woman in Nova Scotia," who some years later gave birth to Cedric. It is odd to think of a woman still in her child-bearing years as elderly. It appears to be a matter more of class than of chronology. The lower orders (e.g. Canadian) were elderly at forty, while Nancy and her friends were perpetually *very* young.

Attempts to keep adolescents and even young adults perennially childish changed with the development of reliable birth control. Now girls are put on the pill as soon as they hit puberty, and plunge rapidly into active sex life. In the sixties, young men and girls were liberated to enjoy sex together. Girls could sleep around, as men had always done, without fear of pregnancy. Relations between the sexes will never be the same again, and forty-nine-year-old ladies find it increasingly difficult to monopolize young men while pubescent blossoms languish, partnerless. If the Seniors can afford it (judging by scenes on the Mediterranean coast) they hire gigolos.

Sexual freedom didn't last long, before AIDS came along to spoil the fun. Now everyone of whatever sex or age is at risk. Women had less than two decades of reckless freedom before it became too dangerous to take chances, and this is the reason many women believe there IS a god, and he is a male, and out to punish women every chance he gets.

Another Generationalsnobfactor is the belief by each succeeding generation that it is the first to discover sex, night-life, drugs, drink, and other forms of reckless living. This may arise from awareness that one's parents knew nothing of these things, but spent their lives breaking the ice on the pitcher, trudging to school through huge snowdrifts, and working for twenty-five cents a day, which they saved to put them through college. On graduation, they married their high school sweethearts, and lived a life of exemplary virtue ever after. I know *my* parents did.

A correspondent writing in *Books in Canada* explained condescendingly that Margarets Laurence and Atwood, Marion Engel, and others of their antique breed, couldn't write about sex because it hadn't yet been discovered: "They all hail from a time when the sex drive was denied and the orgasm constituted a virtual mystery." Bless his heart. Makes you wonder how the race survived, when people were so innocent and ignorant, whereas it not only survived but exploded. Rather surprising in people who denied the sex drive.

Another youthful gent who holds forth on night-life in Toronto for CBC described a restaurant or club or something which stays open all night. And this phenomenon dates back to 1964, "when nobody in Toronto stayed up after eleven."

Oh, Sam. Do some research.

The sixties. The hippies had taken over Yorkville and the permissive society was in full swing. All of the campus area of U. of T. was strewn with bodies all day and all night from April to October, stoned or semi-stoned on various chemicals. Most of them have outgrown such customs, but it's something every generation goes through at one stage of its life, when we are all wicked and blasé and sophisticated, in order to impress our peers and shock our elders.

I once taught in a college over which hung a near-permanent pall of marijuana smoke. The students believed to a man/woman that they had discovered marijuana and all the other hallucinogens, and that teachers in their innocence (except for a few officially Cool Cats) had never heard of such esoteric substances. Every now and then there would be an oblique reference to current practices, and knowing smiles would be exchanged among the initiate; all of this incomprehensible to the simple old teacher.

Such condescension became tedious, but obviously one couldn't stand up and shout defiantly, "I do so too know about drugs and stuff!" Instead I craftily devised some essay topics on Romantic and Victorian addicts, forcing them to read De Quincey's *Confessions of an English Opium Eater*, as well as Coleridge, and some other suspected but unconfirmed cases like Lewis Carroll and Edward Lear.

"Jeeze, what was *he* on?" demanded a startled youth, after we read *Kubla Khan*:

> And all should cry, Beware! Beware!
> His flashing eyes, his floating hair!
> Weave a circle round him thrice,
> And close your eyes with holy dread
> For he on honeydew hath fed
> And drunk the milk of Paradise.

This made it possible to reply, with elaborate casualness, "Opium, didn't you know he was an opium addict?" and explain that the "anodyne" referred to in the introduction to the poem was identified in his Journals as opium.

Sometimes I also introduced Grandma. She died when my father was quite young, but he remembered clearly afternoon tea parties in which ladies added not only cream or lemon to their tea, but a spot of laudanum, a form of liquid opium. It was a quite acceptable social practice: "Would you care for a little laudanum with your tay, Mrs. Smith-Jeffries?" A bottle of laudanum was standard equipment in the medicine cabinet, to be used for toothache and so on. It is pleasing to think of Grandma's guests, many of them well struck in age, staggering away from the tea party, stoned to the eyeballs. So far as we know, no one in the family became addicted, any more than today's respectable suburbanites bear scars of their wild pot-smoking and LSD-ingesting youth.

In the middle of the 20th century, Agesnobbery did one of its turn-abouts and unfashionable old age descended early. Nabokov's *Pnin* (1953) begins, "The elderly passenger ... was none other than Professor Timofey Pnin." We learn later that Pnin was fifty-two, an age which is now considered the prime of life. (For males, anyway; Agesnobbery has always been slanted in favour of males, although of late women have been gaining on them.)

Oh, dear. I shouldn't have brought up Nabokov, who is reliable only for confusing issues. Consider what he did to Agesnobbery with *Lolita*, apropos of which men suddenly became aware of the nymphet as sex object. Before that time, they were regarded as nuisances, who had to be bribed to get lost when a young man came courting their older sisters. Now there is no downward limit on age for sex objects. No child is safe from assailants seeking victims for child porn. This dreary situation has been aggravated by the AIDS epidemic, fear of which prompts sex monsters to prefer infants, as less likely to communicate the disease.

We are all Agesnobs, or Generationalsnobs, in our conviction that our predecessors were all bloodless, cautious, disapproving prudes. But by the time we ourselves reach this stage, we have decided that drugging, drinking, and late hours are a great bore, leaving one exhausted and overhung, and wasting time that could be agreeably spent reading or cursing your computer. I was never vice-prone myself, not because I was either wise or virtuous, but because I invariably got sick if I drank, while drugs did nothing for me but make me feel extremely uncomfortable. The desired "highs" sometimes came spontaneously, with no chemical assistance; my husband claimed I had been born half-stoned and had spent my life in that state, and for all I know, he was right.

It is unwise to indulge in Agesnobbery at either end of the age-spectrum. When it was *chic* to be "mature," life-long enemies were made by elders who sneered and mocked at the young for their immaturity or naïveté. I clearly remember ... but never mind. She was just jealous.

However, when youth is in vogue, it doesn't do to speak rudely to or of old hags who get in your way in the supermarket, or to rail as a certain author used to do at little old ladies in tennis shoes who come to his book signings. I heard him do it on the air several times. Those little old ladies had come there *to buy his books*. He should have licked their little old tennis shoes. Nor is it considered good form to bawl insults out the window at elderly drivers: "Get a hearse, Grandpa!"

We must find better ways of handling irritations arising from survival in our sentimental society of people who have no useful function in a Brave New World. Always remember: you, too, were young once. And you, too, will be old sometime, impossible though it may seem to you now.

12

Ancestor or Ancient Lineage Snobbery

"He looks a proper Ancester," said Ethel.
— Daisy Ashford, *The Young Visiters*.

Ethel was inspecting the portraits in the home of the Earl, who had undertaken to coach the humble Mr. Salteena in how to be "less mere." Their creator, the nine-year-old Daisy Ashford, was an acute and precocious Snob observer, who should be studied carefully by young Snobs.

Ancestorsnobbery was very big in the small town in which I was born during the Great Depression. Everyone was poor, and would no doubt have been classified by Daisy as distinctly mere; we fell back on our ancestors to give us some sense of importance, and hope for better things. I believed for quite a while in the glories of The Family in England, through whom my father might some day inherit a legacy that would end our poverty-stricken exile in Canada. I had a dim idea that some day a letter would arrive from England, blazoned with the Family's coat of arms, which would say something like, "Come back and be dukes." It never occurred to any of us that The Family in England might have other plans for their money, or that from their point of view we were a bunch of colonial poor relations better kept at a distance, on the far side of the Atlantic Ocean.

Periodically forms were received, to be completed for the family tree, and for Burke's *Landed Gentry*. We conferred solemnly over them, with a great sense of importance. Surely they proved the reality of the Family's greatness, and the genuineness of our connection with it?

In my teens, I began losing faith. It seemed everyone in our deprived little town was a displaced aristocrat. If we were so all-fired aristocratic, why were we also so hard up? Most of our local aristocrats were the true heirs to noble estates in England or Ireland, but had somehow been defrauded of their inheritance by unscrupulous uncles, on the pattern of Richard Crookback and King Claudius. There was one particularly eminent Irish family who had lost their title because the father of the rightful heir, who was now a section-hand on the railway, had fallen in love with a beautiful but unaristocratic village girl, and his snobbish parents had driven him off the estate, with orders never to darken their numerous doors again.

The English aristocracy in our town lived in a section known as Little England, where the conversation largely consisted of reminiscences of their former glory over 'ome. The Irish aristocracy lived at the opposite end of town, in The Devil's Half Acre, where there were a great many ghosts and where it was believed that dragonflies (or Divil's Darning Needles) were indeed instruments of Satan which hovered around good Christians with the object of sewing up their mouths so that they couldn't say their prayers.

For some reason, the Scotch (who insisted that they were not Scots, but Scotch) seemed far less vulnerable to rights-doing-out-of; they had settled down and worked as farmers and stone-masons, and didn't seem to care about being aristocratic. By this time they were solidly established and sending their kids to university.

Nevertheless, our loftiest aristocrat was Scotch. He was also one of our least prepossessing citizens: Jake Stewart, who was to be seen all day and every day slumped outside the pool hall, *was the rightful king of England.* He was a descendant of Bonnie Prince Charlie, and if he had his Rights, the current occupants of the throne would be sent back where they belonged (Germany?) and Jake would wear the crown. If you let yourself be snared by Jake, your ear would be bent for hours by a long bitter lament about his tragic fate.

Somehow the thought of Jake as king destroyed my belief in the whole principle of aristocracy. Jake, who had no chin, and only a few yellow fangs in his receding jaw, as well as a severe and chronic case of B.O., in the royal carriage, headed for Westminster, or boarding the *Britannia*, made ancestors an unlikely foundation for superiority, and disinclined me to boast of the splendours of The Family in England.

In fact, none of the Aristocrats believed in the other aristocrats, and Jake's claims were a joke, not only among the general populace but among the rest of the Stewart family, who regarded Jake as their cross.

About this time, I read *Huckleberry Finn*, and found the King and the Duke disturbingly familiar. I wished the family in Canada would forget our aristocratic connections and start trying to make a decent living, instead of sitting around waiting for that crested envelope.

Years later, I did meet some members of The Family in England. I'd been hitchhiking around France and Britain, and one day (stopping for lunch at a pub in Kent) damned if I didn't see the family name emblazoned on a brewery. They brewed beer, that's what The Family did, and had made a good deal of money at it, though none of them showed the smallest desire to donate it to the poor relations in Canada.

Some of them were quite rich, and some were dog-poor; one branch lived in an authentic Stately Home, and another lived in a hellish little third-floor walk-up flat and had to share a bathroom. Some were nice and intelligent and cultivated and educated, and some were nasty and ignorant and religious and superstitious: i.e., they were like most families. Several of them were writers and academics, and we got along nicely. But none of them had done anything particularly brilliant or unusual, except for an oddball who had been a friend of Evelyn Waugh's (a good trick, in itself), mentioned favourably in one of Waugh's journals, and subsequently eaten by a tiger in India. The rich ones had belonged to the pukka sahib class who went out to India to make their fortunes and tote the white man's burden. Our coat of arms had an elephant *passant* on it.

I learned heraldic terminology (far more about it than I had any desire to know) from my cousin Norman, a Snob of the first order, whose specialty was genealogy, a desperately dangerous trap for Ancestorsnobs. Early in our acquaintance I had recognized a rich vein of lunacy in The Family, and even there Norman stood out as a crackpot of the highest order, or the worst type.

Norman was not satisfied with being a member of a good solid middle-class family who had made handsome profits from brewing beer. He had devoted his life to tracing The Family back into the mists of antiquity. He had decided that we were Normans who had come to England with William the Conqueror, although all the authorities denied it, and he had pushed on to tracing their roots in Normandy.

To make a long story short: after the death of King Solomon, ten of the twelve tribes of Israel seceded and set up a separate kingdom, which was overthrown by Sargon of Assyria, in 722 BC. The dispossessed tribes were lost to history.

"They pretend," said Cousin Norman, fixing me with his glittering eye, so that I could not choose but hear, "these so-called genealogists and historians pretend, that The Tribes were assimilated by neighbouring countries. But they weren't. It's a conspiracy, to conceal the truth."

The Lost Tribes had travelled north, eventually winding up in Normandy. They were the last remnant of the true Israelites, God's chosen people; modern Jews have usurped the title, but they are impostors. (Norman was a wicked anti-Semite.) He learned all this stuff from a book on the British Israelites by yet another of our ancestors — a real one, this time. Anyway, our family are the last and only survivors of the Ten Lost Tribes of Israel. There were some others in Normandy, but they all died off, and now we're the only ones left. Beat that, for a pedigree.

Norman told me all this stuff in one of the family's pubs. He kept offering me cigarettes, and I kept telling him I didn't smoke; finally I realized that he was trying to draw my attention to his cigarette case, which was silver, with the family coat of arms — that elephant trotting along (*passant*). It was also on the labels of the beer we were drinking. It was on a crest decorating Norman's blazer. His house was plastered with it, on every impressable surface.

"You have a right to bear the family arms," Norman told me, though I had privately decided that I wouldn't be caught dead anywhere near that silly-looking elephant, however *passant*.

I noticed while we were in the pub that people seemed to be drifting away from our vicinity, finishing their beer and quietly disappearing; on closer acquaintance it became apparent that when Norman walked down the street, people fled as from the plague, to escape hearing about the Ten Lost Tribes, and how we came to England with William the C., and all the rest of it.

In other respects, Norman seemed reasonably sane: he played the piano well, and had been at Cambridge (though he hadn't graduated), and was quite nice looking in a gangling blond Bertie Woosterish way. The Ten Lost Tribes were not dark and swarthy, as Jews are, but tall and fair, like Norman and King David. There was biblical authority for this: "First Samuel Sixteen, it says he was fair, and of a ruddy complexion. You can look it up." I did, and found that Norman had invented the fair part. David was ruddy, and withal of a beautiful countenance, and goodly to look at, but there's nothing to suggest he was blond.

Another thing that I learned later: old Norman had no right to bear the family arms. His connection was through a female line, and he had changed his name from George Commonplace to Norman Family (I won't tell you the real one), causing much indignation among those who really were entitled to bear the silly arms, although why anyone would want that two-stepping elephant on their belongings beats me.

I've told this story at length because it illustrates the terrible dangers of Aristocrat Snobbery. If you can believe the claimants, everybody in the world comes from an old aristocratic family; the poorer and scruffier they are, the more outrageous their claims. I once met some dethroned Hungarian royalty living in a shanty in northern British Columbia, with no indoor plumbing. If you must get involved in genealogy, tracing the family roots, remember that absolutely no one outside the family has the smallest interest in your forbears.

Even living in a Stately Home or a castle is no guarantee that you are genuinely aristocratic: selling them, along with a pedigree, to rich American upstarts was a 19th- and early 20th-century industry in Britain. There is really no way to be a successful Aristocracy/Genealogysnob; you will only bore everyone to death. As old Whosis in "The Gondoliers" (all right, I've looked it up, Don Alhambra) observed 100 years ago,

> When everyone is Somebodee
> Then no-one's anybody.

13

Carsnob

... the upper class, on the principle of archaism, affect to regard the automobile as very *nouveau* and underplay it consistently. Class understatement describes the technique: if your money and freedom and carelessness of censure allow you to buy any kind of car, you provide yourself with the meanest and most common to indicate that you're not taking seriously so easily purchasable and thus vulgar a class totem. You have a Chevy, Ford, Plymouth, or Dodge, and in the least interesting style and color. It may be clean, although slightly dirty is best. But it should be boring.
— Paul Fussell, *Class*.

We have glanced at this fascinating subject in an earlier chapter ("Oldsnob, Newsnob") where I reflected on Fussell's theory and generally rejected it, because I drove a dirty old Ford, and no one ever assumed that I must be a wealthy aristocrat who despised vulgar class totems like good cars. Certainly no humble rustics or coarse mechanicals ever approached me, respectfully pulling their forelocks and asking if they could be of service.

I once had a better car, though it was also a Ford, and dirty, but someone stole it. Before that I drove a dirty Ford half-ton pick-up, which brought me great prestige among small boys, but eventually I was afraid I might fall through the floor onto the road, which I could see rushing by beneath me through the rust-holes. I don't buy Fords because I want to deceive people into thinking I'm upper class, they just seem to happen to me. They are dirty because I don't dare wash them for fear they'll go into shock, and disintegrate on the spot. Not that I'd wash them anyway. I just wait for the next rain.

However, I'm not envious. All cars look alike to me. In my youth people sometimes tried to impress me (they don't bother nowadays) with their BMWs and Porsches, but it was a waste of time. I can't tell a BMW from a Lada. Whatever a Lada may be.

In the dear dead days beyond recall, cars were nearly infallible Snobindicators (except for me, of course). Possession of a Rolls Royce (since first writing bought out by *Volkswagen*? Can such things be?), a Daimler, a Hispano-Suiza, or an Isotta-Fraschini happily proclaimed wealth and quite possibly aristocracy. Rolls Royce, says the *Encyclopaedia Britannica*, "… were prepared to satisfy any request, whether for upholstery in matched ostrich hide with ivory buttons, or for a dashboard in rosewood carrying instrument labels in Old English script … [But] the market collapse of 1929 sealed the doom of the really luxurious motorcar."

That wasn't the real reason. It was Henry Ford who began the decay-process with his deplorable assembly lines, putting the car within the reach of the humblest proletariat and robbing it of prestige. Easy credit — "instalment plan purchasing" in the quaint phrase of the day — finished it. Anyone could own a car. The only recourse for the rich was to pretend to despise it, and regard it merely as transportation, on which no one would waste good ostrich skin.

An acquaintance who once gave me a ride home in an appalling mauve Cadillac asked me what I thought of his car, and I said carefully that it seemed very powerful. However, he said that he was getting rid of it, going to get a Mercedes, maybe.

"What's wrong with this one?" I asked, not adding, "apart from the fact that it's the kind of thing you'd see at a Mafia funeral."

"Every nigger in Detroit has got an El Dorado now," he said bitterly, for he was not only politically incorrect, but the crudest sort of racist; I only rode in his mauve monstrosity because I was stuck for transportation. He expatiated on the expense to which he would be put, buying a car which would be Detroit-proof.

Old Money will thus choose to drive an old Ford or Chevy in order to make Nouveaux in their Cadillacs, Jags, BMWs, and Lincolns look vulgar and anxious. Paul Fussell says they particularly despise the Mercedes, which is "a sign of high vulgarity, a car of the kind owned by Beverley Hills dentists or African cabinet ministers."

The Nouveaux really win in this competition, if they have the courage to defy the Old Money set, because they get to ride in nice new efficient comfortable cars, even though these mark them as vulgar. On the other hand, the Old Money set can save a lot of cash by preferring cheap cars.

The manufacturers are putting up a gallant fight to reverse this undesirable behaviour by Old Money, which is expected to set a good example to the lower classes. An advertisement in *Maclean's* reminds them that they, and they alone, can afford the costly joys of the new "high-tech, high-class, high flyers," which will set them apart from the common herd. After lyrically describing the pleasures of the new luxury cars, in which mechanical connections have been done away with by electronic controls — "it's affectionately termed 'drive by wire' in the industry" — the advertiser guides prospective buyers to realize that spending money on luxury is right for them:

> It's a good thing those of you buying the so-called luxury and sin items, whether it's cigarettes, alcohol, or costly cars, are usually fairly immune to rising prices. Approximately one of every 20 cars sold in Canada is deemed a luxury car, meaning it costs $30,000 and up.

This was obviously written by a relative of our Large Income letter-writer: same philosophical position attributed to potential customers ("We're too rich to worry about rising prices"), same ignorance of good Snobpractice: The rich must always protest that they're quite poor — "I hope you don't mind riding in our funny old car." However, it might work with inexperienced Nouveaux.

Even if a Top Person decides to say to hell with the Cheap & Dirty ploy, he might hesitate before buying something distinctive and expensive. Another class factor enters here: the Criminal Class, which has little interest in old Tempos but can turn a fast and rewarding buck out of a stolen Rolls, Jag, Porsche, Lambourghini, or even a Cadillac.

The attentive reader may recall that I had a Ford stolen, and point out that nothing is safe. True, but mine was stolen by a bunch of teenagers, spaced out on booze and pot, may they nevertheless burn in hell, not by professionals. No self-respecting car thief would have soiled his hands with my car. Car theft is among our busiest contemporary industries, is highly profitable, and the perpetrators are almost never caught. Police generally don't even bother trying. "Too bad," they say, swallowing their doughnuts. "If we tried to catch car thieves, we wouldn't never have no time for nothink else."

A hazard with expensive cars is the habit of the criminal classes, if they can't actually take the car, of removing tires, radios, tapes, and everything portable, as well as stripping the vehicle down to its frame. They then sell all these items, so I am given to understand, and buy drugs. They are evil.

It is activities such as these, rather than honest snobbery, that disincline even the wealthiest to spend a whole lot of cash on cars, because the insurance never covers the real cost and inconvenience, and besides the companies keep raising your rates. Owning an expensive car has become as discouraging and unrewarding as owning valuable jewellery. (See Clothessnobbery.)

We have omitted discussion of the primitive snobbery of speed. This should be, logically, confined to teenage males, but it survives to some extent in adults, or such of them who have continued their adolescent driving habits: "I get in the fast lane, and yah better not get in my way, buddy, look out!" (Literal quotation.) The idea that some kind of superiority derives from the way you press down on an accelerator is so dim-witted as not to merit discussion. However, they frequently kill themselves off quite young, and so do not present a permanent problem, although they're a public nuisance while they last.

I still can't accept the Fussell theory that Top People really prefer to drive cheap & dirties, simply to indicate their contempt for "so easily purchasable and thus vulgar a class totem." I challenge him: how would the serious Snobstudent distinguish between the lofty Top People and the financial incompetent, who drives a dirty old Ford Tempo because it can't afford anything better? The prey of used car salesmen who, on seeing it approach, rub their hands and nudge each other gleefully: "Here's where we unload that dirty old Ford Tempo"? Are Top People, seeing an ancient and unclean vehicle, moved to cry to the driver, "Welcome! You're obviously One Of Us"? No, they aren't.

Actually, the financial incompetent in question doesn't drive it any more because it was costing so much in repairs that she had to give it up. (Okay, it was me.) The garage man said he would try to sell it for me, but they might have to haul it away for scrap. So I had to buy an *other*, as distinguished from a *new*, car. And then the dirty dog of a garage man kept my Tempo himself, repaired all its defects, repainted it beautifully, and gave it to his wife.

This is one of the reasons, along with my feud with the dental profession and Bell Telephone, that I loathe and despise the human race, and as far as possible associate only with dogs and cats. Call me a snob if you like.

A word on Drivingsnobbery, a category which includes absolutely everyone. We all believe ourselves to be good drivers, that in fact each of us is, though unacknowledged, the ONLY good driver on the road. Can I except myself? I don't like driving. If I were rich, I'd hire a chauffeur, except that I disapprove of servants. Or I might make lavish use of taxis? And yet at some deeply buried level, there is a dim conviction that only I am a truly responsible and conscientious driver, and though freeways scare the daylights out of me and I take the train rather than drive the QEW or 401, I am still more than competent at car-handling ... while at some other levels, I'm fairly sure I ain't.

Tailgaters believe themselves to be drivers of such excellence that they can risk the life and limbs of themselves and others because their reflexes are so fast and infallible that they are entitled to drive any way they want, and that the car in front has no right to delay them: it should be compelled to get off the road. It is one of the more lethal forms of Drivingsnob.

I wish to state categorically that tailgaters are by definition the lousiest of drivers, dangerous, incompetent, irresponsible, and sociopathic, who should all be deprived of their vehicles, locked up in unsanitary dungeons, and deprived of sustenance until they vow never again to tailgate. I believe this is the only cure.

A new factor in Drivingsnobbery is known as Road Rage. Actually, it isn't new, but no one took it seriously for years and years. (I did, but who listens to me?) It was terribly un-chic to suggest that driving is a terribly dangerous activity, or to admit that you ever felt terrified of your fellow automobilists, or that cars brought out the absolute worst in most people ... you were supposed to be dashing and blasé and think of it as an amusing sport, and to regard the speed limit as a joke. In fact then as now most people drove along in a towering rage, hating all other drivers and yearning to smash them into mush. But recently a few people have wakened up to this alarming truth, and there is some awareness that you take your life in your hands every time you pull out of the drive.

It is a form of unconscious snobbery, I believe — the conviction that you alone have a right to be on the road, and these intolerable interlopers are trespassing on your property. What's more, none of them can drive (you only excepted) and are lacking in even the most elementary courtesy ... it is only fair, just and your absolute prerogative to blast them off the road.

Some of the guilt for Road Rage must be attributed to the advertising biz, which is still selling cars on "performance," i.e., their ability to travel at illegal rates of speed. We see them blasting along beautiful empty roads at murderous rates: God help unwary animals or even humans who blunder into their paths. But where do they find these roads? Most of the roads in this part of the world are perpetually choked with traffic, and you're lucky if you can move at 10 km/h. And the empty ones are empty for a reason: they're either so twisty and pothole-infested that there's a speed limit of 60 km/h. So what good is your juggernaut?

Furthermore: in this day of energy shortages and overcrowded highways and road rage epidemics, should we be using cars as toys? Should we ever have used cars as toys?

We will return to this scary variety of snobbery in a later chapter. Watch for it! The life you save may be your own.

Snobnote: Carsnob Language. While lower orders, classwise, refer to "my Mercedes" or "the BMW," the Highersnobs often facetiously mention "the gas buggy" or "the horseless carriage." Both of these are kept in *the car house* (see *To Kill a Mockingbird*). They enter a garage only when they are in need of repair. G*arage* is pronounced as if it were French, and is never rendered as gerridge or *gar*adge. You may think this an affectation or quibble, and indeed such niceties are intended only for high-level snobs of whatever specialty.

No self-respecting driver at any snoblevel would so degrade itself as to call its vehicle by some cutesy nickname. There is a stage when everyone in one's age group acquires its first car, usually at about fifth hand. I learned to my pain and distress that all my friends had given their heaps (they were heaps in those days) whimsical names such as Bumpsy or Rootytoot. And what did I call my car? they asked smilingly. I was speechless, because the least unrepeatable thing I'd called it was "You bastard." But in those days, I didn't like to say so at a meeting of the Women's Press Club.

14

Clothessnobbery

Mr. Gladstone, in his old age, paid a visit to Oxford and was horrified to observe the new fashions in undergraduates' dress. In his young days every young man who respected himself had at least one pair of trousers in which he never sat down for fear of making them bag at the knees, while the outfit in which he normally walked about the streets was never worth less than seventy or eighty pounds. And yet, in the time of Mr. Gladstone's visit, the undergraduates still wore stiff collars and bowler hats. What would he have said if he could have seen them now? And what shall we say fifty years hence?
— Aldous Huxley, *Those Barren Leaves*.

Fifty years thence would make it 1975.

Remember the campus scene in those still-permissive days? There was a conspicuous shortage of stiff collars and bowler hats. Notices on buildings warned students that they were required to wear shirts and shoes, and might not bring their dogs to class. The notices addressed students, but had some application to faculty as well; there was more than one prof who habitually brought its dog to college, and occasionally to class.

In sunny weather, as soon as they escaped from class, students removed everything but the legally required minimum: males kept on brief shorts, females shorts and an abbreviated top, while they sunbathed. The attenuation of the ozone layer had not made the news to any extent, nor had we made the equation of suntan = cancer.

In cold weather, students wore an assortment of rags, often covered by an ancient and balding fur coat, though they usually had warm boots. As always, nonconformists suffered: girls who showed up in dresses and heels were mocked, as were men in shirts and ties.

It is difficult but necessary to remind ourselves that only a few years ago, well within living memory, there were people who habitually dressed for dinner every night. Women wore floor-length gowns, with sleeves (décolletage was bad form for dinner) and men wore dinner jackets and black ties, or what the French insist on calling a "smoking," in the belief that they are using English slang.

The world of fashion was once the Happy Hunting Ground of the dedicated Snob. Here display, ostentation, and wasteful spending became virtues, and clear proof of superiority. Clothes were a near-infallible class guide, in the golden days when the very rich could happily flaunt their wealth without being criticized by envious journalists. The rich had the nicest clothes, and the poor had their cast-offs.

This useful criterion has been steadily eroded in the 20th century.

In previous eras, women who aspired to looking fashionable were at the mercy of expensive *couturières*, but in the 1920s flapper fashions made it possible to whip up a modish dress out of a few scraps of chiffon, instead of having to buy dozens of yards of velvet or satin. Sewing machines improved, and paper patterns became easily available. The ambitious clothes-snob, if she secretly learned to sew, could actually be better dressed than someone with twice her income, who bought her wardrobe from Chanel or Schiaparelli (the St. Laurent and Dior of the period).

The low-income Fashionsnob would never admit she made her clothes herself, but would pretend that she had found a "clever little dressmaker," which of course she had.

Everywhere we turn in the fashion world, the levelling effect of the Industrial Revolution and mass production can be observed. From cars to clothes, the prizes which once were exclusive to the Top People have been increasingly appropriated by the Middles and Lowers. High fashion can be reproduced, and mass produced, at comparatively low prices, and the Clever Little Dressmaker can still work her magic. In the beautiful past, with the exception of eccentric misers, one's social status could be assessed at a glance from one's clothes, something that is virtually impossible today.

Another leveller is war. Both of the big 20th-century wars, with their ubiquitous uniforms, blurred class distinctions. In World War II, all sorts of non-U types became officers, much to the horror of the Old Régime, who indignantly pointed out that in their day, officers were supposed to be *gentlemen,* again identifiable at a glance. The problem was particularly severe in the Air Force, where it became apparent that flying skills were not confined to the Upper Class, and commissions were issued to people just because they were good at manoeuvring planes, rather than because they had attended the right schools, lived in stately homes, or had papas engaged in approved professions. It became increasingly difficult to spot Uppers/Lowers on sight.

I once knew a Wing Commander who had by some accident come across an early appraisal of his military potential; it said, "Definitely not officer material."

Sometimes, on the strength of these uniforms, and romantic ideas about war, unwise marriages were made between these non-gent officers and girls from authentically U-families, who failed to research adequately the background of the prospective son-in-law. This was particularly difficult if he came from a foreign country, and could lie about his antecedents.

In the fifties, many of these same ex-officers, their uniforms now history, became Angry Young Men or Beats. Read *Room at the Top* and *Look Back in Anger,* pop fiction for the period, for case histories. The vets, when they entered university after the war, became famous for their slovenly habits of dress (possibly a reaction against years of uniformed neatness) and for their defiant attitudes to social mores, most unsuitable. They refused to pull their forelocks, or make a leg to their superiors, and frequently went without ties, deliberately refusing to try to live down their ignoble origins.

And then, the sixties, when one of the strangest phenomena in the history of fashion, indeed of social evolution generally, manifested itself. Throughout recorded time, the wealthy and privileged had set the fashion; the poor and deprived had struggled along in their wake, trying valiantly (though always failing) to keep up. They imitated their betters, not only in dress, but in speech, manners, everything. They did it very badly, occasioning gentle Upper Class mirth at their expense. Much excellent comedy is based on this pleasant distinction between the Classes, and the amusing efforts of the Masses to imitate their betters.

Now, apparently out of a clear sky, all this turned upside down. Young Uppers began imitating the Lowers. Male and female, they dressed in rags, they stopped going to the hairdresser, and instead of U-language, painstakingly acquired the idiom and vocabulary of the gutter. Fashion trends shuddered almost to a standstill. The awful truth was that the concept of being well-dressed, tastefully dressed, elegantly dressed, well-tailored, etc. all these formerly reliable standards were thrown into the discard.

At first it affected only the young, but soon their elders (ever striving to regain vanished youth) hurled themselves into the movement. The clergy cast aside their dog-collars and defiantly flaunted turtle-necks. In academic circles, some faculty strove to be indistinguishable from students, stuffing themselves into jeans and affecting "message" sweatshirts. Even if they spurned such idiocies, they at least scrapped conventions. One brutally cold day I wore ski trousers, a heavy sweater and knee-high waterproof boots. As these were unbearably hot, I shuffled around all day in sock feet. A colleague wore a long purple velvet skirt, soaking wet around the hem, a wrinkled Indian cotton shirt, and running shoes. A few years before we would both have been sacked for appearing in such *outré* garb, but in the seventies (the sixties didn't really hit Canada until the seventies), neither costume excited a second glance.

Although some girls still wore mini-skirts, the unisex or androgynous look was dominant so that it was often impossible to distinguish boys from girls by haircuts or clothes. A few males took to skirts, but only briefly, and all the girls wore trousers of various descriptions. The most contentious male issue was hair. Young men fought passionately for the right to wear it long, and were in some high schools expelled for refusing to get it cut. Employers refused to hire long-hairs and beard-wearers. Then suddenly, almost without warning, long hair and facial hair became *de rigueur*, "With It," the ultimate in Cool. Middle-aged gents let their greying locks grow long, and identified ardently with the young.

In the good old days, the young had emulated their elders and betters, in the hope of being accepted by the Establishment. Now everything was turned upside down, and the Establishment tried to demonstrate hipness and coolness by appropriating the fashions of youth, in which they looked perfectly frightful and were jeered at by the young, from whom they'd hoped for applause.

James Laver points out that girls in mini-skirts and tights have very much the silhouette of a young man in doublet and hose, at the end of the 15th century. And as for the men …

> … they are no longer concerned to "dress like a gentleman." In other words, the idea of gentility

> which has kept men's clothes almost static for the last 150 years, is no longer accepted; and this represents a real revolution in manners. For nearly the whole of that period, all classes, except the very lowest, aspired to a "gentlemanly" appearance. Even when men adopted sports clothes, the sports were ... [those] of the upper classes. This is no longer true. Many male garments of today seem to be derived from such "lower-class" pastimes as riding a motorcycle, or are altogether classless. What this means is that, in Western society, the whole idea of gentility has broken down ... London West End tailors, whose world-wide reputation, acquired in the time of Beau Brummell, was due to the excellence of their cutting and the fine materials of which their clothes were made [suffered adverse effects].
> (Laver, 266)

The decay of the idea of gentility, Laver admits, has led to hardships for "bespoke tailors." The most admired men in the modern world are not ambassadors or politicians or generals or archbishops, but baseball and hockey players, film actors, and (especially) pop singers, few of whom are concerned with the Savile Row look. President Clinton ominously omitted to wear a hat at his signing in, the first president in history to have appeared on such an occasion minus the once-mandatory grey topper.

The universal, ubiquitous, and indispensable item in any wardrobe is, and has for years been, jeans. Everyone wears them — rich, poor, old, young, fat, thin, tall, short. Regardless of age, sex, race, colour, or religion, the world wears jeans which, now totally classless, have been working-class wear for generations. Jeans began sneaking into middle-class wardrobes, without fanfare, as long ago as the forties. Cheap, comfortable, washable, not requiring ironing, they have changed the whole concept of dress. After you have spent a relaxing weekend in jeans and running shoes, it is pure hell to put on tortures like tights, high heels, skirts ... And gradually everyone has stopped, or is in the process of stopping such masochistic practices.

Hats, once a major item in a lady's wardrobe, were among the first to be abandoned. Such things as girdles and corsets have almost ceased to exist; they had been threatened since the time of the flappers, but led a vestigial existence among the sufferers of middle-age spread. Recently hats have come back, not because of a fashion turnaround but because of environmental forces: fear of cancer from UV rays reaching us through our depleted ozone layer. But they are now practical rather than elegant.

As late as 1969, high school dress codes forbade girls to wear slacks, jeans, shorts, anything but a skirt, to class. Boys were yelled at and disciplined for not tucking in their shirts and not getting haircuts.

The revolution came overnight, like a lightning bolt, an explosion. Only a few years before, restaurants had been rejecting rebellious non-wearers of ties; now they had to put up signs refusing to accommodate the shirtless and shoeless.

In the golden days of the past, the rich were easily recognizable. Every lady had a fur coat, preferably mink or sable, as well as jewels, and recognizably expensive *couturière* clothes. Working girls dreamed of some day acquiring a mink coat. Nowadays if you wear furs, you run the risk of being hit with eggs or sprayed with paint by rabid environmentalists. The only permissible exception is an obviously ancient and tatty muskrat, bought second-hand at the Salvation Army. It is virtuous to wear this, because it looks awful, it keeps you warm, and you are drawing attention to the fact that although you're not responsible, someone was brutal enough to kill a bunch of little animals to feed the vanity of the original owner. But because you are wearing it when it is semi-bald, you are at least drawing attention to the cruelty, so that they didn't die in vain.

No matter how rich you may be, you can't wear jewels, although not for fashion reasons. If you flaunt your jewels you'll get mugged, and you can't insure them because insurance costs as much as the jewels. You might as well forget the loss, and buy some fakes which you can at least wear in public without fear of an attack. You can't even keep them in your house, because they'll inevitably be stolen. The only thing you can safely do with valuable jewellery is keep it in the bank, and what's the fun in that? You can of course wear the fakes, with a sign saying "Fake jewel, do not steal. Real Thing in safety deposit box."

The rich-poor gap is constantly growing, but as it grows, the rich get less and less fun out of their wealth, because the wicked poor steal it. Perhaps if the rich gave some of their money to the poor, the villains would allow their betters to enjoy a little peace and comfort? No, it wouldn't work. There are too many of them, and too few rich. The poor we have always with us, as the Good Book reminds us. All we can do is protect our possessions as best we may, with gated communities and security guards and bodyguards and attack dogs and burglar alarms and ... oh, hell, there's not much fun in that either, especially when you can never completely rely on the incorruptibility of the hirelings (*vide* Princess Steph) and sometimes the attack dogs turn around and attack you, if you startle them, or if they don't know you very well, and haven't got it through their heads that it's to you they owe their allegiance.

It is a difficult time, in many ways, for the rich and snobbish. But as Sophie Tucker remarked, "I bin rich and I bin poor, and rich is better." You must learn to put up with hardships, in the cause of wealth. We seem to have got off the subject of clothes, but as the hippies used to say, everything is connected to everything else. If that isn't classy enough, E. M. Forster said "Only connect ..." Okay. Back to the wardrobe.

In the past there were movements that perhaps foreshadowed the current revolution: in the 19th century the suffragettes produced the idea of "rational dress," notable for the contribution of Amelia Bloomer, whose sensible garments made it possible for women to ride bicycles (the beginning of several revolutions, in transport, in women's sports, and in male-female relations).

In the 1890s, the Aesthetic costume made its appearance. It was worn by only a small section of the community, James Laver tells us, and was intended as a protest against the ugliness of contemporary fashion, with a dash of rational dress thrown in, and some concern for health. (Doctors had been inveighing against the "tight lacing" of corsets which made possible the tiny waists required by the crinoline and bustle.) Aesthetic dressers wore heelless shoes, no corsets, and loose robes, often embroidered with sunflowers: "The Aesthetic dress was attractive enough for those who had the figure for it, but the majority of its wearers were not so favoured ..." (Laver, 200)

But that's something that applies in all fashion trends. Think of the mini-skirt, which was fetching on slender little creatures with good legs, but cruel for the unhappy fat girls with heavy thighs who were forced by fashion to expose their worst features.

Male Aesthetes wore knee-breeches, velvet jackets, flowing ties, and "wideawake" hats. Oscar Wilde made the costume famous when he wore it on his American tour, inspiring Gilbert and Sullivan to write *Patience, or Bunthorne's Bride*. It should be noted that the practitioners of unconventional dress were snobs in their own way, just as contemptuous of the clingers to convention as the other way round.

Other anti-class rebels who fought the ideals of fashion, were the Bohemians of the twenties and thirties, the Beats of the late forties and early fifties, and — its finest flowering — the Hippies in the sixties and seventies. Though diminished in number, and having less publicity value, they are with us still. Yuppies and their variants attempted a backlash, but it was a losing battle. Their polished look was discarded in favour of a new trend, Grunge, which required that one wear rags, often with real or ersatz dirt. It didn't last, but it was significant as a rebellion against the attempted return to elegance.

Clothessnobbery will continue, but the domination of women by the *couturière* houses may be a thing of the past. No woman is going back to wearing corsets, high heels, and the other tortures. At one time, it was a popular cliché to say laughingly that women were willing to suffer any agony to be in fashion; now it seems that comfort is winning. It is no longer unusual to see a woman wearing an elegant costume as far as her ankles, where it is accessorized with running shoes. Okay, *designer running shoes*, but still running shoes.

A form of backlash has manifested itself in such programmes as "Fashion TV," but it seems to be chiefly runway stuff, poorly adapted to the Real World. It is popular with certain audiences because it involves a lot of bared breasts and nearly bared genitalia, but comfortable and wearable it ain't, for the general public.

Environmentalism has also laid its cruel green hand on the favourite forms of display: No one living south of say, Winnipeg, can wear a fur coat nowadays without feeling guilty, or being persecuted. If you want the look of fur, you're told in hectoring tones, you can get a fake fur — just as warm and even more stylish. If you actually live in the far north, or are an Eskimo hunter, or an Arctic explorer, you are grudgingly allowed to wear caribou hide or sealskin. But this takes us well out of Snob influence and becomes a survival issue. Now even fashion models are leading strikes against wearing furs. Efforts to "bring back" furs have met with furious resistance.

The designers do their best, fighting a gallant rearguard action, hysterically raising and lowering hems, but it is in vain. Most women have rebelled against their dictates. You can wear just about anything anywhere, any time. Most of the efforts to educate the public in Snobfashion values have failed, possibly because of the availability of mass-produced goods. For example, designer jeans: they just aren't sufficiently distinguishable from ordinary jeans, unless you wear the label on the outside, which of course people do, but it's a desperate way to prove your superiority.

School kids, I gather, still compete furiously over okay labels, and God knows, clothes are expensive enough, except for mink coats, which have dropped like mercury in winter. Kids' clothes at present writing are required to be several sizes too large, so that the brats look like dwarfs, underprivileged dwarfs wearing the cast-offs of giants. Along with this, of course, the backwards baseball cap, which is at this writing said to be on the way out. We wait breathlessly for its successor.

The older you get, the less this stuff matters. A couple of generations ago, an old or even middle-aged lady would have had to wear a velvet hat, gloves, a corset, stockings, skirts, etc., and a fur coat in winter. Even with the coat, she wasn't really warm, as the wind blew up her skirt, but she couldn't wear slacks or trousers, even though she was freezing to death. In summer, she had to wear a girdle and stockings, and if she went shopping or anywhere else, white gloves, which had to be washed after each wearing.

Today's Senior can be a comfortable slob, without fear of criticism. Jeans, and all varieties of warm trousers are now chosen for cold weather, a cosy parka instead of a fur coat, with no fear of persecution by the animal rights egg-throwers. In summer they brazenly wear shorts, as they have been doing most of their lives, after all, and if they have the odd varicose vein, tough. You don't have to look at them.

As for the young, James Laver tells us what we've always known, that their habits of dress are chiefly motivated by the Seduction Principle, i.e., of dressing to attract the opposite sex, perverse though the style may seem to elders. The other factor once operative in fashion, sometimes in contradiction of the Seduction Principle, was the Hierarchical Principle, by which one dressed to indicate one's position in society, by imitating the Establishment. As we've seen, this is getting harder and harder to do. The Hierarchical Principle may yet vanish altogether, leaving the young to concentrate exclusively on the Seduction Principle, while their elders may relapse happily into the Comfortable Slob Principle.

Exceptions: sportswear is governed by rigorous fashion rules, which can be disregarded only by athletes so good that no one dare criticize them. The complications are terrifying: if you are a beginner, you make an idiot of yourself if you turn out in gear suited only to experts. But you must nevertheless conform to the rigid requirements of the sport. In skiing, for instance, if you appear on the slopes for the first day wearing last year's approved costume, you may never live it down, and your skiing experience may be permanently traumatized. But this is too complex a subject to be gone into at this point.

I will end on a nostalgic note. I read in Paul Fussell's *Class* that George IV condemned Robert Peel as common: "He's not a gentleman: he divides his coat-tails when he sits down." And in this very century, Vance Packard snidely described how a famous actor betrayed his humble origins: "… every time he sits down, he pulls up his trousers to preserve the crease."

What's so base about these actions? A gentleman never thinks of such matters, because he has a valet who will carefully press the crumpled garment when the Young Marster comes home. The rich can *afford* to get rumpled. Alas, there is a noticeable shortage of valets to press those coat-tails and trousers. And if you, as a lofty Snob, suddenly acquire a glorious Jeeves, you are never safe from that soul-destroying article in *People*, to be followed by the brutal biography. Which will be painstakingly footnoted and lawyer-checked, as a specific against libel cases.

Nothing has comparably damaged the idea of gentility so much as this mysterious 20th-century change in fashion. Nothing has previously made life so confusing for the aspiring snob.

Jeans and hats were straws in the wind. Now the levelling process has reached the point where a thoughtful Fashionsnob doesn't know where to turn. *You can't tell U from Prole*.

Snobnote: Toplessness and Nudity. In Europe, as we all know now, toplessness on beaches has long been accepted without remark. No males have gone mad with lust and assaulted topless ladies right and left; if they have, it hasn't made the public prints. And it would have made them, had it happened.

Bare breasts have frequently appeared on the runways of fashion shows, both abroad and here in once-Puritan North America, without producing any epidemics of rape, or indeed causing any particular sensation. They still can shock in less ritualized circumstances, however, and few of us can have missed the sensation when Gwen Jacobs bared her bosom in Guelph, Ontario, a few summers ago, excusing this brazen behaviour by the fact that it was a hot day, and lots of men were going about topless.

The public was divided on the desirability of the practice. There were of course a certain number of sniggering males who still suffer from Peeping Tom syndrome. There were both males and females who argued strongly that such behaviour was evil and would corrupt little children. It was the thin edge of the wedge, these people claimed, and all of society would be corrupted beyond redemption. One woman climbed her fence and assaulted a topless sunbathing neighbour, for exposing herself where impressionable kiddies might see her mammary equipment, and become debauched, depraved, and dissolute, even though they had been breast-fed as infants. As proof of their thesis, they point to a shocking occurrence during the Queen's visit to London, Ontario, in 1997, when a charming lady appeared unclad, with "God Save the Queen" written on her naked back. (So unsuitable.)

Others argued that if it was okay for men to expose their naked chests, why should it be wrong for women? And as far as corruption and incitement to rape was concerned, why doesn't this happen in African states where toplessness has been the rule from time immemorial? It is the forbiddenness of breast exposure which is titillating (these people insist) not anything intrinsic in the nature of the anatomy.

We now learn that toplessness is losing its vogue in Europe, not because everyone has suddenly become prudish, or because of an epidemic outbreak of lechery, or even a change in fashion. It is because of the attenuation of the ozone layer, and the danger of skin cancer. The skin on the female bosom is extremely sensitive and delicate, and can't tolerate exposure to the hot sun. So it's really a silly argument all round.

There are those among us who rather enjoy mooching about outdoors in the altogether, but not in public. After a certain age, depending on the shape you're in, nudity is not really terribly pretty, let alone rape-inducing. But on hot summer nights, a dip in the pool *sans* swimsuit is most agreeable, whether solo or with a congenial companion, and on a lovely clear flower-scented night is ideal for star-gazing.

As for the Puritan prudishness kerfuffle: that's dear old Canadian Protestant righteousness-snobbery. *We're* not a bunch of loose-living immoral *débauchées* like the degenerate Europeans.

15

Educationsnobbery

Thanks to Saint Bothan, son of mine,
Save Gawain, ne'er could pen a line.
— Sir Walter Scott.

As we've seen, acquiring literacy was crucial to women, and not only snobwise. It was the most significant step, prior to the invention of the birth control pill, toward emancipation. Oddly enough, at certain times and places, literacy was disadvantageous to men. Few readers today will be familiar with Walter Scott's *Marmion*, but it was still officially Literature for my father's generation, and Paw could recite yards of it from memory.

In the relevant passage, it appears that Duke Marmion, a bad lot generally, had been sent by the King to deliver a message to The Douglas, who was an earl of something or other, and who was icily polite to Marmion in his role of King's messenger, but with whom he refused to shake hands, because Marmion had forged a letter.

"Did ever knight so foul a deed?" inquired The Douglas, and went on to thank Saint Bothan, see quotation *supra*.

Saint Bothan, my papa explained, was the patron saint of illiteracy and ignorance. Where he got this little gem of recondite lore I don't know; I've never been able to find any record of Saint Bothan anywhere else, though I've searched. (Unfortunately, I didn't start wondering about this until years later, and when I checked my solitary authority, he couldn't remember his source.) Nevertheless, Saint Bothan may once have had plenty of followers, for at some periods, reading and writing were considered rather lower-class, fit only for clerks and priests, not for gentlemen.

The gentry hired a clerk to look after sissified stuff like letter-writing and bookkeeping, just as they hired a butler to see to the wine, and a falconer to look after the hawks. One did not soil one's aristocratic hands with that stuff, but saved them for killing enemies and game, and for horsemanship.

It should be noted, before we leave Marmion & Co., that Gawain, the one who did learn to write a line, made a pretty good thing out of it: he became a bishop at so young an age that he was referred to affectionately as "the boy-bishop."

Gradually, as literacy became the In thing, Saint Bothan lost prestige and disappeared. Universities were established all over the place, as were distinguished schools (for boys) and since these were the preserves of the upper classes, some degree of academic education became almost as important as horsemanship for the aristocracy. It was a long time before literacy was considered important for females, and anyway, the dear little inferior creatures hadn't the intellect to profit by it.

The Renaissance made literacy imperative, and even girls (upper-class girls, that is) were given sound educations. It took a long time for the lower orders to catch up. Eventually in the late 19th century, universal education was grudgingly conceded, although the superior classes fought it bitterly. Educating these creatures would only make them discontented with their station in life, argued opponents of the new order, and they would start demanding other unsuitable privileges.

Many education bills were introduced in the British parliament, but they were all defeated by the Tories, "largely through fear that public education would make servants insubordinate to their masters," according to R. F. Butts, in *A Cultural History of Western Education*. In 1870 the Liberals passed an elementary-education act, of which Sir John Fortescue snarled that it would only produce "a more accomplished type of criminal." Sir John had no use for any form of democracy, which he denounced as "the rule of the half-educated by the wholly conceited."

Universal education has made life difficult for the aspiring Edusnob, who must be very careful when it undertakes to impress its inferiors with its academic distinction, because it is too easy for the prosperous proletariat to respond, "If you're so smart, why ain't you rich?" (See Reverse Educational Snobbery, at the end of the chapter.) One method is to introduce into the conversation matters that refer, apparently obliquely, to years spent in institutions of higher learning, but it has to be done with great care.

"Let's see, when did that happen? Oh dear, I'm afraid this gives away my age, I must have been when I was in Grad School ..."

You have, theoretically, disarmed your audience with reference to your age, and have contrived to drag in the fact that you've been in the School of Graduate Studies. Not actually vocalized is the triumphant, "Beat that, you semi-literates!"

This is very low-level Snob stuff, though not as bad as framing your degree and displaying it over the fireplace, or — God forbid — putting it on correspondence: Ms. Joyce Smithers, BA. Not many actual BAs are guilty of this (though I know a lady who always appends a PhD to her signature) but they sometimes used to have trouble with mothers, who were inclined to display it prominently on envelopes when they wrote to their educated kids. This is no longer a serious problem, as post-secondary education becomes commonplace.

Doctors, dentists, chiropractors, garage men, and other base mechanicals may have their qualifications framed and displayed; they may even be required by law to do it, for all I know. Perhaps the object is to reassure the client that his/her care-giver is legitimately qualified. Unfortunately, fake degrees are readily available at very reasonable prices. A friend of mine, a graduate nurse with very high qualifications *but no BA* grew tired of hearing her associates degree-dropping, and sent away for BEAUTIFULLY ENGRAVED AUTHENTIC PARCHMENT DIPLOMAS, as advertised in one of the supermarket tabloids. For $5 she acquired a BA, and for $10 an MA. "The PhD was stiffer," she warned us. "Twenty-five bucks."

I don't have a PhD myself, and perhaps I'm just jealous. (I did all the course work for one, but never wrote my dissertation, for reasons which I will not go into here, because it is bad for my health to get into rages, but partly because I ran out of money.) However, I know a gent who, about forty years ago did achieve the pinnacle, and has expected ever since that the world will fall down and worship him for his certified education. The world did not co-operate, and he is still furiously dinning into deaf ears the fact that *he* has a PhD. (Or *is*?) He is apparently unaware that the number of PhDs has multiplied astronomically since his day, and some American universities graduate them by the bushel in such esoteric disciplines as Religious

Knowledge, Metaphysics, and Crystal Therapy. (This last may be a lie, told to me for leg-pulling purposes, just to see me react.)

Frustration about non-recognition of PhD importance can cause severe psychological trauma; at one time there were three PhDs (though only two people, one of them had two doctorates) in the same room at Toronto Psychiatric Hospital. Both were patients, not healers or therapists. Incidents of this type do not enhance the prestige of post-graduate work.

I once lived just outside a university town in a village which had been to some extent taken over by representatives of the higher learning: "Our little university colony." It wasn't exactly The Groves of Academe; more like its tulgy woods. For all their learning, most of them were pretty hard up, and they boosted their self-esteem by creating a sort of fantasy village which had very little resemblance to the actual one, though they occupied the same physical space. The real village was a mixed bag of real farmers and hobby farmers (who regarded each other with mutual contempt), pensioners, business people, tradesmen and professionals of various persuasions: the garage man, the proprietor of the local store, two ministers of rival churches (who regarded each other with mutual contempt), a doctor, a retailer of farm implements, factory and clerical workers, salesmen/women, a music teacher, a journalist (me), several unemployed drunks, and one authentic millionaire whose flamboyant private life provided us with an unfailing source of stimulating gossip.

The fantasy village invented by the academics was quite different. It was inhabited by simple rustics borrowed (I suspect) from Thomas Hardy or even P. G. Wodehouse. They were horny-handed and unschooled, but they looked up with simple rustic awe to the learned, educated folk who had come into their simple rustic midst.

The professors adored hanging around the local store, where the proprietor, recognizing a good business ploy when opportunity offered, pragmatically installed first a pot-bellied stove (though with no fire in it, since the stove pipe ended at the ceiling) and then a cracker-barrel, which he pronounced cracker barl, to amuse the audience. It was pure theatre.

One of the profs wrote amusing little essays which he sold to various academic journals and to the CBC about his quaint rural neighbours. Another one simply acquired conversational fuel for dining out and party-going. According to him, the quaint rustics came to him for advice, and for wise judgements on international affairs, and so on. "Say, Dawk [Doc]," was the opening gambit of their quaint rural questions. The real-life rustics might have addressed their medical doctor as Doc, or even Dawk, if they happened to have that kind of accent, though they didn't; but it would never have occurred to any of them to give the honorific doc to a mere PhD (in Modern Languages, yet). The quaint conversations were almost completely imaginary, although some of them may have been hung on a fragile peg of fact. It was useful party fare, though, because it gave Dawk a chance to register his PhD, and to regale the audience with his wise answers to the simple rustics' questions.

This was fairly successful Snobtechnique, until you caught on to it, and heard it used too often, and also until you got to know the villagers, especially the sardonic proprietor of the village store. Because it was convenient, and saved his customers the nuisance of driving all the way into town for stuff, he was able to charge outrageously inflated prices; he made it clear that no one was welcome to sit around the pot-bellied stove or dip into the cracker barl unless they were justifying their presence by buying something, and not just a package of cigarettes, either.

The error of the academics — a wilful error, originating in wishful-think — was to believe that the locals were impressed by university degrees. But most of the local kids were going to university, or had already graduated; there was no romantic mystery about it, as the Dawks liked to pretend. One of their wistful and quite vain dreams, when they threw a party, was that the passing rustics, observing signs of festivity, would mumble in their quaint local dialect, in awed tones, something to the effect of, "There be grand doin's, up to t'Great House," even though the academics didn't live in t'great house, which was occupied by farmers who had inherited it from their grandfather. However, they never had grand doin's.

The academic set were not pleased when the children of the quaint rustics showed up in their classes. They spoiled the fun. The profs secretly felt that university education spoiled the charming simplicity of the rustics, who might not look up to their wiser neighbours with the uncritical worship which they wanted to believe in. They particularly deplored rustics whose kids turned out to be brighter than the prof's kids, which sometimes annoyingly occurred.

A related form of snobbery, which perhaps should have a category of its own, but which manifests itself particularly in education, is British Snobbery. Of course I'd run into it before, but I met an exceptionally fine specimen once, and have been treasuring her memory ever since. (I knew she'd come in handy for something, some day.) I knew her before I lived in Fantasy Village, and before I had embarked on my abortive career as an Incomplete PhD. In fact, I was just on the verge of returning to university to embark on that ill-advised enterprise, and this lady came to take over my job.

"So you're going to work on your master's degree," she said, smiling at me condescendingly, and I said no. I'd done the master's, I was going on to the next level. (I still believed in this stuff, way back then.) She smiled condescendingly again.

It turned out that all Canadian degrees were meaningless, because our system was so utterly, intrinsically inferior to the British one that all this messing around in graduate schools was the merest self-delusion. We simple-minded Canadians might *think* we were being educated, but we weren't really. No one could be educated unless they went to British schools and British universities.

Nevertheless, her husband was working on his PhD in a Canadian university. Why he had thus lowered himself, wasting his precious time and intellect, I never did find out. I was having so much difficulty in restraining myself from saying, "If it was so great over there, why don't you go back?" that I could hardly trust myself to speak.

Mrs. British did not have her children in Canada, but went home to England because Canadian doctors do not know how to birth a baby. There is no good bread in Canada. There is no good cheese in Canada. The meat in Canada is no good. The milk isn't as rich as British milk. The eggs are produced in egg-factories, not from free-range hens, like British eggs. I once brought her a loaf of absolutely superb rye bread, which I bought in a small bakery right around the corner, as evidence that good bread can indeed be bought in Canada, and she announced at once that it wasn't Canadian: it was obviously made by immigrants. The reason she found Canadian bread so unsatisfactory was that she bought sliced Wonder Bread at the supermarket. She thus had evidence to prove that there was no decent Canadian bread, regardless of the fact that I got gorgeous rye and a delicious crusty baguette at my bakery every day.

One day she came in the office in a white rage. The university had returned her husband's doctoral dissertation, on the pretext that it was inadequately researched and would require more work before it was acceptable. *How dared they*? A vulgar little provincial university with no standards. (If they have no standards, how come they returned your husband's thesis? I silently inquired.)

"And it isn't as if Canadian degrees mean anything," she added, though she knew she was talking to someone whose degrees came from those meaningless sources.

One day I asked her which university she had attended, in England. Are you ready? *She hadn't gone to university at all.* She had gone to a school with standards of such astronomical height that, having attended it, one simply had no need for higher education. There *was* no higher education.

"How pleasant for you," I said, and by George, I meant it to sting.

I'll bet you think I'm making her up, but I'm not. She was real. One of her daughters showed up in one of my own classes, years later, when I was teaching in a college. How could her daughter get an education in a place like that, with an incompetent teacher like me?

Britsnobbery is a fascinating phenomenon in itself, and perhaps I'll return to it later. Right now I've got myself in such a tantrum, thinking of how I let that woman get away with such stuff, a hundred-odd years ago, that I can't do it properly.

There is a great deal of inside snobbery among scholars; consider the treatment of high school teachers by university professors. The teacher may have as many and as good degrees as the prof, and may be an infinitely better teacher, but he will always be, by definition, inferior, and will be condescended to, even by the lowest serf on the university faculty, with no recourse.

But even Oxbridge dons, who may be at the top of the heap in the Edbiz, are small beer in the bigger world of Socsnob; remember Lady Montdore's deprecation of them in *Love in a Cold Climate:* all right for dinner, but not for really important functions. And never let a high school teacher presume that he's all right for dinner, even though he has 98.7 degrees from Fahrenheit. Don't even mention public school teachers.

A longstanding Snobcompetition exists between the scientific side (the mechanicals) and the humanities (pipe-dreamers, or worse) but C. P. Snow dealt with this exhaustively long ago, and the interested should consult his tome, if they can endure the style.

Reverse Educationsnobbery

There is an anecdote, possibly apocryphal, about a self-made man of legendary wealth who had been startlingly successful in spite of early poverty which had compelled him to leave school at age eleven. A reporter asked him once if he had any regrets about his truncated education.

"Yep, I got regrets," sighed the millionaire wistfully. "If I'd a quit when I was eight, I coulda made twice as much money if I hadn't wasted all them years foolin' around in school."

I wouldn't have given much credit to this story if I hadn't known the ineffable Charlie Carter, mentioned earlier, whom I immortalized in my novel, *Flitterin' Judas*, published by McClelland & Stewart, who gave it absolutely no publicity or promotion, because, I believe, they had not yet assimilated the fact that people have to know a book exists before they're likely to buy it. (See chapter on Literary Snobbery.) It was thus one of the most inconspicuous immortalizations in literary history. Nevertheless, I think, it's a very funny book, and it's sad that no one read it.

Charlie shaped my life in many unanticipated ways. He was a self-made man, who with his brother owned a construction company, where I worked one summer as stenographer, payroll clerk, and Shakespeare authority. There were a hundred or so students working there, and when they attempted to impress the boss, subtly, with their academic superiority, he would sigh and remark, "Ain't it a sonofabitch, dear? Here's me, a poor ignorant bugger never got outta Grade 8, and I got all you educated bastards workin' for me. Makes you think, don't it?"

The camp was subjected to frequent inspections by representatives of various levels and departments of government, who were misled by Charlie's four-letter vocabulary and casual ways into thinking he was a simple creature. They enjoyed condescending to him, in a genial way.

Charlie's way of dealing with them was beautiful to behold. First he listened to them seriously and respectfully, looking suitably awed; then he got them drunk. Then, as they began to blather in their cups, he would somehow communicate the fact that he, Carter, though a poor ignorant etc., was the contractor on a big operation. "Hey," Charlie would tell the big shots, "a guy as smart as you, I bet you could run your own business."

The next day the big shot would be wan and hungover, trying nervously to remember what indiscretions he had committed, and almost licking Charlie's boots in his anxiety to ingratiate the man who did in fact own his own business: "I'm the President, but I ain't stuck up." I longed to be able to do something similar, but it isn't as easy as it looks. You have to be gifted.

Charlie told me how he got his start in life. He and his brother Paddy were poverty-stricken farm boys, who went to Edmonton and got jobs as truck drivers with a contractor. Then Paddy knocked up the boss's daughter, was forced at gun-point to marry her, was taken into the business, and got Charlie in. Together they pushed his father-in-law out of the business and took it over, with Charlie as president and Paddy as general manager.

"See, what you do when you got no schoolin', dear, you hire some poor educated bastard and let him do all the hard work."

Other Varieties of Edusnob

There are of course thousands of variations. A favoured one is "My degree is better than your degree." This is not as highly developed in Canada as in Britain and the U.S., where the distinction between ivy-league and red-brick is overt: "Southern Methodist? Is that some sort of religious cult?" and on an international level, as in the languid Oxbridge query, "Harvard? What is that?"

But don't let us kid ourselves: it obtains in Canada as well. The University of Toronto condescends to all other universities, within the Province of Ontario and without; if you go from say, one of the western universities for graduate studies at U. of T., you are treated rather as if you came from Lower Slobbovia: "Sas-katch-ew-an, did you say? How interesting! They have a university there?"

There is also a minor but growing prep-school snobbery, following the Brit model of Eton and Harrow. Here we have Appleby, Upper Canada, U.T.S., Ridley, not forgetting St. Mildred's, Havergal, Hillfield-Strathallen, Bishop Strachan, and I forget the rest. The snobtechnique here is much like that of the U. of T. to its inferiors: "Oh, you went to — uh — Burlington Central? Is that a tech school or a real — sorry, I mean an academic school?"

Serious Edusnobs will not send their children to any of the above centres of learning. They will get busy early and get the boys into Eton and Harrow, and the girls into their equivalents (I don't know their names) or better, to finishing schools on the continent, preferably in France or Switzerland. It is desirable that the children be forced to wear a school uniform, so that photos of them can be displayed, and that the curriculum should be — so far as scholarship is concerned — at least 100 years behind the times. Girls, for example, should be taught music, riding, French, and if possible, needlework. They should also be able to sweep a curtsey, against the day when they are presented. Any suggestion of utilitarian accomplishment is deplorable. We're right back to the barbarian insistence on the deprecation of productive labour: "A knowledge of good form is *prima facie* evidence that ... the well-bred person's life has been worthily spent in acquiring accomplishments that are of no lucrative effect," to quote Thorstein V. once again. If a girl goes to the right Snobschool, she can get a job in advertising, publicity, fashion-writing, television, anywhere it's not a question of mastering skills but of knowing the right people.

There are growing university snob cults by which the exponent hopes to suggest that his school had a special, perceptible distinction: "I knew you were a Queen's man the minute I saw you. One can always tell, can't one?"

People who have not been to university should not allow themselves to be intimidated by such techniques. They should study the Charlie Carter method, outlined above, or other approaches can be developed. For example, you can say, "I'm afraid I only went to a community college. I'm quite beneath your notice." This will make the university snobs scurry desperately about, trying to prove that they are NOT university snobs; they will tell you that some of their best friends went to community colleges, not because they couldn't get into university, but because they wanted to study fashion design, or to become a security guard.

A classic case of Educationsnobbery was that of Captain Hook, in *Peter Pan*. Hook was a public school man, and in consequence lived in a state of perpetual anxiety about good form. The fear that haunted him constantly was whether it was bad form to worry about good form? And of course it is, the worst possible. Good form is only achieved when you are indifferent to questions of form. Thus, Hook suffered gratuitous anguish from the fact that his enemy, Peter Pan, was always in good form, though he had never heard of Form, good or bad. Even worse, Smee (the lovable pirate) also had good form *without knowing it*, which is the best form of all.

Hook struggled to reassure himself: "His shoes were right, and his waistcoat was right, and his tie was right, and his socks were right." Unfortunately, he realized that Peter "did not know in the least who or what he was, which is the very pinnacle of good form." Hook longed to see Peter betray bad form, but he never did, until at the end, Hook trapped him into form-dereliction. Defeated by Peter's swordsmanship, driven to the bulwark of the boat, he bent over suggestively and invited Peter to kick him, and Peter couldn't resist.

"'Bad form!' cried Hook jeeringly, and went happily to the crocodile."

It is difficult but essential to understand that there are still unhappy individuals, most but by no means all public school men, who are similarly obsessed. Concern with good/bad form is a rather pathetic type of snobbery. A similar stricture applies to good/bad taste. So watch it.

Another technique for dealing with Edusnobs is a silent one: it is simply to remind yourself that anyone who has to work as hard as all that to prove he/she, I mean it, is educated, has missed the boat. Properly educated people are not Educationsnobs.

At one time many of us had a dim idea that universal education would save the world from its mad behaviour: if only people were informed and able to make intelligent judgements, we would stop having wars, destroying planetary environment, and so on. It doesn't seem to be working, though. For one thing, schools aren't very good at educating: they keep graduating people who can't read, write or do arithmetic. Only a short time ago I met a lady with a master's degree in (I think) psychology. We chatted briefly and, on parting, she said, "Sure was nice to meet youse."

A specialized form of Edusnob in recent years has brought the whole establishment almost to a dead stop. This was the Whole Language vs. Phonics competition. As anyone with half a brain should see at a glance, we need both systems to learn English, but we need Phonics to start. Then Whole Language slides in naturally. But the Whole Language freaks were determined to chuck Phonics altogether, though it had been doing a good job for hundreds of years in teaching people to read and write. Nevertheless, out went Phonics, and in some schools, teachers were forbidden to use it.

"I still teach Phonics," a courageous rebel told me. "I close the door, of course. God knows what they'll do if they catch me."

The result of this banishment of a good working system was that kids by the thousands began graduating from school unable to spell. The Wholelanguagesnobs then declared that spelling wasn't important anyway. Some people never learned to read, in spite of having spent twelve years in school. I had a twenty-two-year-old man who couldn't read in a college class, and he wasn't stupid, either. He was quite alarmingly bright at some things.

In contrast, consider the cases of Homer Bateman and Sally Cartwright, who were the village idiots when I was a child. We still had village idiots in those barbaric times, though they soon turned into the retarded, and would now I believe be intellectually challenged. Homer came from a good family, and was "simple," because he had been dropped on his head as an infant. (This accident happened frequently in those days; its function was to prove that the condition was not hereditary.) Homer talked to himself, in public, and to trees. Sally came from a very poor family, and was "not all there," no extenuating drops on head.

Nevertheless, both Homer and Sally learned to read and write. Homer could be seen every day in the post office, collecting the newspaper for his Mummy. He read it aloud to himself in the post office, breathing heavily and running his finger along the line, until someone told him it was time to leave. He often stopped on his way home, and read a news story to a maple tree. He could read the Prayer Book, too, and did so loudly in church, defying his family's attempts to suppress him, while cheered on by juvenile church-goers.

Sally's rather elegant signature appeared on buildings all over town, in chalk stolen from school. I suspect that Sally probably had a reasonable IQ, but had no guidance in behaviour from her truly deplorable family. Neither she nor Homer finished public school, but they were literate as many high school graduates today are not.

In earlier generations, when people had to pay to go to high school, the majority never went beyond Grade Eight or Nine. They nevertheless had a command of reading, writing, spelling, and grammar which some university graduates haven't achieved under the present system.

I gather that the Whole Language monopoly is on its way out, but the harm it has done will never be undone. Some of its victims will go unlettered to their graves, and it isn't their fault. It's the evil-doing of Whole-Language Edusnob.

A splendid letter in a Burlington newspaper was headlined "Phonics is key to reading fluency": Condensed, it argues that for too long, too many students have been negatively affected by whole language. Many studies prove the necessity of a foundation in Phonics, and there is no such evidence to support whole language. Without Phonics, students get stalled at a grade three or four reading level, and often graduate at that level. The states of California, Texas, and Wisconsin have made it mandatory to teach Phonics, while Canada sticks with Whole Language, and Phonics is neglected. It is not taught in teachers' colleges, and so graduates don't know how to teach it, though it is the foundation of reading fluency. There are only 44 sounds to learn and out of 26 letters only 10 vary in sound.

But how can "word recognition" deal with our millions of words? And their numbers are growing every minute.

Snobnote: Teachers have always scored low on social approval. Read *The Legend of Sleepy Hollow* if you don't believe me. Poor Ichabod Crane was an object of ridicule *because* he had wasted his life on getting educated, instead of doing something Real such as farming, like his successful rich rival.

Parents furiously demand good teaching, but resent paying a living wage to teachers, good or bad. Further, there is no reward for good teaching. Suppose a teacher is a marvel. It knows how to arouse the kids' interest and enthusiasm, stimulates thought, inspires students to work together and independently; shows them the relevance of their courses to their lives; is in fact a teaching genius.

Fame of such a teacher spreads. Everyone agrees he/she/it should be rewarded, encouraged. But *there's no way of promoting a teacher,* qua *teacher.* All teachers are equal, good or bad. The only way to promote a teacher is to shift him into administration, which is by definition more important and prestigious than working in the class-room. So the class-room is robbed of a genius, the very person who can do the most for students, and the administration gets someone who probably isn't particularly good at administering, and is bored frantic because it misses contact with students.

There is still a strong, sometimes unconscious, prejudice among the general public against all teachers, who as we know, are overpaid, underworked, lazy, and irresponsible. They're through work at 3:30, after which they loaf around smoking pot. In their long vacations, they go to the Bahamas and squander their substance on riotous living, while the taxpayer has to do without the comforts of life to pay their exorbitant salaries. And it isn't as if they could play football or hockey or anything important like that.

When the teachers went on strike against the educational mayhem of the Harris government (1997), this section of the population became extremely articulate, voicing their outrage on radio talk shows and in letters to the editor. One woman inveighed contemptuously against the teachers' need for preparation time: after all, they've taken their subject at university, isn't that enough preparation? Nothing changes in history, geography, math, grammar, astrology …

Does nothing really change? Tell me, ma'am, what and where is the Soviet Union today? What are its boundaries and capital? Is it permissible to use *like* as a conjunction? And *astrology?* Well, astrology probably hasn't changed much. On the other hand, it's never been on the high school curriculum, though who knows? It may soon take its place there, along with Creation Science, God help us.

16

Foodsnobbery

"Where for the land's sake *did* you get these amazin' pickles?"
— *Huckleberry Finn.*

We had lunch not long ago with a young man who had ambitions, God knows why, to be considered a gourmet. Unfortunately he got terribly mixed up over morels and sorrel. He hadn't a clue what they were, except that they were considered arcane delicacies and were expensive. He explained to me that "sorrels" (which he pronounced incorrectly with the accent on the second syllable, as in morel) were exotic mushrooms.

Now although I am the most self-effacing of Goodfoodsnobs, I do know something about both morels and sorrel, not because I'm a gourmet, but because I'm (a) an old wild-food buff and (b) stingy. Both morels and sorrel grow wild, and *only* wild, morels because no one knows how they reproduce themselves, and sorrel because it grows wild in such profusion that it's treated as a weed. Morels are a fabulous delicacy, and sorrel can be made into an elegant soup (called The Queen of Soups by Ludwig Bemelmans, a soup authority). Simple country types, therefore, can easily be experts on exotic items over which uptown sophisticates embarrassingly fumble.

Morels are little mushrooms which are found in spring, around May 24th in our part of the country. They look rather like mini-sponges, and are theoretically found in old apple orchards. However, they've also been found under pine trees, on river flats, in unfrequented lanes ... I once found one growing out of a railway tie. Although they are not easily confused with other mushrooms, it's a good idea to check them out in a mushroom book, if you are an edible-fungus tyro.

You can sometimes buy them dried, at hideous expense, but they can almost never be bought fresh, though once I saw a six-quart basket of them at the big waterfront market in Seattle. According to Euell Gibbon, who wrote *Stalking the Wild Asparagus*, you can easily go out and pick "a peck basket full." This is a lie. Don't trust anything Euell says; he claims that skunk cabbage is edible.

There is, or used to be, an Alberta firm which collects various wild edible fungi, preserves them in brine, or dries them, in which states they are not bad, better than nothing, but obviously nothing like fresh-picked morels.

Generally if you want morels, you have to go out and hunt them yourself, on foot. Experts and amateurs have tried in vain to domesticate them, so New York sophisticates are unlikely to be informed about them. On reflection, you're much better off NOT to go out morel-hunting. They are addictive, and once you're hooked, you spend the rest of your life in a state of morel-deprivation. The season is very short, and the supply meagre. You can tramp for miles, wading through long grass, getting caught on barbed-wire fences, bitten by bugs and shot at by farmers in whose orchards you are trespassing, without finding a one, or worse, finding one that has been eaten into rags by snails. Leave them for me. I'm used to hardships.

If you order them in a restaurant, you are almost certain to get dried or tinned ones. Further, restaurant chefs can't resist gilding the lily: they serve morels stuffed with paté, and otherwise messed up in ways that kill their delicate flavour. I read one recipe which called for stuffing them with a mixture of frozen green peas, garlic and sausage meat. Blasphemy.

The right way to eat morels is, as Mrs. Beeton would say, first catch your morel. That's the hard part. Then cut them in two, removing resident woodlice, earwigs, et al., wash them (the morels, not their occupants) in cool water, and then cook them gently in butter, and only the best butter, like that used in Wonderland watches. Morels deserve only the best. Salt and pepper cautiously, using freshly ground black pepper, no substitutes. Eat them reverently, with a baguette of lightly buttered, very fresh French bread.

It would be all right to make soup, if you happened to have a ton of them. But no one ever has a ton of morels, no one ever has enough. There is no such thing as "enough morels." Trying to improve them with fancy sauces and stuffing is evil, and should be forbidden by law. Wasteful and ridiculous excess, like casting another perfume on the violet. Most of the foregoing also applies to chanterelles, although they come later in the summer, in these parts.

Now to sorrel, accent on first syllable. Unlike morels, it presents no scarcity problem; it grows wild all over the place, and likes to riot in gardens. It is an attractive little plant, with a small yellow blossom and heart-shaped leaves like clover. The lower orders call it sour-grass, and eaten raw, it has an agreeably sharp, sour taste, pleasant in salads.

It is the main ingredient of Germiny à l'Oseille, Ludwig's queen of soups. Recipes can be found in uptown cookbooks, particularly French ones. Its Snobvalue doesn't derive from a shortage of sorrel, but from the nuisance-value of cooking it: leaves have to be stripped from the stems, as the stems are covered with long fibres, which if they are allowed to stray into the soup, make it look as if the cook has moulted. Most restaurants don't want to bother with it, and you will probably have to cook it yourself. This is what gives it gourmet quality and Goodfoodsnob appeal.

I don't grudge sorrel soup to appreciative Foodsnobs, but it is unwise to waste morels on them. I always feel that no one truly appreciates morels as I do, and unless I'm with someone for whom I feel the deepest affection and respect, I tend just to eat them all myself.

Just in passing, my husband proposed to me after I had fed him morels cooked in butter, served with French bread. They were the first morels he had ever tasted, and he didn't dast lose touch with the only source of them he was ever likely to find.

Since writing the above, I ran across a restaurant review, describing a place which claims to specialize in morels. They have "a team of gatherers who search the woods for the delectable fungi." One way they are presented to the diners is "with chèvre goat cheese in puff pastry with a port, apricot and chocolate sauce." This is an indecency. The delicate flavour of morels would be smothered in all that glub. And Harvey — chèvre means goat, so what you've said is goat goat cheese.

MORAL: Don't try to sound Classy. See chapter on Wordsnobbery. Read *In Defence of Plain English.* (Advert.)

Foodsnobbery II: Caviar

Caviar is of course the definitive Snob delicacy, and for one reason only: it is expensive. Okay, it's rather nice, but it shouldn't be eaten and only Badfoodsnobs will go on doing so. However, this form of snobbery is on its way out, along with Servantsnobbery, and for the same reason. Sturgeon will soon be extinct, along with practically all other fish. Every time you take that little spoonful of caviar, you're wiping out approximately 100 potential sturgeons.

What's more, I suspect that many of its professing admirers don't really like caviar. If it's so good, why smother it with sour cream, and onion, and other flavour-disguisers? Caviar-eating is the ultimate Snobactivity, and I'm using snob here in the most denunciatory sense; it's also ecologically criminal. Save those sturgeons!

We have arrived, you will perceive, at a Goodsnob/Badsnob division. Badfoodsnobs will eat something just because it's scarce and expensive. A good many species are being wiped out because they are believed to have aphrodisiac qualities — a certain kind of bat, a little monkey whose brains are eaten raw, as well as the stuff we all know about, like rhinoceros horn and bear gall-bladder. Goodfoodsnobs, even if they liked the stuff (which is improbable) would never touch any dish which contributes to the decline of a species.

Foodsnobbery III: Peppers, Cinnamon, and Zucchini

Food vogues are transitory forms of Foodsnobbery, here today and gone tomorrow. They are indefatigably promoted by food columnists in newspapers and magazines, and by that weirdest form of journalism, the Restaurant Review. ("I ordered the smoked salmon, my companion chose sushi.") Recently these scribes have been under a mysterious compulsion to force all of us to ingest impossible quantities of eggplant, zucchini, and peppers of several types.

Eggplant is a beautiful purple egg, which looks delicious, but in fact has no taste at all; it can only be passed off as food by dipping it in crumbs or batter, frying it, and smothering it in sauces, or baking it under truckloads of cheese. Zucchini is tolerable raw, in a salad, if it's good and crisp, but cooked, it's a tasteless white flab. "It takes on the taste of the vegetables it's cooked with," everyone urgently assures me, as if that were a recommendation. If I want something tasting of tomato and onion, I'll eat tomatoes and onions, no need to mess about with flabby zucchini. This alleged vegetable is an absolute menace in the garden; it takes over the space you need to grow real vegetables, like green peas and new potatoes. There's no getting rid of it, once it's in, and it produces its monster fruit in fearsome abundance. You can't give them away, you can't possibly use them all, and don't bother suggesting zucchini loaf to me. Gack, is all I say for zucchini loaf, and don't bother sending me your recipe, either.

Another food obsession, still going strong, is to load everything with nutmeg and cinnamon. I used to rather like these spices, mildly, if they were used judiciously, possibly in apple pie. But nowadays every course is polluted with them, from soup to dessert; they're even in the salad. I've come to hate them. I sometimes like to taste a flavour OTHER THAN nutmeg and cinnamon, goddammit.

The current fixation is on peppers. Just try to find a restaurant meal that is not contaminated with jalapeño peppers, banana peppers, red and green bell peppers both sweet and hot. Sometimes there's no other vegetable, just piles of pepper strips, raw and fried. As with cinnamon, I used to like peppers, mildly, but I'm beginning to hate the sight of them, and even the sound of them.

Joanne Kates' column in *The Globe and Mail* pullulates with red peppers: "When they put the red peppers vinaigrette on the table with the pesto-brushed breadsticks, you know this is where you want to be." A few sentences later, we've reached the antipasto: "fresh figs, prosciutto, marinated red peppers, eggplant and mushrooms, artichoke hearts ... an astonishing red pepper custard ..." Among the other appetizers, "Goat cheese is baked with fresh herbs and served with oven-roasted tomatoes, peppers ..." Next sentence: "Sweet red peppers ... are everywhere ..." and finally, the main course, "... a superlative stew of [guess!] roasted red peppers, sun-dried tomatoes, capers, olives and mushrooms." So if you weren't sick of red peppers before you started, you damn well must be before it's over.

The final item at present dominating cooking columns is allegedly fresh or smoked salmon. The allegedly fresh must be so lightly cooked as to be raw in the middle. Raw fish is very In. If you aren't scared of parasites, go ahead. Personally I like my meat and fish well cooked. It's terribly un-chic, but it's a hell of a lot better than trichinosis and related entertainments. Salmon used to be despised, because it was cheap and easily available everywhere. Now it's expensive, and consequently has great snob appeal. It will probably soon disappear from menus, or become as prohibitively priced as caviar, as will practically all fish, and for the same reason: we've pretty well wiped them out with irresponsible fishing methods like factory ships, bottom dredging, and drift nets.

Foodsnobbery IV: Asparagus

Every spring when the asparagus comes in, the cooking columnists go cuckoo, inventing new and ridiculous ways to ruin this glorious vegetable. They bake and fry it, they dip it in batter, they chop it up with (guess what?) peppers, they put CURRY on it ... anything to disguise and murder that delicate, delicious flavour. Actually, most people don't even know what asparagus really tastes like, because the stuff you buy is hours or even days away from freshness. And with asparagus, as with so many delicacies, Freshness Is All. The true asparagus epicure will not touch store-bought, canned, or frozen impostures. The only way to get really fresh asparagus is to gather it yourself. The epicure will have his own asparagus in his garden, or failing that, will go to a Pick-Your-Own place and rush home with it at top speed. There IS another way, but you have to be hardy, dedicated, and obsessive: you go tramping along railroad tracks, along obscure little country roads (if you can find any obscure little country roads, in these degenerate days) or in fallow fields. Asparagus grows wild in these places, and since it's a perennial, once you have discovered a plant, you have a fair chance of finding stalks in season every year. We go cross-country skiing in likely places, and spot last year's plants, making careful mental notes of their location. They're easy to see against the snow. It's an odd and interesting thing: I have normally no sense of direction, I can't find my way out of shopping malls or paper bags, and am chronically in a state of panic through inability to remember what I did with my car keys or reading glasses, but I can home in like a guided missile on places where I spotted asparagus plants years previously. We do of course have it in the garden, but we never seem to have enough — there is no such thing as enough asparagus — and so we still go hunting. Besides, it's fun. As is morel- hunting.

The Goodfoodsnob treatment of asparagus is this: gather your asparagus, wash it, put the water onto boil. Put your asparagus in a steamer basket, and cook it over boiling water for six minutes max. Serve plain-buttered to accompany your main dish, or with a lovely cream sauce on toast, as a main dish itself. It is permissible to sprinkle with crisp bacon. These are the only ways in which the true asparagus connoisseur will tolerate its favourite vegetable to be treated. Curry, indeed.

Another form of Badfoodsnobbery which is closely related to lunacy is the Rare Steak Syndrome. It has long been considered a mark of the gourmet to demand that one's steaks be hardly more than warmed over the barbecue or under the grill. If you say "Well done" in response to "How do you like your steak?" you are invariably subjected to a very rude sermon, or diatribe, by your companions and by waiters, explaining that your taste is atrocious and that anyone with true respect for food and for their palate will not ruin a fine piece of meat by over-cooking. I have always loathed underdone meat, and have been known to faint away at the suggestion that I eat steak tartar.

At one steak dinner to which I was unwillingly dragged (because I knew I'd be subjected to the medium-rare sermon) I nevertheless stuck to my guns and feebly stipulated "Very well done"; the waiter looked at me with loathing, and the next guest — casting me a glance of withering contempt — demanded in a deep bass voice that her steak be "Bloody!"

I'm forever indebted (in more ways than I can or will tell) to a scientific friend who seconded my request for a well-done steak, and listened stoically to the accusations of barbarism which followed. It isn't like underdone pork, which can cause trichinosis, they scolded us. Becoming bored after a bit with this display of Gourmet Snobbery, he asked if he might explain why he preferred well-done beef. He then described how, as an undergraduate, he had taken a course in parasitology, and had learned that underdone steak may carry a parasite which induces a condition called toxoplasmosis, the symptoms of which are enlarged glands in the neck, enlargement of the liver and spleen, rashes, fevers, and general malaise. Sometimes the parasite will attack the liver, lungs, heart, and central nervous system; it can cause impairment of vision, and (in children) recurrent convulsions and retardation of mental development.

The company sat frozen in horror during this recital, and when their rare steaks were brought to the table, they were as one sent back to be charred into safety. My scientific friend's steak arrived next, and although it still had tinges of pink; he nevertheless chomped into it cheerfully, and on being questioned about this inconsistency, explained that beef parasites occur less frequently than pork parasites, and he was too hungry to wait for further cooking.

It was a salutary lesson for the Raresteaksnobs, but when their steaks were brought back, along with mine (blackened by the sadist in the kitchen), none of us had much appetite, especially when our helpful friend gave us a little lecture on insufficiently cooked hamburgers, from which one acquires something called "hamburger disease," which tends to strike children with such symptoms as bloody diarrhoea, nausea, abdominal pain and bloating, and high fevers. It can affect the kidneys and the blood-clotting system, and is in some cases fatal. All from undercooking, our expert explained cheerfully, finishing not only his steak, but plans among his hearers for happy barbecue parties. And a good thing, too.

Foodsnobbery V: Restaurants

Restaurants have always been the resorts of Foodsnobs, because there you have an audience for showing off to. Large dinner parties serve the same function, but their prestige has more to do with the display of servants and table-settings than with the food, which is often pretty foul since all the effort and expense have gone on conspicuous waste instead of on good cooking.

Restaurants are not what they used to be, for showing-off purposes, because the starring role, once monopolized by exigent customers wearing mink coats or smoking cigars as the case might be, has been usurped by a new breed of waiter. In the old days, the waiters were supposed to be unobtrusive, their function to cater to and ingratiate the obnoxious guest, to rush about lighting their cigars, refilling their glasses, etc.

Now the waiters are front and centre. They are usually male, often university students or actors between engagements. The actors manifest themselves at your table with a flourish, often actually bowing, and employing an exaggerated French accent (sometimes fake, sometimes authentic).

"Good evening! May I introduce myself? Please call me Gérard. And I learn from our Reservations that you are Mr. and Mrs. Costive? May I take the liberty of congratulating Madame on the élégance of her toilette? You are an ornament for our little restaurant, Madame! And now may I guide you through tonight's menu?"

The university student's approach is breezy and straightforward.

"Hi, guys. I'm Ted. Actually, I mean, I'm like, a student at York, engineering, second year, and geeze, y'know, it is TOUGH. So I gotta make like a waiter weekends or I can't swing it. But it's great, see, cause you meet like lots of great people, only you don't have enough time to study. Anyways, you don't wanta hear my troubles, I mean, I'm here to help *you*. Well, what we got tonight is, like …"

Most of Ted's pitch is aimed at screwing the largest possible tip out of his victims, by presenting himself as needy and deserving. Gérard is no doubt thinking of that too but he is also deeply interested in his dramatic performance. There's a wonderful waiter in a book called *The Last Page* by an unrecognized genius named Bob

Fenster. The waiter is called Perkins, and he sees his role as guide, historian, and chef-booster:

> "Two specials tonight," Perkins said. "The Scallop Linguini Maria. Maria was Chef Ramone's first lover of the new year. Maria, who left Chef for the baker at the Café Fritz. It's a lovely dish, exuberantly creamy with a tragic touch of tarragon to remind us all of the romance and sorrow that make exquisite dining possible ... The Lamb Steak Wilette for the woman who tried to swim the Panama Canal. Chef Ramone has honored her with garlic purée and hazelnut crème."
> (Fenster, 32)

He also urged, for those in a more casual mood, the Hamburger Jim: "Jim blew into town a few weeks ago, made everyone examine the dark side of their souls, and then he was gone. Chef has captured Jim in bleu cheese with a fleck of jalapeño to hint at something deeper." (Ibid.)

Later, as he pours the wine, he praises the customers: "Chef is pleased with your orders tonight. He senses that you are establishing a deeper friendship that in the long run will be more satisfying than any short-term diets."

However, he was deeply disappointed in them on another occasion when they declined, in spite of his urging, to "explore desserts today," because Chef had been doing profoundly significant things with whipped cream. The perceptive reader will immediately pick up on the transmission of the vocabulary and tone of art criticism to food. Perkins was a pioneer in the field, a daring experimenter. Not many waiters, even in the flossiest establishment have the courage or skill to do well at this, though one can detect the stirrings of its approach.

The writers of dining-out columns are in a state of extreme doubt and uncertainty right now. At one time, they were simply restaurant critics, hard-nosed exposers of the lukewarm soup, the burned stew, the tinned custard. Now they are betraying anxiety and insecurity: they're beginning to wonder if they, like Perkins, should be performing the role of art critic. One such exponent is Sara Waxman, whose descriptions of food pullulate with Rich, Beautiful Prose:

> The green salad is a scattering of fresh leaves that crunch and burst into a symphony of natural flavors, casually tossed with walnut chunks for texture and shiny with the slick of extra virgin olive oil and a hint of wine vinegar and mustard. Grilled steak comes with pungent green peppercorn sauce, a pile of crisp golden pommes frites ... Ah, the good that can come from a humble potato ... and a dab of Bearnaise. Total $14.50. These are the foods a midsummer night's dream are made of.
> — *Toronto Sun*, August 8, 1993, 24.

And so on, for several more lyrical paragraphs. The exquisite flavour of tarragon. Atmosphere of a cosy French cottage. The simplicity of brown butcher-paper on tables. Now I'm all for simplicity, and there's nothing wrong with butcher-paper. But is it something to write poems about? At other times the diners-out become hysterical about the joys of truly civilized dining, with starched table linens (napery, in Snobspeak), sparkling crystal, and silver.

There are the specialty snobs, who make a production of eating only approved kinds of cheese or chocolate. The ones who lecture you on the okay dishes, and display their cosmopolitan taste and expertise in ordering, often causing their audience, or victims, to behave obstreperously and say (pressed to have *Abbachio alla Romano*) "I'm a vegetarian," or "Gimme a grilled cheese."

The Winesnob is a special study, of course; we have glanced at him under "Briefly Noted." His object in life is to command an admiring audience. This turns off many of *nous autres* (*tr.*: we others, i.e. outsiders, Nonwinesnobs) eliciting such defiant rudeness (after a learned exposition on why one should order a particular Pouilly Fuissé) as, "I guess I'll have a beer."

Once, after an especially trying performance by a Winesnob (long consultation with Edouard the waiter, calling in the *maître d'*, judicious sampling and knowledgeable "tasting", while the rest of us waited in agony, fearing he was going to send the bottle back), I heard myself demanding a Coke, and I *loathe* Coke.

Yet another form of restaurant snobbery is the proprietor's desire to have only seemly customers on display in his establishment. We once found ourselves inflicting severe pain on the headwaiter in a really quite ordinary restaurant; his anxiety to keep us out of sight was touching. We were perfectly clean — exceptionally clean, having been in the water practically all day — and adequately covered, though admittedly a trifle moist. We had been canoeing, and just as the expedition was coming to an end our dog, a large black Lab who was sitting in the bow, saw a duck. He leaped out of the canoe, and we both inadvertently leaped after him, or rather were bounced. We had worn our bathing suits all day, but had just got dressed in anticipation of heading for the nearest food source. We wrung ourselves out as well as we could, and were comparatively dry, if a trifle *mal soigné*, when we reached the restaurant, starving. The waiter took one look at us, and beckoned us toward a dark and unattractive little den at the back of the restaurant, blacker than midnight, though it was only about six o'clock of a summer evening.

"I'm not sitting back here," I said, "I want to sit by the window. There are plenty of tables."

His agony at the thought of us sitting by the window was such that we decided not to torture him further, but took ourselves off to the nearest drive-in.

Ludwig Bemelmans tells fascinating hotel stories about the snobbish tyranny of head waiters who sentence undesirable guests to tables adjacent to the kitchen, where waiters will come and go all night, bumping them and spilling things. So we paused before leaving the restaurant to inform the waiter that, though we might look a smidge dishevelled at the moment, we were persons of most respectable connections, our brother-in-law in fact haberdasher to Mr. Spurgeon. And by George, we meant it to sting.

Finally ... unless I think of some more later ... there is the snobbery of being recognized by the head waiter. It is particularly tedious when someone drags you into a restaurant and you have to stand around feeling embarrassed as he and the head waiter fling their arms about one another and shout, "Georges!" "M'sieu Klootz!" while they do both-sides cheek kissing. Jesus.

Foodsnobnote: The following beautiful lyric was sent to me by two husbands (not mine) who had overheard me fulminating against the excess of peppers and zucchini currently on the menu. They had suffered from it because their wives, though normally excellent cooks, had unwisely accepted the pepper and zucchini dogma so that all their meals were contaminated with these growths. They had been writing a poem on the subject. It wasn't finished, but they would like my opinion. With their permission, I have added a few touches of my own. It's called,

Down with Peppers and Zucchini

We are tired of peppers and zucchini
We are bored insensate with peppers and zucchini
If you're invited out to dinner, you can bet every dish will contain peppers and zucchini
Cooking columns know of only two vegetables: peppers and zucchini.
If you go to a restaurant, Lucien will tell you tonight's soup is *crème* de Pepper and Zucchini
The roast guinea hen is stuffed with peppers and zucchini.
The walrus flipper and octopus *en brochette* are garnished with pepper and zucchini,
Or perhaps you'd prefer road-kill opossum braised with peppers and zucchini?
And for dessert, Chef recommends zucchini *mousse*, garnished with peppers, on zucchini loaf.

We were once tolerant of peppers, though never strong on zucchini
Rather liked a faint flavour in soup of fresh green peppers, though not of zucchini,
To which every sensible eater prefers something tomato-y or bean-y.
But now we say, Down with both peppers and zucchini, and we don't mean down the hatch, we mean down into oblivion,
And the hell withy'em.
Cooks and chefs
Have worked peppers to deaths.

Whether or not you think we are meanies
We must tell you that pigs turn up their noses at zucchinis.
Even though we are doomed to become social lepers,
You should know that horses sneer at green peppers.
Whether you offer them a red, a sweet, a hot or a jalapeño
They will equally disdain yo.
They will not give you a civil hello

If presented with a yellow.
And will grudge a friendly mañana
To the bearer of a pepper miscalled banana.

Oh ye hostesses, ye chefs, ye cooking column writers,
Ye are of the hands that feed you the biters.
Have you forgotten the flavour of spinach, lightly steamed, with a lemon juice squeeze,
The divine bouquet of lightly cooked green peas?
Parsnips or cauliflower creamed in sauce
Baby carrots in parsley or mint to toss,
Broccoli served with hollandaise
Will elicit from us hymns of praise;
Give us baby beets with lemon and butter
And cries of gratitude we'll utter.
Salads of boston lettuce with green onions, ripe tomatoes and radish
Are far from baddish.
Buttercup squash and yams
Sweetly complement hams.

With all the glories of the garden out there to arouse an appetite in we,
Why in hell can't we have anything but peppers and zucchini?

Foodsnobnote II: Goodfoodsnob practices. Goodfoodsnobs are often vegetarians, their fodder preferably home-grown and organically fertilized, but those who do eat meat insist on free range birds and beasts. Goodfoodsnobs like bread with a hard chewy crust, and despise sugary stuff.

Badfoodsnobs try to show off by eating the scarce, the rare, and the endangered, chiefly because it's expensive. They are heavy on meat and fish. Lower-class badfoodsnobs are nuts on sweets and soft stuff, and have had a pernicious influence on food purveyors, who believe everyone likes their food contaminated with sugar and of a flabby consistency. The result is a continual degradation in food quality. Breads that start off with good chewy crusts gradually get softer and softer, and everything gets sweeter. Horrible example: corn. Everyone loves sweet corn, on the cob or off, but that doesn't mean they want it to taste like candy. Every new variety is more and more sugary, and it was already sweet! They make corn syrup out of it! Canned corn, which used to be quite a decent vegetable, has so much sugar in it now that it's nauseating. No wonder so many people have diabetes.

Final Foodsnobnote: Wide-ranging readers may have seen advertisements in the backs of obscure periodicals offering morel spawn for sale at astronomical prices. We tried it, following the instructions to the letter, with no results although we had lavished the most quintessentially splendid soil on it, and tended it assiduously. Not one morel. So in September, rather than waste that lovely earth, we planted it with onion sets, and some left-over lettuce and radish seeds, all of which did brilliantly until the lettuce got frost-nipped in late October. We were still harvesting onions and gorgeous radishes in December, and this is the unvarnished truth.

17

Herosnob

In the new erotic writing by women, sex is a cruel, even murderous business, and men, for the most part, are brutes.
— Lee Siegel, *De Sade's Daughters*.

A peculiarly Canadian Snobphenomenon can be observed in the work of contemporary female novelists. There is an extraordinarily frequent occurrence of a very sad and unfair situation: none of them have much fun in bed with men.

With other girls, yes. All alone, yes. With animals. Even with spirits. But with guys? Few or no favourable reports. This position is supported by publishers, several of whom specify particular interest in books by lesbians and feminists. Same-sex relations are almost guaranteed publication, even in this age of ruthless amputation of expenditure on arts and letters.

Reviewers and critics, who are obsessively fearful of appearing reactionary or what we used to call "square," wax rhapsodical about practically anything except conventional heterosexual activity, which has no *chic*.

But is this snobbery? Well, it does betray an invidious attitude toward the entire male sex, surely? Granted, women have several millennia of invidiousness to catch up on, but it still strikes one as a smidge perverse, especially as many of them nonetheless get married (to men) and insist on having children ("essential to the realization of their full selves").

The hero has disappeared from women's literature.

Many heroines are seriously unhappy in any circumstances, of course; they are often like Margaret Laurence's Morag, described by an admiring reviewer as "a misfit … numbed by booze and cigarettes." Morag, Vanessa and the other Laurence girls have love affairs with men, but *they're no damn fun*. Sex is a dismal, gloom-inducing business, although it is described in unnecessarily careful detail, as if Margaret feared her readers didn't know how it was done, and needed a sort of exercise manual.

"Margaret!" I often wanted to yell, ploughing through painful details of what he did to her and she did to him, "you don't have to draw a diagram! We know how! *Everyone* knows how!"

Birds do it, bees do it, even educated fleas do it. It comes naturally! It's easy! Too easy. That's why we've got a population explosion.

It's not only easy, *it's fun*. The risks can be awful, but the sport is terrific. Otherwise, why bother? But to the orphan misfit heroine, numbed by booze and cigarettes, it seems to be some kind of gloomy duty. It is ironic that the Laurence canon has been condemned by the religious right for these graphic descriptions, because in fact they are far from pornographic or even erotic. They do not arouse lust; they're more likely to put an impressionable reader off the whole thing.

Another numbed orphan misfit is Marion Engel's heroine (she had only one, who appeared in various guises in all her books). She gave up on men completely, to have a love affair with a bear. Some readers found these scenes hilarious, but apparently the intention was serious, even solemn. Bear was exciting on the hearth rug, but no more reliable than human males, not a good provider, and an abysmally bad communicator. (For a generation hooked on communication between lovers, he was the pits.) What's more, I simply don't believe in Bear's desirability as a lover. An ursine coupling filmed on a recent "Nova" programme was far from romantic. Mind you, a female grizzly bear can look after herself, if the attentions are unwelcome, but it still seemed a sadly brief and ungallant encounter. No messing about with courtship or gestures of tenderness. Nevertheless, *Bear* was so much to the taste of the literary establishment that it won a Governor General's Literary Award.

Critics are now claiming that the bear was *mythic*, symbolizing woman's deep bond with Nature, or something like that. All that rolling around on the hearthrug was deeply spiritual and mystical. Uh huh. Marion Engel was of course extensively interviewed when the book won the GG, and I personally heard her explaining why she had chosen a subject as unusual as a romance between a girl and a bear. Nothing mythic there at all.

Someone had challenged her to write a pornographic book. She had almost decided it was impossible, since porn was now out in the open, the market was saturated with it, and of course part of the appeal of porn is its forbidden element. Was there any kind of porn that hadn't been over-exploited? Ha, she thought, how about bestiality? Of course it's been done and done, but almost always with a human male taking advantage of some other species of female. (Faulkner's idiot and that cow, shepherds and sheep, goose and duck abusers.) But human females and male beasts had been neglected, so that gave Marion the material for her pornographic book, which really isn't very pornographic, but perhaps that's a question of individual taste.

In *Judith*, Aritha Van Herk's eponymous heroine also eschews association with the human race, preferring pigs, but it's a platonic relationship, praise God. Judith managed her sex life unassisted. There is a masturbation scene which (depending on your frame of mind) is either blush-makingly embarrassing, or gut-busting unintentional comedy. But I suspect it's what won the book the Seal First Novel Award. There's still a deep conviction in the publishing fraternity that nothing sells like dear old sex, in however dismal a form. Judith's was just about as anaphrodisiac an exercise as can be imagined, and she performed it simply as an act of hygiene.

Jane Urquhart's heroine in *Away* falls in love with a shipwrecked sailor whom she finds dying on a beach in Ireland. She embraces him, he says, "Moira," and dies. But she knows she has found her only love. She changes her name from Mary to Moira and dithers about for years in a prolonged trance or walking coma. (These fey states are endemic in Ireland. Anywhere else they'd call in a shrink.) Eventually she comes out of it, marries a school teacher, has two kids, and they emigrate to Canada. And who do you think shows up? None but the spirit of that dead sailor! Well, sort of. It's unclear whether it's the soul of the sailor, or whether a water spirit ("faery," in Urquhart-speak) took possession of the sailor's body, at or before his death, or what the hell is going on. Mary/Moira immediately dumps her husband and children, explaining to a mystical aboriginal that she lives with the spirit of the lake: "... this lake that shares my name — Moira ... I will stay near him until I die. I am loved by him and he is loved by me."

What was the spirit of a Canadian lake doing in Ireland, messing about in the body of a drowned sailor? Did it know while living in Canada that Mary was its fated love? Somehow got into a sailor's body in the hope she would find the body and fall in love with it? Was it hanging about waiting for a body to enter so that it could say "Moira," with the idea that they would meet at Lake Moira many years later? Classically, nature spirits are confined to a fixed locality, and can't go moithering about in other people's bodies, way across the sea. (Who's minding the lake?)

What died, there on the beach, leaving Mary loose in the flue — the sailor or the spirit? Did it influence the Canadian move, which would bring her into the Lake Moira area? Why did it disappear for all those years, and let Mary give another guy a bad time, just when he needed her to help bring up the kids? Not one of your better class spirits, if you want my opinion.

You may protest that I am bringing crass material standards to a magical mystical mystery, but I say the most magical and mystic of mysteries should make *some* kind of internal sense. The strain on the suspension of disbelief is intolerable. Still, this awful nonsense, written in a kind of pseudo Celtic-twilight prose, received enormous critical acclaim, and won the Trillium Book Award. Peter Gzowski solemnly assured the author that she was a mystic. Big praise in this Age of Spirituality, see Religsnob.

In *Abra*, Joan Barfoot's protagonist gave up not only on men but on the human race, with a not very convincing return to nature and self-sufficiency, arranging her life to avoid speaking to anything sentient from one year's end to the other. No bears, no pigs, nothing. It had all the pace and suspense of paint drying, but it won the *Books in Canada* First Novel award.

If men experience their deepest emotional attachments through male bonding, the Can-lit heroine finds them with other women. In Susan Swan's *The Last of the Golden Girls*, the heroine, though she spends a great deal of time on her knees performing fellatio on a variety of males, discovers that her most important relationship is with her girlfriend Bobbie, with whom she played sex games in adolescence. In *The Wives of Bath*, Swan reconsiders the Freudian theory of penis envy, with the protagonist a student at a girls' school, in love with her room-mate. To further the romance, she masquerades as her own brother, in which persona she works as the gardener's assistant. This would seem to require her to be in two places at once, but no one suspects for a minute. However, she urgently needs to demonstrate masculinity, so she murders the head gardener, cuts off his penis, and glues it on herself. This turns out to be a bad idea, as almost anyone could have predicted. Barbara Gowdy says on the cover that it's "... one of the most powerful depictions of adolescent female sexuality" that she has ever come across. "Such audacious honesty of perception and spirit is achieved only by writers of the highest order."

And Daniel Richler compared it to the St. Trinian's classics: blasphemy.

A lay member of the reading public reports differently: "I spent years in girls' schools and women's residences and I know them well. But I didn't believe in Bath Ladies College for five minutes, neither girls or teachers." Another failure in the requisite suspension of disbelief.

One of Barbara Gowdy's girls, in a short story called *We So Seldom Look on Love*, gets her kicks from cadavers, claiming they give off tremendous energy, which I somehow doubt. That's the distinguishing feature of corpses: they ain't got NO energy. We get explicit instructions on how to have sex with a corpse, although for some of us this has a fairly low priority. Gowdy won the Marion Engel Award for 1996, and Swan a National Magazine award for fiction.

Still, it can't be long until lesbian novels will have as much trouble finding a publisher as heterosexual ones do today; surely their shock value must be wearing off. Once the world accepts homosexuality as a fact of life, and not a mysterious and glamorous Sin; when everyone but a few nuts on the Religious Right takes it for granted, then it must inevitably become just as ordinary and predictable as heterosexual love. Not ordinary and predictable when it's happening to one's self, naturally, but tending in that direction in literature. Love of all varieties is wildly exciting and absorbing in its early stages, but the high temperatures cannot be sustained; they have to simmer down to something less hectic or we'd all go up in flames.

A gay friend recently complained that he sometimes pines for the old days of persecution in the closet, when life was dangerous and love forbidden. Now that everything's out in the open, everybody so tolerant and understanding, he mourned, all the dramatic tension has been lost. "One might as well be heterosexual."

E. M. Forster couldn't publish *Maurice* in his lifetime: he would have lost his job. Now it's all over the place. Proust had to disguise all his boys as girls. Now he's blatantly required on university curricula, with no secrets left at all.

What about the corpses, spirits, and other nut stuff? Will otherwise undistinguished writing be hailed with awe and admiration just *because* of the kinks? Are we driven to the conclusion that editors and critics need a course in Emperor's New Clothes theory?

I don't yearn for a resurgence of the Warrior Hero, with his axiomatic assumption of the inferiority of women, but some of us still prefer men (live, human) to any of the unappetizing options so far offered by contemporary literary stars. If you have to get your kicks from corpses and spirits, you must be pretty desperate.

The hero had a sadly brief life-span in women's literature. In men's, as we've seen, he was for several millennia the Hunter-Warrior. A modification was the introduction of the Parfitt Gentil Knight who was a gent as well as a warrior. The Sir Philip Sydney type. Then came the melancholy hero, with Hamlet the prototype. (See Sicksnob). He was still a warrior hero, but he was also an intellectual who saw the futility of it all. Later variations: The 19th century brought the Poor Little Me (PLM) hero — the sensitive artistic child with rich unfeeling parents who send him away to a ghastly school where he is treated brutally by beastly boys; Samuel Butler's Ernest in *The Way of All Flesh* is prototypical; also John Ruskin in his autobiography *Praeterita*.(I must admit this one made me cry.) There are elements of PLM in Joyce's unpleasant Stephen Dedalus, who makes me sick. The 20th century brought the working-class hero, who modulated into the Slob Hero (Kingsley Amis), the Beat Hero (Kerouac & Co.), the Angry Young Men (John Osborne and contemporaries).

And through it all the Hunter-Warrior stamps on, in the form of Rambo and others of the Raging Brute fraternity. Male authors' heroines, if any were necessary, were flawlessly beautiful, with golden hair, and nothing to say for themselves. Occasionally there was a bad girl, with a good figure, flashing black eyes, and no principles. She always came to a sticky end.

Women's heroes have been less varied, possibly because the majority of us were kept effectively illiterate until the late 18th to early 19th century. Then the ladies' great and almost-only hero burst upon a hungry world: The Great Dark Man (GDM). He was tall, dark, handsome, rich, rude ... but underneath that intimidating exterior beat a heart of pure gold, only waiting to be discovered by the Right Girl. And that girl was not the gorgeous dish of male fantasies. She was often a plain little thing, like Jane Eyre, or you, or me. But he saw her true worth, and ditched the rival glamour girls for her. Then she could put her little head down on his shoulder, and never worry again about anything, because he would always take care of her, faithful unto death.

Jane Austen's Mr. Darcy was for many years the king of the GDMs, and all the Brontë heroes were cut from the same cloth. Interestingly, they were all atrocious snobs to begin with, but were reformed by the love of a good woman. The GDM was pure fantasy, modelled on a (quite false) image of Lord Byron, who was every girl's dream prince. No GDM has ever existed in boring real life. He reached his peak and climax in Rhett Butler, and then disappeared, except from Harlequin romances and the like, where I believe he still flourishes.

A minor hero appeared briefly in women's literature in the twenties and thirties: the whimsical detective. There was a flock of these — Lord Peter Wimsey, Mr. Campion, Roderick Alleyn ... their name was Legion. They were all much given to quotation from *Alice*, Edward Lear, Hilaire Belloc and the like, a habit (I must reluctantly admit) that I too find appealing. On examination, they all turn out to be simply the dear old Great Dark Man, in whimsical disguise.

The GDM was equally fascinating to homosexuals, if we can trust Quentin Crisp, and I do, utterly. It was Quentin, and not a disillusioned female writer, who one day in the sixties sat up in bed and cried desolately, "There is no Great Dark Man!" He was almost immediately followed by all the women authors in the western world, and since that time, the Hero has in effect ceased to exist in women's writing. We have been obliged to face up to the awful truth: men are human and fallible and scared and incompetent, just like us. They are all secretly looking for a great big capable Earth Mother who will take them in her strong arms, and they can put their tired little heads down on her big kind bosom, and they'll never have to worry again, ever, because she will always take care of them.

Was this a form of revenge on the part of women writers, to make up for a couple of thousand years of Hunter-Warriors and Raging Brutes? If we can't have a Great Dark Man, we won't have any heroes at all?

It is pleasurable for me to be able to record that my hero, William Makepeace Thackeray, saw all this coming long ago, when he wrote *Vanity Fair — A Novel Without a Hero*. Actually, there is a hero — old Dobbin, humble worshipper of dear little Amelia, who kicks him around like a soccer ball with her tiny little slippers. But Dobbin is not a romantic figure. He's a good steady honest devoted hard-working self-made man, but such a hog for punishment that one almost sympathizes with Amelia.

> [She] had a way of tyrannizing over Major Dobbin … and she ordered him about, and patted him, and made him fetch and carry just as if he was a great Newfoundland dog. He liked, so to speak, to jump into the water if she said "High, Dobbin!" and trot behind her with her reticule in his mouth. This history has been written to very little purpose if the reader has not perceived that the Major was a spooney.
> (Thackeray, 662)

Of course, the Major asked to be kicked around, just as Amelia herself had been kicked around by caddish but handsome George Osborne.

> He had placed himself at her feet so long that the poor little woman had been accustomed to trample upon him. She didn't wish to marry him, but she wished to keep him. She wished to give him nothing, but that he should give her all. It is a bargain not infrequently levied in love.
> (Thackeray, 670)

Most young gels, at some time, acquire a devoted lover like the spooney Major. The temptation to kick him around is irresistible. We read the foregoing passage with rather enjoyable guilt. We had behaved outrageously, true; but oh, wasn't it fun?

Oddly enough, it was wicked Becky Sharp who valued Dobbin, though he despised her, disapproving as he did of wicked girls. "Ah!" she thought, "if I could have had such a husband as that — a man with a heart and brains too! I would not have minded his large feet."

Becky had seen enough of handsome cads (including Amelia's George) to know what bad bargains they were, and how poorly they compared as husband material with Dobbin, who had not only heart and brains, but money in the bank. Still, if she *had* got him as husband, she would quite certainly have jeered at his large feet, and criticized him for stepping on her toes when dancing.

I started out this rather digressive disquisition with Canadian women novelists, and their negative views on heterosexual love. I haven't really checked up on non-Canadian novelists' views, but an *Atlantic Monthly* article (February, 1997) by Lee Siegel, suggests that things may be even gloomier south of the border. Reviewing a variety of allegedly erotic books by females, he finds that everybody is abusing somebody else. "We are all deviants, and a belief in normalcy wreaks the cruelest perversions of all … coupling is always … hurtful, selfish, punitive …"

Interestingly, the solemnity we noted in Canadian writers also characterizes U.S. authors: "If [she] were not so solemn about it, the scene could be an arch satire of sexual revenge. But she *is* solemn."

Well, it's a solemn subject, sex is. No laughing matter. Get that grin off your face.

In the books reviewed, heroines are raped, beaten, tortured, decapitated, stabbed to death, in "public caricatures of private acts, monotonous rituals unfolding along inexorable lines," Siegel mournfully concludes, commenting that "… if the measure of literary art is the fullness of response to it, these books have not found their readers." Surprise, surprise.

I know I'm a stuffy old thing, but for some strange reason, the new erotic writing doesn't turn me on worth a damn. I've said it before and I'll say it again: if sex is as dismal and dangerous as the allegedly "erotic" authors would have us believe, why bother?

Snobnote (Lord Byron Division): Poor old Byron had the unfortunate distinction of looking like a dreamboat — tall, dark, handsome, brooding, melancholy, etc. In fact he was neither strong nor silent, though he was a good swimmer, a good athlete in spite of being lame, a famous conversationalist and a great poet. Voltaire said he didn't like heroes because they made too much noise, but the girls went bats for Byron, and pursued him all over hell's half acre.

> A virtual synonym for the greatest of lovers, he was passive toward women, sodomistic, sado-masochistic, fundamentally homosexual, and early disgusted with all sexual experience anyway. Outcast for his incest with his half-sister, he nevertheless seems to have gotten beyond narcissistic self-regard only in relation to her … In Italy in the autumn of 1817 he enjoyed an orgiastic season in Venice involving many scores of women but … settled down from 1819 to 1823 in a domestic relationship with the Countess Teresa Guiccioli [until] weary of his life, he went to Greece to seek a soldier's death [after] a last bitter frustrated

> homosexual passion for his Greek page boy Loukas …
> — *The Oxford Anthology of English Literature*, Vol. II, 285.

But as a romantic Great Dark Man, a bust.

His closest equivalent, in modern times, though it may sound profane, was Elvis.

18

Home Sweet Home (House and Garden Snobbery)

Showing off used to be the main satisfaction of being very rich in America. Now the rich must skulk and hide. It's a pity.
— Paul Fussell, *Class*.

There's a great deal of Snobtraining to be done in the matter of house ownership, and Nouveaux must take extreme care if they don't want to be figures of fun. A great deal of the pleasure of wealth has been spoiled by the environmental movement, with its tiresome attitude toward big cars and monster houses, both of which have been condemned as environmental obscenities. If you let this get to you, and it's hard to ignore it completely, you will lose all the pleasure of having anything that is bigger and newer than your neighbours, although this is the instinctive Snob tendency. In fact, it's what snobbery is all about.

If you are going to have a very big, very new house, then you must firmly decline the temptation of Olde Englysshe styles. There has been an outbreak of pseudo castles and mansions that must be deplored and avoided at all costs. Absolutely *no* turrets, towers, barbicans, moats, keeps, drawbridges, or anything at all savouring of feudal, medieval or Tudor influences. We have a rash of these horrors in rural southern Ontario. There's one not far from us with a portcullis, and another with machicolations (openings for hurling missiles, and possibly dumping boiling oil on attackers). It also has its own airstrip. Another fortified castle has a ready-made Ruin, of classical flavour, vaguely Graeco-Roman. Crowds of ecstatic Oldmoneysnobs gather on Sundays and holidays to point out its vulgarities and absurdities, and fall down laughing in the middle of the road.

The rebellious Nouveau may cry that if he can drive a Mercedes, he can damn well have the kind of house he likes, too.

Well, he can't. A car you can get rid of.

If he insists on building one of these frightful hybrids (with an exercise room and showers in the dungeon) he will be a laughing-stock, and will never live it down. His children will be ashamed of their Lovely Home, and will move to Toronto as soon as they're sixteen, to live in condemned warehouses.

It's safer for the insecure Nouveau to buy an established Classy house, but if you are determined to have a new house, the wisest course is to make it uncompromisingly 21st Century, conforming with the strictest environmental rules. It should have the latest thing in solar technology for heating both house and pool.

Your house should be furnished with gorgeously comfortable modern stuff. Don't fall into the antique trap. As we all know, if we've any sense at all, there are no genuine antiques left. The stuff in the shoppes has been manufactured for the market, at outrageous prices. Besides, it looks silly in a contemporary house. And again besides, it's uncomfortable.

If you fall into the Monster trap, it will be expensive to keep clean, and you'll find you're not using half of it, simply because of the dear old Servant Problem, which continues to rear its ugly head, even when there are no servants left to create the problem. Well, that *is* the problem. If you say damn the expense, and hire servants anyway, they'll soon have you bankrupt. So don't build a monster house, even a modern one, because you will be despised for it, and you'll either have to spend most of your life cleaning the damned thing or spend most of your money paying other people to clean it.

There are special rules about television sets. Old Money considers television vulgar, and pretends never to watch it, though they may officially have a set for the servants. Actually they watch it just as much as anyone else, but refuse to admit it. They used to spend a good deal of money and ingenuity on devices to camouflage the set as something acceptable, like bookshelves or a bar. In more recent years the trend has been to have a special room set aside for TV watching, and this is a secret carefully guarded from their friends and social equals.

Intellectualsnobs also disdain TV, but can't afford a special room for it, so they keep it in the study, or even in the living-room, but they claim never to watch anything but "Masterpiece Theatre" and opera on PBS. Neither Intellectuals or Old Money are allowed to have one of those dreadful dishes in the garden. ("Backyard" to Nouveaux.) Warning: Never say "backyard" in rural Britain or any County area, where a backyard is a prole hole full of old tires and men spitting tobacco. What you mean is *in the garden*. The garden comprises all the outdoor property, not just plant-growing bits.

Nouveaux who are resolutely defiant of Old Money and Intellectual standards can enjoy every refinement of modern technology, and will all have enormous dishes. In the backyard. They will also have a multiplicity of sets: each member of the family will have its own set in its bedroom, and indeed practically every room in the house will have a set. They will not be piddling little portable things, but great big expensive coloured jobs, each equipped with its own VCR and every other refinement known to the ingenuity of man. This will be deplored by non-Nouveaux, but will inspire admiration and emulation (sincerest form) in other Nouveaux.

Let us step outdoors. Please note that lawns are not discussed in this chapter; they are a study in themselves, and have their own space. We will look first at the pool, which should be enormous. Small pools are a waste of money, even for non-snob reasons, because you have to keep turning around all the time. Lap pools are good Snobvalue, if you make them really long, and I mean Olympic size or thereabouts. The true Poolsnob has an austere attitude, regarding its pool as a place for healthy discipline, not as an amusement for the kiddies. (They can have a kiddies' pool; only good swimmers will be allowed in the real pool.) It is considered bourgeois to use the pool as an entertainment centre, though it is probably utopian to imagine it can be stopped entirely. Small pools are for suburban backyards, not Snobestates or even Snobgardens. Above-ground pools are in the unmentionable category, Snobwise. Better have no pool at all.

A large pond or small lake has better Snobvalue than a conventional pool, but you can have an indoor pool as well if you like, and a small sailboat, rowboat, or canoe on the lake. Power boats are unthinkable on your own lake, and are always, everywhere, categorized as Nouveau. Old Money will touch nothing but sailboats on the big lakes or the ocean. On rivers, a canoe is both environmentally virtuous and okay snobwise, *vide* Pierre Elliot Trudeau, *supra*.

If you are unabashedly Nouveau, you can have a great big powerboat, just as you can have a BMW or Mercedes. You will be despised by both the Olds and the Environmentals, but you don't let it get to you.

Now for the garden and its décor. For some mysterious reason, statues that might look pleasing in Britain tend to be preposterous in North America. Eschew particularly anything with a religious element, or which appeals to your appetite for the quaint and whimsical. (You must repress this appetite brutally, as you would a taste for doughnuts or little cakes with green and pink icing.) It is permissible to be defiantly Nouveau, but you don't want to be Lower. So you must sternly banish all decorations like gnomes, mushrooms (humorous or otherwise), any kind of animal or bird figures, especially ducks with or without a clutch of cute ducklings. Real ducks on the pond are good Snobvalue, but not if you like to go in your bare feet, which is well regarded, Rural Snobwise. Ducks are charming to look at, but they do not toilet-train well. Avoid Canada geese, live or artificial, like the plague. We trust it is unnecessary to mention flamingoes. Picturesque shepherdesses and all that sort of things must be rigorously excluded. Defy these rules and you will find yourself shunned by your neighbours, and jeered at as suburban: you can't want that, surely? It's worse than honest prole. If you find yourself confronted in a shop with, for example, a whimsical gnome and thinking, "Isn't that cute?", run, do not walk, to the nearest exit.

If you hunger for decorations, you may plant things. You can have a greenhouse if you like; the glasshouse has the blessing of a long British U-tradition. Again, though, there are traps for the unwary: it is considered rather poor form to grow orchids, I'm not sure why; perhaps it's something like driving a Mercedes. Camellias and freesias are okay. You should also have a cutting garden, or cottage garden, with things like roses and carnations, shasta daisies, daffodils, tulips, and so on. No petunias, zinnias, or impatiens, which are lower-middle to prole.

There is a new Snob trend among floral colours: white, blue, and yellow flowers are much better value than the "hot" colours, which are unsubtle. Also, frequently, less expensive. If you are an Envirosnob, weeds and wild-flowers are beginning to be big, and you should cultivate a condescending smile for flowering crab and plum trees. (Suburban.)

True snobs must plan on having fresh flowers in the house at all times, or at least whenever you are expecting guests: whether you really like flowers or not, tasteful bouquets are a sign of Good Taste.

However, you should avoid pink or red carnations, unless you grow them yourself, in the glass house. Store-bought carnations are terribly bourgeois. Of course fresh flowers are a filthy nuisance, for they keep wilting, and the water in the vase begins to smell if you don't change it frequently, but you must NEVER yield to, you must never entertain, the thought that plastic flowers would be a lot less trouble. Snob (and environmental) suicide. Environmental because manufacturing plastics is ecologically evil, and it means you're not growing good oxygen-producing green plants.

Plastic plants or blooms indoors are only exceeded in vulgarity by their use outdoors. Do not succumb to the convenience, or the pretence that you can hardly tell them from real ones. They are absolutely beyond the pale, even on a balcony where the sun broils live plants. If you succumb, you are courting ostracism by all snobs of whatever caste.

There are many unsuspected traps for the unwary and uninformed would-be Snob in the garden. I just read a British murder mystery with a heroine in the plant nursery business. Now you'd think that she'd be all in favour of people buying bedding plants, wouldn't you? She gets an order for plants, to make an instant garden, which is going to mean big bucks. Is she pleased? Not a damn bit of it. The book is full of sneers and jeers at her customers and their vulgar habit of buying bedding plants. I must admit I don't understand what's so vicious about it, but I submit it for the record.

A small reward will be paid to any knowledgeable reader who can tell me why it's so offensive to buy bedding plants from a nursery. Perhaps it's a shameful admission that you don't employ a gardener?

As I trust has been made clear, whimsy (in the form of the gnome or mushroom) in the garden is universally frowned upon, and is a kind of declaration of lower-class tastes. However, equally deplorable is aggressive aestheticism and declarations of sensitivity and spirituality through and about your garden. This tendency was once called "greenery-yallery"; I heard it designated by Lister Sinclair as "God-wottery," from a very sensitive and spiritual poem, "My Garden," by one Thomas Edward Brown: "A garden is a lovesome thing, God wot."

Snobwise, this kind of picturesqueness is considered regrettable. It is refained. Much better form to be tough-minded and hard-headed, gardenwise. While it is god-wottery to rhapsodize about your roses, it is good Archaic Principle to boast about your leeks and brussels sprouts.

The following poem was written as a corrective to T. E. Brownery.

Summer Complaint

This hibiscus
Has had the hibiscuit
The foxglove is wearing mittens;
The catnip has bitten the kittens.
Nastiness and inertiums
Afflict the nasturtiums.
Sweet William is known now as Willy the Stink
Inglorious mornings dawn not Heavenly Blue but
Purgatorial Pink.
This garden is a loathely spot, God rot it:
Polluted pool, grunged grot, it
Might be dismissed by a philosopher with a tisk-tisk, but
This hibiscus has had the hibiscuit.

Snobnote: Bathrooms. A special Snobwarning must be issued on this delicate subject. At present, there is no denying the fact that the world has gone bathroom-cuckoo. We know from Angela Thirkell (see Servants) that in her day one bathroom per household was considered ample, because the housemaid would carry up those buckets and jugs of hot water. Now the occupants of monster houses feel abashed if they have fewer than six bathrooms, one per bedroom, plus a main-floor powder room and a shower in the utility room for people coming in from the lake or garden.

This is not considered excessive among Bathroomsnobs. More dubious is the tendency toward a kind of Roman Emperor attitude regarding the bath, which now requires a very large room equipped not only with the latest plumbing, but with luxurious sofas, arm-chairs and tea-tables, complete with china tea-pots, cups, etc. These offer the desirable Snob image of the bather, wrapped in a gorgeous robe, relaxing on her sofa with a cup of fragrant tea. Brought by a servant, obviously. No Roman luxury if you have to boil the kettle yourself.

Stop there. As we've seen, servants are scarcer than hen's teeth. As we've also seen, practically everybody today works at some kind of job. When are you going to find the time to loll around on that luxurious bathroom sofa? If you do find time, when will you use the *chaise longue* in your bedroom? And the one in the garden, and in the conservatory? When will you use the ostrich skin sofas in your sitting-room and family rooms? There are only twenty-four hours in a day, at last count.

Another cardinal error in the bathroom-sofa trend: one illustration of a "truly elegant" bathroom showed the sofa and tea-table in surely undesirable propinquity not only to the bidet but *to the toilet*. Does one really want to lounge, drinking tea, so close to that essential but unattractively functional article? No, no, it simply won't do. The sofa, tea-table, etc. in the bathroom suggest vulgar excess, or a too-plausible plumbing salesman. Save the money and give it to the poor, or to the environmental movement. Perhaps your sofa lets you feel like a Roman emperor/empress: you're asking for a decline and fall.

Here is one department in which we can usefully learn from the French, both Canadian and European. They have always segregated the toilet from the rest of the plumbing, except for the *bidet*. Even in comparatively humble homes, otherwise quite unostentatious, one can have a bath in uninterrupted comfort without denying others access to the indispensable utility.

19

Lawnsnobbery or
The Revenge of the Lawn*

(*A small inexpensive prize will be given to anyone identifying the source of the [stolen] chapter title.)

One of the quaintest and yet most significant forms of snobbery in the contemporary scene is Lawnsnobbery. Its origins have been explored with careful scholarship by Snob-Expert Thorstein Veblen, who else, and I wish I could quote the section on lawns in full, because it is highly relevant to our subject, and also gorgeously funny, written with a deadpan irony that fills me with pure ecstasy. In the interest of brevity, however, I'll paraphrase.

Western society (invented, according to Veblen, by a race of dolichocephalic blond pastoral herdsmen) finds pleasure in contemplating "a well-preserved pasture or grazing land." Cows were the source of wealth, the badge of success: therefore cow-pastures were beautiful. That's what it boils down to — the lawn is a cow pasture. As civilization advanced, and snobbery blossomed, it became rather gauche to be associated visibly with thrift and usefulness: "... the use of the cow as an object of taste must be avoided." Why? We should all know it by heart by now, but I'll repeat, for the slower students and those who have skipped classes.

It's an essential of snobbery that we scorn the base degrees by which we did ascend. At one time you could boast about your cows; but with greater Snobsophistication, you despised anything that smelt of utility, as cows manifestly do, among other smells. Anything carrying the faintest whiff of usefulness or thrift or manure became deplorable, and was relegated to the lower classes. Interestingly, in the non-aristocratic U.S.A., utility and thrift were permissible until comparatively recent times. A 1920 photo shows the White House lawn being cropped by the White House flock of sheep (black sheep, curiously enough), and this a century after the invention of the lawn mower.

You will recall from reading Jane Austen and her peers how lowering it was to be associated with anyone who was (ugh) *in trade*. Gentlemen inherited money and/or land, and while they might direct the business of the estate from their office, they never soiled their hands with mud or manure. In consequence, they often didn't know much about their ostensible duties, were robbed by their stewards, or mismanaged things so vilely that before long the ownership of land became a burden and, by definition, a losing proposition.

As we've seen, work other than war, hunting and sport continued to be a lower-class activity until well into the 20th century in some circles, though it gradually gained some degree of respectability.

The passion for the cow pasture as a gauge of beauty continued even though the utilitarian cow had to be banished from it. The wealthy in England found an answer: instead of a good practical cow, they had the grazing done by an otherwise useless animal. Herds of deer were favourites, at least in Britain. Lawns didn't have nearly as much appeal in France, and still don't — look at the Tuileries. We have been trained to think deer are more beautiful than cows, as their only practical value is for sport (stag hunting is still big in Snobcircles), and venison has much higher Snobvalue than beef.

Desire for the non-functional cow pasture has become an obsession with suburbia. It is assumed to be axiomatic that cow pastures are intrinsically beautiful. But if one examines the unconscious motivation, it will be easily perceived that the motivation for lawn-hunger is pure snobbery. A well-groomed lawn was the trademark of the landed gentry, who could afford not only the deer to crop it, but gardeners to groom and cosset it. Somewhere deep in the unconscious of every suburban dweller is a belief that, if you have a flawlessly smooth lawn, people will think you are rich and powerful, able to afford a herd of deer and another herd of outdoor servants. Probably none of them has ever consciously *thought* this, but it's at the root of Lawnsnobbery.

The lawn, as presently constituted, must be one of the most ridiculous of human inventions, since it requires incessant work, with damn-all return, because (as we'll see) no one gets any fun out of it, because of the ever-present danger of *spoiling the lawn*.

Before World War II, lawns were pretty well on their own, because the mowers were powered only by human muscle. In my childhood, most of our lawn grew up in orchard grass. We mowed the area in front of the house, a patch in the back for alfresco dining and socializing, and a lumpy rectangle that served as a badminton court. No one put fertilizers and pesticides on lawns; it was considered rather pretentious even to water them. May beetles, or white grubs, or June bugs were left to the care of the birds and skunks and moles. They made holes in the lawn, but didn't do it any permanent harm. Sometimes in August the grass looked a trifle brown, but it always came back.

After the war came the power mower, and everything changed. By the 1950s even my father, who had resolutely fought against every encroachment of the Industrial Revolution, succumbed to the allure of the motorized cow. Otherwise, we left our lawn pretty much to itself; it had managed without coddling all those years, why change now?

Suburbia, however, went nuts. Lawn-addicts lost all sense of proportion. They competed viciously as to who would have the smoothest, most perfect lawn, with the result that many streets looked as if they were bordered by indoor-outdoor carpet. If a skunk or mole digs a hole, the 'burbites go mad, and start putting out poison bait, which also kills cats, dogs, and birds. However, most lawn freaks hate cats and dogs, because they are not always respectful to lawns.

In pre-pesticide days, people lived philosphically with weeds, and even liked some of them. There was very little spraying, of anything. There was no market for the chemicals, but where there is no market, the resourceful (if ecologically unscrupulous) marketer simply creates one. After the war, manufacturers of pesticides, seeing their chance, bombarded the public with propaganda to make them believe that the presence in the lawn of anything but grass was akin to the Sin against the Holy Ghost (whatever that is; I'll look it up in a minute). Dandelions in particular are evil. Veblen observes,

> By further habituation to an appreciative perception of the marks of expensiveness in goods, and by habitually identifying beauty with reputability, it comes about that a beautiful article which is not expensive is accounted not beautiful. In this way it

> has happened, for instance, that some beautiful flowers pass conventionally for offensive weeds; others that can be cultivated with relative ease are accepted and admired by the lower middle class, who can afford no more expensive luxuries of this kind; but these varieties are rejected as vulgar by those people who are better able to pay for expensive flowers and who are educated to a higher schedule of pecuniary beauty in the florist's products; while still other flowers, of no greater intrinsic beauty than these, are cultivated at great cost and call out much admiration from flower-lovers whose tastes have been matured under the critical guidance of a polite environment.
> (Veblen, 132)

Snobtest: Identify flowers esteemed by lower-middles. Answer at the end of chapter. No peeking.

Since there's nothing easier in the world to grow than dandelions, and nothing cheaper, since they're free, they are by definition offensive weeds, even though they're quite as beautiful as daffodils or tulips. You can eat them in salad in spring; they are much esteemed as a cooked vegetable in Europe. They produce micro-organisms in the soil which combat fusarium wilt, a fungus which attacks tomatoes.

On the other hand, the pesticides that lawn-freaks spray on their acres of green desolation have caused all sorts of environmental damage; the fertilizers seep through the soil, and get into our waterways. Typical sewage effluents contain from 500 to 1000 micrograms of phosphorus per litre of water; a desirable proportion is 20 per litre, or less. This is the stuff which promotes the growth of algae, making the water cloudy green and scummy. When the algae die, they sink to the bottom, where their rotting consumes the oxygen supply in the water. This process, called eutrophication, starves fish and other marine life of oxygen. It very nearly killed Lake Erie, and is still threatening our lakes and rivers. We should prevent the chemicals from getting into the system in the first place, ideally, but if efficient technology were developed to extract chemicals from sewage effluent, recycling them back to the agricultural system, vast sums could be saved, and the chemical manufacturers would lose millions, both good things. See what Lawnsnobbery does?

My information on this process comes from a professional limnologist.

Ecology-freaks have preached this loud and long, but the Lawnsnobs are addicted to their chemicals, as incurably as any cocaine freak to his. Another interesting factor: the pesticides don't work. Eventually the sprayed lawns turn a scaly brown. They have to be periodically dug up and replaced with new turf. The lawn-freak's incessant torture of his lawn kills the soil bacteria. Further, the insects build up resistance, so that the poisons don't work — at least on the bugs. They can still poison small animals.

We once had all our lawn chores done by my son's horse (alas, now deceased) at no cost: he loved the work. What's more, he could get into difficult places that no lawn mower could reach, nibbling right up to trees and fence posts. He also mowed the corn and the carrots and my painted daisies, and he was obsessively determined to wipe out the pear crop before we could get any, but he was non-polluting, and a provider of organic fertilizer. The re-al thi-hing. It is also true that his work did not meet suburban standards: our lawn was a disgrace to the neighbourhood.

A uniform stretch of grass, the suburban ideal, is otherwise poor ecology. Nature favours diversity. Lawns are much healthier with a mixture of all sorts of plants, including dandelions, and especially clover. Lawnsnobs cannot endure the idea, of course. Last year a worried lady phoned to ask what she could do about clover in her lawn. The conversation was confused for several minutes, as I assumed that she wanted to grow clover, whereas she wanted to get rid of it. She had been educated out of using pesticides, and had been trying to kill the clover by pouring boiling water on it. This didn't work too well, as she had several times scalded her legs, and by the time she got the water to the offending clover, it was off the boil. The clover didn't seem to mind a bit. I told her I'd call her back, went out and ran around the block several times so that I could stop laughing, and then explained that clover is a natural (and free!) nitrogen-fixer, providing the very stuff to make your grass grow green and lush, naturally. Besides, I said, it's pretty. Why kill it? Because, she moaned, it spoils the lawn.

Another Lawnsnob acquaintance, sitting in the garden with me one day, was entranced by a small flock of goldfinches that were dancing about the place. She adored goldfinches, but they never came to her garden. No mystery: they like dandelion seeds, and she had conscientiously poisoned the hell out of all her dandelions (they spoil the lawn).

In view of these strictures, how can lawn-freakery continue? It will, because it has now attained the status of a religion. To deny the virtues of the suburban lawn is indeed the Sin Against the Holy Ghost, which I have now looked up: It is the wilful denouncing as evil that which is manifestly good, thus betraying a state of heart beyond divine influence. Obviously one's interpretation of what is manifestly good is highly subjective, so that the ecologists think their position is virtuous, and the Lawnsnobs believe passionately that a flawlessly neat lawn is manifestly good while a messy one not only is an affront to God, but pulls down real estate values.

On Sunday morning, the dedicated mow their lawns instead of going to church. (They also wash their cars; car-worship is another form of religion.) They have taken to decorating their lawns with icons — gnomes, flamingoes, ducks, comic *trompe-l'oeil* mushrooms which are also old ladies displaying their drawers; and interestingly, of late, small cows and sheep. Banished in the flesh, they have become quaint, and are permitted as art objects, and/or icons. The above are of course hopelessly lower class. More tasteful lawn-worshippers acquire tasteful statuary, often classical reproductions. I recently saw Michelangelo's David and either the Virgin Mary or Psyche. Very very tasteful.

A sad consequence of Lawnsnobbery/religion is that many hard-working lawn-slaves have no leisure. Every free moment, when they're not washing the car, must go to poisoning, fertilizing, drowning, or scalping the grass. There is no quiet in suburbia. No matter how early or late, nights, Sundays and holidays, someone is mowing his lawn, and the howling of the motor drowns out birdsong, conversation, music, and the screams of children being abducted by sex-maniacs. The obvious answer, one would think, is Astroturf. Developers should consider this: after they have scraped all the topsoil off their development, instead of putting down turf (most of which will turn brown and die) they could save no end of work and noise by putting down artificial turf, bordered with plastic flowers.

In its early days, as noted, lawn-possession was a prerogative of the wealthy estate owner; after the invention of the non-powered lawn mower it was chiefly a suburban obsession. The big sit-down mower made it possible to mow acres of turf without much effort, though it is far from being fun, accompanied as it inevitably is with incessant noise. One would think it was a dreary chore, but in its early days it had great Snobvalue because it was expensive. Many suburbanites with pocket-handkerchief lawns invested in sitdowners, presumably for prestige, since the work could easily have been done with a handmower.

Men often feel diminished by a machine they have to propel: they seemed to be serving it, rather than the other way around. This violates a cardinal Veblenesque Snobrule: Productive physical labour is associated with subjection to a master (whether it's a man, a woman, or a machine), and therefore is a mark of inferiority. But with a sit-down mower, there's no question of who's boss. It also proclaims one's ability to pay, especially if it's far bigger and more expensive than need be, as well as one's superb contempt for thrift — always a sure sign of inferiority unless you are a millionaire, when miserliness becomes cute.

Today, in Ontario at least, strip development has taken the prosperous suburbanite into the country, and it is commonplace to see miles of monster lawns on which no one strolls or sits, their only occupant the lonely man on his motorized cow. Even farmers, who at one time were too busy to mow anything but a small patch around the house, have fallen victim to the mania. It is difficult to imagine a more egregious waste of time and money. If there's anything useless in the world, it's an unbroken stretch of undiversified grass. Children can't play on it because it's saturated with chemicals; rabbits, if they know what's good for them, would be advised not to nibble it. It can't be used for grazing, for the same reason.

Conspicuous waste is its only function. Many lawns are forbidden to children as play space, for fear a game of baseball or soccer will make holes: "YOU'LL SPOIL THE LAWN!"

Astronomical sums are spent each year on chemicals, on machinery, and on gas to fuel them. Chemical firms have made fortunes, and the lawn-obsessive has forfeited all leisure. Practically no one nowadays can afford gardeners, and for awhile this meant drudgery for the lawn-owner, even with his sit-down mower, since the task of maintenance is unceasing except in the winter. You finish mowing one end, only to find that it's grown an intolerable inch at the other.

Then a few astute entrepreneurs saw their chance, and formed Lawn Maintenance firms. They take over all the work. They spray poisons and fertilizers, they mow and water. They can do the job without the odious imputation of being servants, since they have contracts, and cost the earth. They won't tolerate trees or flowers or shrubs except along the border; they must be able to blast right through without impediment, and God help the foolhardy wild flower that dares to raise its head in the path of the juggernaut. If you have a shrub or flower-bed that interferes with their passage, you may be required to take it out. If you don't, it may take a serious beating. One recalcitrant employer who refused to have a bed of hostia removed found them mown down. Many lawn maintainers now claim to use only "organic" pesticides, whatever that means. Strychnine is organic. No matter what they use, they upset the soil balance by the continual dowsing with chemicals of one kind or another.

Still, the lawn-firms make it possible for the estate-owner to contemplate his acres of ersatz cow pasture without giving up every moment of leisure to its maintenance. The lawn-man doesn't lend as much prestige as a real servant, but he's the best the Lawnsnob can do in these trying times, and he can be referred to as "our man" in a casual way, as long as he's not in hearing distance.

Answer to Snobtest: Petunias, with impatiens upcoming.

20

The Perversity Principle in Literary Criticism Snobbery

They used to walk through a pleasant wood of young birch trees which were just coming into bud. The stems reminded him of phallic symbols, and the buds of nipples ... The distant hills reminded him of a pair of large breasts. God, but those rhododendron buds had an urgent, phallic look! He pointed out that he and she were walking on seeds germinating in the womb of the earth. It made him feel as if he were trampling on the body of a great brown woman, as if he were a partner in some mighty rite of gestation. Flora sometimes asked him the name of a tree, but he never knew.
— Stella Gibbons, *Cold Comfort Farm* (slightly condensed).

An important element of all forms of Critsnob is a mysterious process in which the critic professes to discover transcendent artistic beauty in something which looks to the average poor slob like a hunk of junk. This proves the critic's superior sensitivity, awareness, and trendiness, and allows it to condescend to the poor slob. In the next chapter we will glance at its role in the GirderDrop school of sculpture, and the Dribble and Slurp movement in painting. Perversity Principle (PP) critics also see sexual significance in absolutely everything, as in the nature interpretations of Mr. Mybug, *supra*. In this chapter, we will consider The Perversity Principle in Canadian Literature.

The PP in Elizabeth Smart

My first instance of Perversity is Elizabeth Smart's *By Grand Central Station I Sat Down and Wept*, henceforward abbreviated to *BGCSISD&W*. Original title: *Images of Mica.* (*BGCS* etc. dictated by George Barker, q.v., *infra.*) It was first published in 1945, when it received cool reviews. *The Times Literary Supplement* commented on a "gift for poetical phrase which is occasionally arresting" BUT "her heroine's self-absorption is so intense that it produces a revulsion of feeling in the reader [and] has wasted a great deal of poignancy on a trivial and undeserving subject." Cyril Connolly complained of the "magnificent humourlessness [which blinded] her to the moral situation and also to all general comic or ironical attitudes." But then Brigid Brophy wrote, "It is a cry of complete vulnerability ... a work of art ... I doubt if there are a half dozen such masterpieces in the world." It was also praised for its "total disregard for contemporary social conventions" and its "lyrical prose."

A film was made of it. It's had mountains of near-hysterical adulation piled on it. I waited for months to get a copy from the library, licking my lips with anticipation, looking forward to something of the stature of Joyce's *Ulysses*. That's what the paeans of critical panegyric had led me to expect. Elizabeth had told *Vogue* that she wanted to see if she could write a book "as considerable as something by Jane Austen, the Brontës, or George Eliot."

It was a rather slim volume to carry such a weight of encomium; 128 pages, of which 13 were taken up by a Foreword by Brigid Brophy. (The first edition, because of the post-war paper shortage, was squeezed into fifty-eight pages.) But after all, one does not judge literature by bulk, I said.

The Empress has no clothes on, I said a short time later.

First the lyrical prose. Ms. Smart was one of the early exponents of the Historic Present (HP) ("I am standing on a corner in Monterey, waiting for the bus to come in.") This is still believed to be a sign of literary brilliance, like using fuck and shit, and editors have told me that I have to stop writing in the deplorably antiquated narrative past tense (NPT); all its potential has been long since exhausted, and the only way to write these days is in the historic present, which I have come to think of as the hysterical present, because it so often associated with a kind of irrational gibbering. I've also been told that the HP is intrinsically superior to the NPT because it has *immediacy* that the old-fashioned past tense simply cannot achieve.

There is nothing intrinsically superior about the Historic Present, and it frequently involves you in difficulties with tense progression, though many of its exponents don't know what tense progression is. Further, there's nothing new about it: Lawrence Sterne used it in *Tristram Shandy* for complicated reasons of his own — he was, or possibly is, being born for the entire duration of the book, and so the HP becomes, in his hands, a complicated sort of joke.

The truly great exponent of HP was Damon Runyon, whose nameless narrator lives only in the present and, according to E. C. Bentley, editor of my collection, and author of its brilliant Introduction, in all the Runyon stories there is one single instance of a verb in the past tense. He said it was in a story in that very book, but he would lay plenty of 6 to 5 that it is nothing but a misprint. And since reading that, I am going through that book many times, no little and quite some, and I am unable to find it. Still, anything which Damon Runyon may do is aces by me.

But I digress.

Back to Elizabeth Smart, who has otherwise nothing in common with Damon Runyon, for she is totally devoid of a sense of humour, an affliction from which contemporary exponents of the HP frequently suffer. Let us consider the famous lyrical prose of *BGCSISD&W*. Most of the lyrical stuff is not really original with her, but is imported through quotations from the Bible and Milton. Nothing esoteric, familiar quotations which would come easily to any Ontario child forced — as most of her generation were forced — to attend Sunday School and church, and memorize verses. Well, you wouldn't learn Milton that way, but if you took English 205 in second year university, you would.

Perhaps I have a blind spot. I find "lyrical prose" or "poetic prose" too damn close to "purple prose." We all write it ourselves in our youth, often in love letters, or in undergraduate assignments, and it is very embarrassing to read in later years. It is, I protest, an adolescent form of expression. It is a bastard form, neither prose nor poetry, and therefore free from the disciplines of either. Elizabeth, of course, did not believe in discipline of any kind. She needed total freedom, something frequently invoked by the slothful and slovenly.

Style is, I suppose, very much a matter of taste. How about content? *BGCSISD&W* is one long wail of self-pity. Elizabeth wants another woman's husband and can't get him. Oh, how tragic. The heart bleeds. How brutally the world has used Elizabeth, in not making George give up his wife to embrace the great tragic epic love. Brophy speaks of the author's "vulnerability," but Elizabeth has damn all concern for other people's vulnerabilities, and contributes materially to exacerbating that of her lover's wife.

The book opens with Elizabeth waiting for that bus, which is bringing George Barker and his wife for a visit. She has invited them. "I am their host." This hospitality is not disinterested, since she intends to seduce the husband. Once they've arrived, she and the Mister spend a good deal of time copulating, practically under the wife's nose.

Our dear Elizabeth, daughter of a wealthy Ottawa family, fell in love with British poet George Barker in 1937, and for years thereafter tried by every dirty trick and sneaky manoeuvre possible to steal him from his wife. An indulged rich brat, she was used to getting her own way, and she succeeded sufficiently to produce four children by George; however, she never managed to detach him from his wife. And yet George was not much of a prize. He bragged of how he was seduced by a boy in a print-shop: "A boy with green eyes and long lashes, whom I had never seen before, took me into the back of a print-shop and made love to me, and for two weeks I went around remembering the numbers on bus conductors hats."

Elizabeth's response was to "withdraw into the dark with my own obstreperous shape of shame, offended with my own flesh which cannot metamorphose into a print-shop boy with armpits like chalices."

Oh, poor baby. Stuck with one sex.

This historic romance, this epic love, went on for years, with interruptions such as that of the print-shop boy with his classic armpits. George had approximately fifteen children (no one knows how many for sure), by four or possibly five different women. First wife Jessica left him, and he contracted liaisons with several other "wives" but he didn't marry Elizabeth, though she went right on chasing him, and screaming, and nagging.

A biography, *By Heart*, by Rosemary Sullivan, tries nobly to present Poor Liz sympathetically, in spite of which she emerges not as a great tragic figure but as an obnoxious insensitive self-pitying monster, who lived all her life on an allowance from her parents, while chronically bitching about their insensitivity, how they didn't understand her, or value her precious George as they ought. So callous. What's more, her mother didn't give her the love she needed. *Poor* Elizabeth! Well, my mother didn't give me the love *I* needed. In fact, I've never met anyone whose mother gave them the love they needed. It's the universal complaint in psychiatrists' case histories. But Elizabeth seemed to figure she had been cruelly singled out for maternal deprivation.

George is a fragile figure to bear the weight of this monumental passion. No great dark man there. He was a poet but not a very good one, though he believed that the world owed him a living, and "he belonged among the great." He unabashedly bummed money from everyone he could possibly touch, and never paid it back; they owed it to him, as a poet. The biographical note on Barker in *The Penguin Book of Contemporary Verse* (1950) describes him as a cross between "… a clumsier Dylan Thomas and a less intelligent Spender." Only two short poems are included in the collection, both of them in my opinion sloppy imitations of T. S. Eliot.

George not only had the morals of an alley-cat, but he bragged about his conquests, causing Elizabeth to suffer monumental pain, which she trumpeted to the world. He seems to have been something of a draft-dodger: when all his contemporaries in England were out fighting Hitler, George was modestly hiding out in America. He was not a good provider. He had run-ins with the coppers (how scathing is Liz on the insensitivity of policemen!) and was at least once in jail: "They have hung that marvellous face … in the criminal's gallery. He is straightjacketed to the bed."

He calls her foul names, he sends her out at midnight on New Year's Eve to get him a thermos bottle. He abandons her: "My love, why did you leave me on Lexington Avenue in the Ford that had no brakes?" (Get that poetic prose!) She angrily quotes the insensitive questions of her family and friends: "If he needs money, why doesn't he get a job?" "What does he know of Love that lets his country down in her Hour-of-Need?" What did *they* know of love? Elizabeth asked contemptuously.

She's pregnant: "I am the last pregnant woman in a desolated world." Wrong, dearie. Just one digit in the population explosion.

At last, though, she has to admit that George has "sinned against love." She doesn't explain exactly how, but one gathers that the sin was in not leaving his wife for her, Elizabeth. What's more, he's still sleeping with his wife: how base can you get?

George needs women, but he believes they are inferior creations: "… the woman exists in a lower category of spiritual consciousness," he says in his novel, *The Dead Seagull*, and later in an interview in which he criticizes *BGCS* as "kerfuffle, what you could read in any women's magazine," he airily explains, "Women don't have souls."

Elizabeth's entire published *oeuvre* couldn't have added up to three hundred pages, a rather wobbly foundation for the worship she has been given. If she really had a great literary talent, how come she wrote so little? Her two novels (*BGCS*, *The Assumption of Rogues and Rascals)*, a slim volume of poetry called *A Bonus*, and *In the Meantime*, a VERY brief anthology (about twenty poems, three short stories) complete the canon. I hadn't read any of Elizabeth's poetry before, and it startled me because it was so very, remarkably, unconscionably bad. Some of it is doggerel (i.e., it rhymes, though it has no rhyme scheme or consistency in pattern) and most of it is verse so free as to be licentious. It is really not poetry at all but bad prose. A worse quality still is its pretentiousness. It pretends to profundity. Technically it is far below the level of most student poetry, far worse than the poems which still sometimes appear in rural weekly newspapers.

The Assumption of Rogues and Rascals came out in 1978. Auberon Waugh reviewed it in *The Statesman*, under the heading, "Heroine in a Terrible Mess!"

> … her book has no story or characters. The heroine is not remotely interested in anyone else, and she can't be bothered to remember people, places, or things in the course of this terrible concentration on herself … The answer to her agonized questions ["What's it all about? What's it all for?"] … is surely that Miss Smart wishes to exhibit herself … The most endearing thing about her is that she seems to be under no illusions [that she is not a complete mess]. If the spectacle of a young woman so obsessed with her emotions is likely to revolt, the spectacle of an older woman still wallowing in them 30 years later will scarcely be found more appetizing.

Of Elizabeth's defiant determination to "… leave the washing up and take a look around" he suggests, "I really think she should get the washing-up done."

On the strength of *The Assumption of Rogues and Rascals* and a Canadian edition of *BGCSISD&W*, Elizabeth was invited to Canada to act as writer-in-residence at the University of Alberta. She thought she was going to "enrich the lives" of the lower orders in "… the Bible Belt, the Suspender Belt," but it turned out to be Hell. "Why this is Hell," she quotes Mephistopheles, "and how shall I get out of it?"

The hellishness may have resulted from her habit of getting, in the words of a woman member of the English Department, "skunked." At a Faculty Club party, she "… drank everything in sight and main-lined martinis and house wine until she lapsed in incoherent babble and made passes at both me and [a male undergraduate]. We finally poured her into her apartment … After that I avoided Elizabeth … others in the department also attempted to befriend her and had comparable experiences so that she seldom received a second invitation."

Elizabeth, as a proponent of Passion, would no doubt have described her behaviour as Dionysiac abandon, rather than getting skunked. But in fact, no matter which you call it, if someone gets drunk, makes passes, throws up, etc., she is unlikely to receive a second invitation. We aren't all into Dionysiac abandon and Passion, once we've grown up. If this was the "enrichment" she planned to offer Edmontonians, it wasn't the kind they'd hoped for.

None of this affected the Smart-cult critics. Alice Munro and Michael Ondaatje recommended her for a Canada Council grant, so that she could stay in Canada for a year and write. She stayed in Canada, but failed to write anything, except self-pitying notes in her journal: "Lonely & bored. Unstimulated … Complaining, explaining but not being able to explain. Getting fat, lethargic, hopeless, like an unloved child. Sorry for myself. For the first time ever …"

The first time ever … Lady, every word you've written has reeked with self-pity. But the critics went on lauding her.

Philippa Toomis wrote in *The Times* of how *BGCSISD&W* describes "… a love both despairing and triumphant upon which the reader may gaze, awed, appalled, or even perhaps, envious …" Wrong, Philippa. Does one really feel awe and envy for the self-obsessed whiner who has no interests beyond her selfish frustrations? Maybe there are others who have had babies, or lusted after another woman's man, but they aren't important. They aren't sensitive like Elizabeth, they don't suffer like Elizabeth. The world has an obligation to give Elizabeth whatever she wants, and if she wants something that belongs to another woman, well, too bad for the other one. It's significant that *BGCS* was published in 1945, but its author never mentions that the most terrible war in history was devastating the world. What does that matter, compared to Elizabeth's unhappiness?

A friend in the British Labour party once remarked on the fact that she wasn't interested in politics. "Not in the great issues and underlying ideas." Elizabeth replied that she wasn't interested in politics *because* she was "only interested in the big things." In practice, Elizabeth was uninterested in anything that didn't centre around Elizabeth, the ultimate Big Thing. The devoted Sullivan mentions the war as "the backdrop against which Elizabeth pursued her ethic of love."

Sullivan is less a biographer than a votary. Elizabeth is faultless. Her every word, however offensive, however trifling, is sacred. Even a request for disposable diapers is conscientiously recorded, as if it were literature. If one read only *By Heart*, without consulting Smart's work, one would believe she belonged with George Eliot and Virginia Woolf, neither of whom allowed themselves the self-pitying, self-indulgent, undisciplined antics of Ms. Smart. Further, the biography is longer than the life-time production by Ms. Smart.

In an effort not to be unjust, I read *Autobiographies*, which an editor, Christina Burridge, patiently stuck together from a mess of journals, loose paper, fragments of letters, etc. Like *By Heart*, it's a devotional work. By the time I'd finished, I'd begun to dislike Poor Elizabeth so much that it was difficult to maintain any detachment. She was a lush, she chain-smoked, she sniffed glue, she slept around with both men and women, and she was nasty as hell. Sullivan's hero-worship excuses all her faults, explaining repeatedly that she was A Writer, which is (apparently) justification for anything and everything. Well, many writers have been fairly unpleasant human beings, it's true; we forgive them if their writing is so good that we can't resist them. Shelley may not have been a good husband, but goddamn, you have to forgive a man who can write the "Ode to the West Wind." Elizabeth's writing is just not good enough.

Anyone who is critical of Smart is invariably advised that she doesn't understand (or is afraid of) Passion. Myself, I'm with Hamlet. I say, Give me the man, or possibly woman, who is not passion's slave and I will wear him/her In my heart's core.

For my sins, I've had to read a great deal of student poetry, much of which was bad. But almost all of it was better than Smart's. Hers is without doubt the worst poetry I have ever seen published with a pretence of being serious. Nevertheless, Sullivan is so infatuated with her subject that she believes it is brilliant. All of Elizabeth's writing is sacred and inspired in her biographer's eyes, from childish scribbling and teenage maundering to fashion writing and advertising copy ("This Christmas You Can Enjoy Your Guests") and such masterpieces of advancing years as "Trying to Write." Every line she wrote is seriously listed in the Index, under the heading "Works," including "Birth of a Genius," written at age fourteen, and the kind of baby-books that every mother keeps.

"With four children and grandchildren, she was able to write books that sent a mad look careering into eternity," writes Sullivan. She did? Well, where are they? I've read everything she wrote, and I've yet to see anything that answers that description.

In *BGCSISD&W*, Elizabeth piously pretends to deep sympathy for George's wife, Jessica. But in real life, she was agitating for Jessica to get a job, somewhere that she wouldn't be in the way of George and Elizabeth, and where she could support herself instead of being an expense to George.

In a 1943 notebook she wrote, "… Jessica []: that noble creature who is so good herself that she can't believe in the bad motives of anyone else! Balls."

> Balls to you, Jessica, with your astute line of the abused. The reason you manage him so cleverly is because you don't love him. He's *your* husband and *your* honour is at stake. You like the pose of the faithful wife. But you anticipate prizes.

The birth of Elizabeth's children was a celebration of love, but Jessica, it seems, had no right to have babies. She had twins the same year that Elizabeth's second child was born — referred to as "Jessica's two wrong reason twins."

I have a strong suspicion that self-pity and greatness are incompatibles, antipathetic. Freud discussed the difference between the "meagre day dreams" of the non-artist, and the way the true artist "… elaborates his day dreams so that they lose that personal note which grates upon strange ears, and become enjoyable to others." Elizabeth never learned that skill. Her day dreams of no-goodnik George grate upon the ears, and no flowery poetic prose can disguise his no-goodness or her wallowing self-pity.

I don't feel awe or envy, Philippa. I do feel a strong urge to administer a good kick in the backside. Several backsides.

Now I've used up a whole chapter on Ms. Smart. Still, she's the best example of the Perversity Principle in Literary Criticism we're likely to find. Just remember, as I forgot, that to be a successful snob, you must practise the Perversity Principle and pretend to admire such masterpieces.

Snobtest:

> "Dawn creeps over his window like a guilty animal." Lyrical prose from *BGCSISD&W* (1945).
>
> "Dawn crept over the Downs like a sinister white animal ..." Parody-lyrical prose from *Cold Comfort Farm*, by Stella Gibbons (1929).

Cold Comfort Farm is a deliciously funny book; if either Elizabeth Smart or Bridget Brophy had read it, they couldn't have gone on writing Rich Beautiful Prose and eulogies thereon. *CCF* is a satire on this type of literature, which abounded in the twenties, though E. Smart's admirers don't seem aware of the fact. After Ms. Gibbons' hilarious parody, its creators felt too silly to write any more of poetic prose for years. The *New Statesman* called it "a wicked, needed Baedeker," a guide to readers "who are not always sure whether a sentence is Literature or whether it is just sheer flapdoodle." Gibbons marked the "finer passages" with one, two or three stars. "It ought to help the reviewers, too."

Snobnote to Perversity Principle in Literary Criticism: A few years ago, my local newspaper had a review of a book by some Hollywood commentator. It was an absolutely rotten book, the reviewer said, without one redeeming feature. A waste of time and paper. No one could possibly want to read it. Nevertheless, the review took up a solid half page in the newspaper, with a large photo of the author.

So I wrote them an indignant letter. Why waste space on a review, if only to say the book is junk, and recommend that no one buy it? Here I was, a local writer, and my last book hadn't received one measly mention in my local daily. It was a serious book, non-fiction, and represented years of painstaking research.

The editor explained that the rotten book was "news," because the writer of this, and other lousy books, was a big name in the U.S., and anyway they'd mentioned my (then forthcoming) book in a review of the one before last.

An old familiar rage possessed me. My first book (a novel) came out at the same time as *Princess Daisy*. Remember that masterpiece? The newspapers were full of it, and its demerits. They deplored the fact that such garbage should be published. Other books were squeezed out, since there simply wasn't room for them if *Princess Daisy* was to be properly demolished. A critic whom I knew told me he regretted not being able to review my book. He thought it was very funny, and well written. But after all, *Princess Daisy* was News, because it got a record-making advance (millions!). So it was a contemptibly lousy book, so what?

Publishing Snobbery illustrates the profound belief by publishers that book buyers are not concerned with the quality of books, but only with the authors' names. Once the writer is famous, it can write ever so lousily but its every word will get published. If it is famous enough, it will get advances that put it in the tax bracket with lottery winners and baseball players, for unwritten books.

More than one editor has read a brilliant manuscript which has come over the transom; they have taken it excitedly to their bosses, urging that they have found a potential literary genius.

"What else has he published?" languidly ask the Great Powers, and on learning that he hasn't published very much, because he is still very young, refuse even to look at the work. It costs too much to launch a new writer. "If he's got what it takes, he'll be discovered."

Yeah? He may be ignored all his life because he doesn't know the right people, or be so blighted by despair that he dies of it. Meanwhile the wheeler-dealers, the mass-producers, turn out their awful semi-literate stuff every few months, hire a professional editor to knock it into readability, and get huge advances which leave inadequate cash to finance publication of the gifted writer who doesn't have lowest-common-denominator appeal. Publishers won't read manuscripts unless they're submitted by agents, who won't read unpublished authors. (Catch 22.)

Anna Porter, of Key Porter Books, interviewed by Sheila Rogers on CBC about her latest mystery novel, gave a blood-chilling picture of the publishing world. It's concerned only with sales. An author is judged not by literary ability but by appearance — photogenic enough for TV interviews, i.e., a "promotable personality." If you're plain, if you photograph badly, if you're shy and inarticulate (and writers often are) you're a liability for promotability. You may write like a new Shakespeare, but no publisher will look at you. But if you're a "name," with good promotability, the marketing machine will go into high gear. All your reviews will be favourable, your books will sell like crazy. Porter described books which had been on the bestseller list for 20 to 30 weeks as "extraordinarily bad." No talent is involved for authors, there is no longer a supportive relationship between editors and authors, and the role of the publisher is now simply a peddler of goods, not a developer of literary gifts. Readers may be secretly disappointed, but they don't dare admit it for fear of being thought stupid, even fearing that they *are* stupid, since everyone else says it's a masterpiece.

It's the great age of hype, and the hype-artists (Badsnobs all) whether writers, agents, publishers, or reviewers, are winning everywhere. Writers and readers are both out of luck.

Snobnote: The Promotable Personality. Since writing the above, I've remembered another occasion where the Promotable Personality cropped up, to the detriment of female authors. On this occasion, a Great Man of the publishing industry was addressing a chapter of the Canadian Women's Press Club. He explained to us that nowadays publishers looked for literature by photogenic females who would catch the eye on television; who would be decorative on book jackets; who would draw admiring crowds at book signings. He didn't actually say that he chose his writers for their bust measurements rather than their prose, but the implication was unmistakeable.

By these standards, it's dubious that Jane Austen or the Brontë girls or George Eliot would ever have made it into print. They weren't ugly, but they were no crowd-stoppers. And many serious writers fail to hit their stride until they're pushing forty. (That's in years, not bust measurement.) It's not like fashion modelling, you know. I can't help feeling that a long apprenticeship and the development of a good literate style, while having little value for a fashion model, is desirable in a writer of whatever sex.

There were no similar requirements for male writers. He didn't mention male writers.

His female audience sat stunned. There were some attractive women among us, but not many looked like the Promotable Personality who (as he went on) became increasingly visible in our minds as a nineteen-year-old bleached blonde with a forty-inch bustline.

Finally I decided that he couldn't be allowed to get away with it. Supposing, I asked, trembling with fear, his firm received a book of such unquestioned literary merit that it couldn't be overlooked, even if the author looked like Vladimir Nabokov instead of Elizabeth Taylor in her prime? He seemed taken aback. Apparently this possibility had never occurred to him: surely a writer should have a forty-inch bosom, if she hoped for publication? Then he pulled himself together and said oh yes, of course, unquestioned literary merit ... always room for that.

It had taken a lot of courage to question a big shot in the trade, to question *critically*. I thought my fellow journalists would respect me for having the guts to stand up to this defamer of literary femininity. Instead, the chairwoman smilingly declared the question period was over, and we were *so* grateful to Mr. Big for giving us his valuable time. (He didn't *give* it, he got paid.) I found I was being shunned. Later the chairwoman spoke severely to me about my tactless behaviour to our distinguished guest. So no wonder women writers get pushed around, except for the forty-inchers.

I suppose nowadays they can get silicone jobs, which will make their personalities more promotable.

21

The Perversity Principle in Criticism 2: Painting and Sculpture

I am against Art.
— Quentin Crisp.

... "for art's sake" alone, I would not face the toil of writing a single sentence.
— G. B. Shaw.

Rapid changes in Art vogues make Artsnobbery extremely tricky. In my student days, it was completely unacceptable to admire anything that was done in the 19th century, whether by writers, painters, or musicians; indeed, among the young, it was appropriate to mime nausea at the mere mention of a name: "Sisley? Bleaggghhh!" Indeed, it was perfectly correct actually to spew up at the mention of Gustave Doré or Alfred Lord Tennyson. But recently there has been a perceptible change, and I've heard some academics laughingly admit that Tennyson's *Tithonus* shows a great deal of technical ingenuity, and Sisley — although the unhappy wretch never sold a picture in his life, and was turned down flat by a shopkeeper when he tried to trade a painting for something to eat — is now absolutely okay, and selling for large sums. Now it's too late to keep the poor slob from starving.

The icons of my time (Picasso, Braque, Chagall) are probably objects of derision among advanced artsnobs. I had a guilty secret passion for Salvador Dali, but never dared admit it.

Clive Bell, an influential Snob of the Bloomsbury era, enunciated a fundamental Snobprinciple: "Art and what the grocer thinks he sees are not the same thing." He had great success with this. Not many people today remember anything about Clive Bell, but they're still quoting him on what the grocer thinks. If you (or the grocer) thought what the artist was doing was tripe, you betrayed your grocer-nature. "Grocerish" became a contemporary abuse term. Either you thought like Clive Bell, or you were a tasteless grocer, who couldn't understand any art more demanding than cute pictures of pussy-cats in baskets, or puppy-dogs peeking out of boots.

The grocer theory of art, and the Perversity Principle make possible such *oeuvres* as Girder Dump, and Voice of Fire (see below, I mean of course *vide infra*) as well as work by a movement which a painter friend, Madeline Francis, described as the Dribble and Slurp School. She was not a dopey amateur, nor even a lady grocer, but an accomplished painter who studied under A. Y. Jackson.

The graphic and plastic arts offer severe difficulties to the aspiring Artsnob. In sculpture, there was a vogue a few years ago for what a friend calls the Spilled Load, or Girder Drop School of Sculpture. We were driving along the lakeshore one day when he shouted "Look — over there! See that orange stuff?"

I caught a glimpse of what I thought was a work site, possibly in preparation for the erection of yet another hideous building which would further block any view of the lake for the passing citizenry. It looked like a pile of steel beams or girders, painted for some unfathomable reason a bright orange, but then what do I know about construction *or* sculpture, for that matter?

"When I first saw those," said my friend, "I thought there'd been an accident. I thought a truck with a load of girders had got in a crunch, and the girders had fallen off, and been pushed over on the grass to get them out of the way of traffic. But they were still there, a couple of weeks later. Then I found out that it wasn't a truck accident, it was sculpture."

Later I saw a similar work in another town: smaller scale, and black instead of orange, but obviously inspired by the same muse as the Girder Drop or Spilled Load. At first glance I thought they were a pile of railroad ties which had been dropped there, awaiting disposal (shortly the section gang would come along and load them on the jigger?), but several weeks later they were still there, and worse, there was no railroad. Suspicion filtered through my brain: they were in a park. Would the railroad be allowed to dump a pile of ties in a park? Could it possibly be another Work of Art?

I stopped and checked. There was a plaque explaining it, for the benefit of the uninstructed and aesthetically insensitive. This pile of railway ties marked a turning-point in the artist's work, a departure from the volumetric character of his previous sculptures to one in which the emphasis was placed as much on void as on mass. Thus, slight changes in viewpoint result in dramatic changes in negative/positive compositions. The objective was to dramatize the changing relationship between the elements and the spaces they define, to make the void visible.

Gawrsh. And here I thought it was a pile of old railway ties, such as you can see in quantity if you walk down a railway track. But they weren't just piled up in a stack, the way the CNR does it, and of course they weren't really railway ties, but red cedar logs.

All contemporary sculpture and most of the painting has to have these explanatory essays attached, because the public is so stupid; without the essay, they might just think the sculpture was a pile of junk. Odd that Praxiteles and Michelangelo didn't have to attach expository notes on their works: possibly they thought that works of art should speak for themselves? But what did they know, after all? Crude representationalist stuff they did.

Later I called the Arts Centre and asked for some enlightenment on the girders (they *are* girders, too, no evasions there). The art comes in the way they are arranged. Oh. Then does the sculptor arrange them himself, or does he hire a crane and yell instructions to the operator? And if so, who is really the artist? Suppose the crane operator secretly decides to throw in a little inspiration himself, and even comes secretly back to re-arrange the girders? He may have rebelled silently at the philistine, or grocerish, failure to understand the medium all through the operation. And would the original artist notice the difference, if they were re-ordered in his absence? Why should a crane operator, who after all knows his instrument, not be the best exponent of girder-art? This is tricky stuff.

(Of course I didn't actually suggest any of this stuff at the time. I thought of it at three o'clock the next morning.)

The structure is symbolic of the Centre itself, with its different guilds, and the functions of the arts, the expert explained. I decided to play the heavy philistine.

"When I first saw them," I said meekly, to test her, "I thought there'd been an accident, and a bunch of girders had fallen off a truck."

My mentor was cheerful and uncensorious.

"Most people think that," she said. "That's why we're here — to help the public to understand it. To help them learn the language of art."

My first reaction was similar to that inspired by contemporary poetry: just as there should be some way of distinguishing poetry from bad prose, even the humblest layperson should be able to tell a work of sculpture from an accident in the building trades.

Sometimes, waking uneasily in the too-early morning, I wonder if indeed there is any future for the plastic arts: they reached such peaks in Grecian times, and during the Renaissance, that everything since has seemed faintly redundant and anticlimactic, if not downright ugly. (Indeed, Ugly seems to be an essential of contemporary art.) Are we to be reduced on the one hand to abstractions in concrete and aluminum which cannot be distinguished from industrial disasters or (on the other hand) to coarsely representational statues of politicians to uglify parliamentary lawns, surely something which should be prevented by law?

The thought of an endless parade of Clarks, Mulroneys, Campbells, Chrétiens et al. occupying the vanishing green space around the Parliament Buildings is too distressing to contemplate. (In their three-piece suits, or would they wear tails and top-hats? Kim coyly bare behind her gown? Consider the three-dimensional improprieties. It must be prevented, before it's too late.)

An interesting, if appalling, variation on this theme is the Fat School. In downtown Calgary they have built a rather attractive pedestrian mall on Eighth Avenue. Essential artistic uglification was provided by a bronze of two fat businessmen, slightly larger than life-size, shaking hands. It symbolizes something or other: co-operation between business and the arts? Another Fat Businessman appeared on The Esplanade in downtown Toronto. This one was stepping through a doorway: get the symbolism there? The doorway is Opportunity, and the Fat Businessman as he steps through will lead us all to, perhaps, Prosperity? Or it may remind us of the famous door in the wall in H. G. Wells' story, which Symbolized Mystic Experience through which we move to a different Plane of Consciousness, and all that jazz. It was an interesting story, but we know now that mystic experience is a biochemical rather than a spiritual event, which may enlarge our experience but doesn't really change our natures or move us to a different Plane of Being. Read my two *Ghost* books. (Sorry about all those capital letters, but they're mandatory in discussing Symbolic Significance in the Arts.)

The last time I was on The Esplanade, I didn't notice the Fat

Man. Has fat lost favour, or has he been promoted to a more distinguished location? In passing, Fat sculpture is by no means confined to Canada. A Columbian sculptor named Fernando Botero has (according to *Time*) enraptured Paris with his cheery sensual (also voluptuous; rotund, whimsical) statues. But to many Parisians, as to New Yorkers threatened with importation of them, they're just Fat. A monster nude torso with bulging belly and gargantuan thighs is called "Woman (Bronze)." Is it cheerful? Not many women would feel cheerful about a load of flab like that. So far I haven't read anything pretending they have Important Symbolic Values.

There is also a rash of Very Very Significant sculptures of penises and vaginas, with titles like "Fertility" or "Gaia"; the 1993 stage set for *A Midsummer Night's Dream* in Stratford featured both of these Very Significant Symbols. Perhaps there really is nowhere for the graphic arts to go, nothing for them to say? one asks fearfully.

This is the wrong attitude, if you aspire to be a successful Artsnob. You must carefully follow all the new trends and schools, and master the appropriate vocabulary.

Always bear in mind our previously stated Snob-caveat: you have to be really careful, and keep up to date, or you will find yourself admiring the wrong stuff. It will have gone out of fashion, or you will betray yourself by using outdated terminology. Are you ready?

It is fairly well established that the basis of successful contemporary art, as in criticism, is *perversity*. All that stuff about beauty and truth went out the window a long time ago. When you see a work of art that seems to you silly, or ugly, or more like bathroom tile than a painting, you don't EVER exclaim scornfully, "For God's sake, my five-year-old nephew can do better than that!" This is the unmistakeable mark of the philistine or, worse, of the naïve, and you will see a pitying smile curving the lips of the *cognoscenti*. (Dat's a good woid to use in situations of this type, but be sure you pronounce it right: look it up in the dictionary, or you'll excite yet more pitying smiles. And while we're at it, you should begin practising before the looking-glass on your own pitying smile.)

Let's take a concrete example. Not quite as concrete as those girders, though these are really aluminum, but tangible enough to elicit cries of anger from taxpayers.

A few years ago the National Gallery of Canada bought a painting called *Voice of Fire*, which consisted of three broad stripes of colour: blue, red, blue. Simply this, and nothing more. For this the Canadian taxpayer had to stump up nearly two million dollars, and there was a loud yell of outrage from the non-art-experts, or philistines, a.k.a. taxpayers. They said, among other things, that any house painter could have done it as well, or better, in an hour or so, at a charge of perhaps twenty bucks at the outside. They said their six-year-old nephews could have done it just as well, if on a smaller scale, for although the painting looks simple, it is extremely large, so at least we have our money's worth in quantity, if not quality. MP Felix Holtman said *he* could have painted it himself in ten minutes, with a roller and a couple of pots of paint.

How does the aspiring Artsnob perform in such a situation as this? Have you got your pitying smile well polished up?

All right, you listen to the outraged howls, and you smile your pitying smile. Then you explain condescendingly but gently that perhaps the painting is not quite as simple as it appears. Perhaps it seems uninteresting to you because you haven't quite learned the language of contemporary painting. (That's a very good one, that learning the language ploy, and I believe it has many years of useful work in it still; you'll recall it was also applied to the Spilled Load/Girder Drop exhibit.)

Of course, you explain, you can't apply the same standards to *Voice of Fire* as the decorations you choose for your living-room wall. That will make them anxious about the paintings they've chosen; if you think you can get away with it, if they're the least bit insecure about their artistic judgement, you can add that of course *Voice of Fire* isn't at all the same *genre* as a picture of cute puppies or a basket of pussy-cats. Obviously, this implies that they are so stupid and non-artistic that their idea of a picture is cute-cat-peeking-out-of-boot.

Now that you have insulted and unsettled them, you move in for the kill: *Voice of Fire*, you explain, reaches archetypal memories buried deeply in the unconscious mind. By the very simplicity of its design, the starkness, the purity, it drives all contemporary preoccupations from your mind and lets imagery from the childhood of the human race well up into your consciousness. It takes you back to man's discovery of fire, the beginning of his upward evolutionary climb. You can stick in references to Jung, who is still fairly fashionable (Freud is hopelessly Out) or better, Oliver Sacks.

Many people suffered acute pain at finding themselves in agreement with Felix Holtman. They still insisted that though the artist must indeed have freedom to express itself, the taxpayer shouldn't be stuck with paying for artistic freedom. Let the artist find a patron, as in Renaissance days. Get Conrad Black or Frank Stronach to stump up for it, why not?

Voice of Fire inspired the founding of a group called the Committee for the Removal of Artistic Pollution (CRAP). Its president, Ray Stone, offered a practical criticism of another $1.8 million purchase, Mark Rothko's No. 16: "How do you know it isn't upside down?"

A juried art exhibit in Grimsby, Ontario, was obsessed with corsets. Well, to the uninstructed eye they were just corsets, but not if you looked at the layering of different levels of meaning: "Are these laces, straps, or the sutures of a wound?" Some of the corsets were painted, but in one work, classified as sculpture, they were just three canvas corsets suspended on aluminum hangers on an aluminum rack. "... the work appears at first to be humorous, but ... secondary images of bondage, even of a meat cooler, come to mind."

"Is it really sculpture?" carped a grocerish visitor. "Hanging corsets on a rack, is that sculpture?"

The Hamilton area, it seems, was hooked on corsets. (You might make a joke out of that, said the Gnat.) The week after the Grimsby show, an article by Paul Benedetti in *The Spectator* breathlessly described the work of artist Vesna Trkulja who is deeply involved in corsets, bodices, vests, and cage crinolines: "body armour." Some of the dresses can actually be worn, but "I want the pieces to stand up as sculpture," says their creator, who is shown in a Cage Gown, peering between the slats of something that looks like a panel fence made of metal.

O God! O Grimsby! O Hamilton-Wentworth!

Perhaps the biggest art-furor in recent times arose over the exhibition of *The Meat Dress*, or to use its official title, "Vanitas: Flesh Dress for an Albino Anorexic." It was, and possibly still is, a sleeveless dress made from $300 worth of raw beef. Mr. Holtman suggested that this is a wicked waste of meat, in a world where people are going hungry.

The sculptor, Jana Sterbak, responded irritably that there was no actual shortage of food in Canada, and that her work followed the late medieval and Renaissance convention of depicting perishable objects such as fruit, flowers, or foodstuffs in various states of decay. (But they did them in paint, Jana, whereas "Vanitas" has to be renewed with fresh meat every few days, at a cost of $300, or the smell — let alone the flies and maggots — would drive away viewers.)

The Renaissance artists did this, the artist claims, to remind the viewer of the inconstancy of earthly possessions and worldly power. But does it work? We cleaned out the fridge the other day and had to throw out some superannuated cottage cheese and moribund celery. "God!" I didn't cry. "This sure does remind one of the inconstancy of earthly possessions and worldly power!" What I said, resentfully, was that if it wasn't so much trouble, I'd take the cottage cheese back to the store, because the "best before" date wasn't due for another three days.

A critic in *The Globe and Mail* was vituperative in defence of *The Meat Dress*. The unsigned article is worth serious study for Snobpurposes, as it gives useful Snobvocabulary. First the writer points out that there once was a hierarchy of materials: oil paint and bronze were art, glass and pottery were craft, and raw meat was not on the list. Artists now defy those limits by using unconventional materials, often those that by decaying during exhibition push the definition of art beyond that of collectable object.

If you are working on your Artsnobbery, the question may arise of what you do with the uncollectable object, which can't be used for decoration in the old sense? I simply don't know the answer, but perhaps you can find a solution. (There's a good Artsnobexercise for you.) If you can't think of anything plausible, you can simply groan and say, "For God's sake, must you always be such a philistine? Does Art have to be — " groan of contempt — "useful?"

Sculptor Sterbak is part of a strong feminist school that struggles to find entirely new ways of speaking about women in a field of images dominated historically by the nude, and now by the anorexic models of advertising. This will of course be met with the argument about how there were plenty of male nudes in the past, and now plenty of male models in advertising, Sunshine Boys and their equivalents.

Again, it's a difficult one. Unless you can somehow demonstrate that the use of women models is more exploitative than that of male models, you may have to exclaim that male exploitation, too, must be stopped. Was the model for Mick Angelo's *David* bitter and humiliated at being used as a sex/art object? He looks rather complacent, actually.

Get off the subject as quickly as possible, or they'll start telling you that both male and female models LIKE what they're doing, and would be dismayed at the threat to their jobs if you rescued them. The only ploy here is to remind them that the minute they get a wrinkle or a bulge, the job will be over, and there'll be nothing left for them but prostitution. Now back to *The Meat Dress*:

> Will someone please tell Holtman [snarls the columnist] that Sterbak's work is not a waste of its materials, but rather a comment on our society, its images of women and their resulting obsession with their bodies? ... That part of its power — for the more open-minded viewer — lies in the variety of interpretations one can put on it? Some will quickly see the dress as a comment on the practice of killing animals to wear their fur, or more generally on the extremes of fashion. Some may see the process of decay in the work as a parallel to the aging of the body. Other viewers (including this one) may remember that Sterbak has often addressed issues of women's experience of pain, and perceive the bleeding dress as a body turned inside out, raw flesh exposed.

Doesn't this violate another art-crit law? *Art should never teach or preach*. It should just *be*. But there is a powerful strain of the didactic in the works we've been examining. Later I talked to another art expert who told me that *The Meat Dress* was "very poignant," and that it forced its audiences to think about people who are treated as meat, rather than as creatures with feelings, and about the violence in our society.

This is good Snob dialectic, and aspiring Artsnobs would do well to study it carefully with a view to poaching, in arguments with philistines. I must admit that I had a lot of trouble with *The Meat Dress*. I'm a not always consistent vegetarian. I can see the logic of the carnivore position: what, for example, happens to the male calves of milk herds? We can't keep them entire, because bulls are dangerous, and steers, while milder tempered, are expensive and awkward to keep as pets. Really there's not much you can do with them but eat them. We can't give up keeping milk herds, can we? No milk, cream, butter, cheese, yoghurt. The poor milk cows would not be better off, for unless we keep them they will be extinct. Cave-people killed animals for meat and hides, though perhaps not primarily because they were obsessed by fashion.

I've faced up to it, people are going to eat meat, though I prefer to avert my eyes from it. I don't think beasts should be killed for anything but absolute necessities. A few days ago I was driving along behind a truck in which a poor cow, or possibly a bullock, was being transported. It looked back with an expression of bewildered terror that struck me to the heart far more than any art exhibit could do. If I thought that poor thing was being killed to drape a meat dress, I'd be tempted to perform an act of desecration on the sculpture, if not on the sculptor.

There is another highly successful Artsnob ploy which should be studied by the hard-working snob. It's old, I can remember hearing it as a teenager, but it stands up well. The purpose of art, you explain kindly, is not to imitate nature or to create lifelike images: photography can do that as well, or even better. (This handsome admission disarms would-be critics.)

No. Art has a more rigorous, a sterner function, a social duty to fulfill. It is *to shock*. The object of every artist whom I knew in my youth was to shock the bourgeois out of their complacency.

I remember a conversation in early days, when I was a young housewife and mother, slogging my way through diapers and formula-preparation and all the rest of it, and an artist friend of my husband's was expounding the Shock Theory of Art. I snapped at him. (He was sitting with his feet up, enjoying a drink while my husband got dinner and I put the baby to bed.) I said daily life gave me all the shocks I could cope with, and if that was the function of art, it was redundant, because I didn't have any complacency to be shocked out of. How pityingly he smiled! That's when I learned the technique, and how infuriating it can be.

You see how the Perversity Principle works? Any klutz can enjoy a good book, or picture, or piece of sculpture. It doesn't take any brains at all to admire Michelangelo's *David* — or Bernini's, which is really a better *David*; Mick's is too pretty and unperturbed, while Bernini's is all clenched up to fight a goddam giant twice his size. So anyone can see they're good, with half an eye. You don't have to have taken Art History or Aesthetics 102 to see that. No merit badges.

But to admire Girder Dump, or *Voice of Fire*, or corset sculpture, all of which are pretty silly and pointless, you have to see things imperceptible to the ordinary unschooled eye. You have to penetrate subtleties, and perceive archetypal image-arousers that go right past the non-Snob. Professional critics deal in a very special form of snobbery, as any reader of the arts pages of newspapers and magazines is quickly aware. A very specialized form is found in art catalogues, which have their own arcane vocabulary.

If you find yourself stuck for an argument, there are some useful phrases which you can drag in to confuse your opponent: "I believe it's a case of abstract minimalism," you can say, or "… of seminal aesthetics" … "of indeterminate semiotics." You don't know what they mean? What difference does that make? Neither does anyone else. "Post-modernism" is always handy, too. No one knows what it means, either.

One element in all Crit-snob work is name-dropping — a casually implied easy acquaintance with the rich and famous: "As Barbra said when we were looking at the Basquiat exhibit together …" "Hillary thought it was a mistake to let *Voice of Fire* go out of the country; she's afraid Canadians won't understand it."

There is a disturbing influence at work in art criticism, though, by a renegade named Robert Hughes. He writes for such periodicals as *Time* and *The New Yorker*, and a few years ago published a book called *Culture of Compliance: The Fraying of America*. He's out to spoil honest Snob fun.

He has a nasty habit of looking at pictures, and sculptures and so on, and making tactless remarks about inadequately clothed emperors. He recently described the reviews of a retrospective of the works of Jean-Michel Basquiat as "the purple haze of hype."

Some samples of the purple haze: "Who killed Basquiat, ask the artist's friends and foes alike. Art dealers? The white world? Self-serving collectors? The excesses of the 80s?"

In response, Hughes snarls: "The plain truth — that Basquiat killed Basquiat, that nobody but he was sticking the needles in his arm — is not going to get much airing at this solemn farce of heroic victimology."

Another, and my favourite, critic extolled Basquiat's heroin addiction ("that punishing régime of self-abuse") as part of "the disciplines imposed by the principles of inverse asceticism to which he was so resolutely committed." That is, he took heroin not out of self-indulgence, but for his art, and for the benefit of the public, you and me. This is very high level Artsnobtalk.

"Heroin seems to have played some role in the formation of the discontinuous maps of mental states that are his paintings and drawings. Heroin seems to have helped him fuse his line with his nerve endings as they responded to, parodied and sought to heal a disturbed culture."

That's not only unselfish, that's self-sacrificing, that's heroic. To become a heroin addict in order to heal our disturbed culture! Oh, it's so inspiring! I wish I knew how to show my appreciation.

Old spoil-sport Hughes wonders if our culture is any less disturbed for his sacrifice, and he also points out that Basquiat was often too zonked on horse to work, and so used to hire another painter at $15 an hour to do the actual painting. Hard to decide who should get the credit for the artistic achievement — Basquiat, hired hand Rick Prol, or just heroin. There's always someone like Robert Hughes who grudges the artist his tribute, probably out of envy: "He had no idea of how to discipline himself ..."

That's the Artsnob's cue for a dissertation on discipline, an idea that's appropriate only to the school marms of the art world. What the artist needs is not discipline, but absolute freedom.

After you've said that, go and get a drink and refuse to discuss the matter further. Your opponents will be temporarily floored by finding themselves manoeuvred into the position of condemning artistic freedom. Once they think through its implications, they'll be looking for you to continue the argument, so get out fast while you're ahead.

Dysfunctional Family Ties

The tortured artist agonizes over his masterpiece, a work in space-solid contrasts with strong sexual components (note prominent erection element) sprung from the Spilled-Load School, late CNR period. This brilliant work (here unfinished) has unfortunately been lost to posterity as the artist's cruel stepmother, motivated by sadism, sold the raw materials (twenty-five cents per tie) saying that the composition "messed up the yard." (cf. Lawnsnobbery). She added that she was sick of listening to his bitching and moaning. "Him and his dysfunctional family. If he don't like living in this family, why don't he get out and get a place of his own?"

Is not this symbolic of the guilt of our societal whole?

The artist's struggle continues in spite of our boasted "enlightenment." However, he may yet triumph over philistinism: he is finding everywhere new material for artistic exploitation. A recent highway accident strewed the road with batts of fibreglass insulation: thrilling colour (bright pink against the green of the grass verges), amazing shapes, and a challenging comment on structure in the post-modern dwelling-place. A visit to a landfill site excited him by the potential for artistic expression of disposable diapers and green garbage bags. He was also much moved by a demolition site, which he believes would lend itself to significant manipulation for landscape art.

22

Poemsnob

I too can hunt the poetaster down.
— Byron.

We have adverted to this subject under the Perversity Principle in Literature, but perhaps we might be allowed another word or two, because some discussion is gravely needed. It would be easier if we could illustrate our thesis with examples, but for the danger of being sued by infuriated poets. However, you can consult any Little Magazine or Slim Volume of poetry written in the last twenty years for examples.

As I write, an alleged poet is reading from The Works on radio. Except for the fact that he is reading in a soulful and tragic voice, a tone which implies immense (if vague) significance, it sounds exactly like prose, and not very good prose, either. Oh I do so want to know: what makes this stuff poetry?

How often have I read a hunk of undistinguished prose, perhaps having nothing unusual about it except that it has discarded punctuation and sentence structure and capitals, is pervaded by a certain pomposity of tone and is written, for no apparent reason, in irregular lines. The trouble is, it's supposed to be poetry. If you breathe a whisper of criticism, you're told brutally that anyone who can't tell the difference between this masterpiece and prose is a crass lout, OR a simpleton who can't understand anything more profound than Edgar Guest and Joyce Kilmer. They may smile their patronizing smile and kindly explain that a piece of writing isn't poetry just because it rhymes.

Yer average modern poet, we submit, is merely sloppy, and is not writing poetry at all, but bad prose in uneven lines. However, you'll get nowhere in Snobcircles if you talk like that. You must insist that poetic form and discipline are bilge, that nothing matters but "feelings," and that the most dismal stuff conceals great profundity that is only enhanced by its apparent ineptitude.

We've seen how the Perversity Principle works: a mysterious process by which the expert professes to discover transcendent artistic beauty in something which looks to the average poor slob, or grocer, like a hunk of junk, whereas anything for which one feels spontaneous enjoyment, or immediate response, is dismissed contemptuously. The non-pro reader is intimidated, and humbly accepts that if a Work of Art seems just plain ugly or stupid or pointless, it is not the fault of the Work but of that same non-pro customer, who isn't an expert and so can't trust his/her, oh dear, I mean its, own responses. That's what the phoney artists are banking on.

Things have come to such a pass in the literary world that it is pretty well impossible for a poet to get published if it insists on writing stuff that CAN be distinguished from bad prose. One would think by this time everyone would be rather bored with the lower-case non-metrical effusions which are currently designated as poetry. But no. Publishers of Little Magazines and Slim Volumes still disqualify a poem if it uses any kind of rhyme scheme or metrical pattern, although it must be obvious that the non-disciplined stuff is terribly easy to write: just throw out punctuation, capitalization etc., and write prose, preferably ungrammatical prose, in irregular lines, and well decorated with fuck, shit, and asshole, for Significance. Read it aloud in a pontifical voice, and you're on the way to poetic acclaim. You should also work in some Mystic Symbolism. You can wonder where the lions are. No one will ask you *what lions?* because that will stigmatize them as philistines. The lions are mystic symbols.

Just for the hell of it, let's *be* philistines, and ask the poet "Symbols of what?" He will tell you you're an insensitive clod if you can't understand the symbolism, and that poets do not have to explain their work. Keep asking questions like these and the poet will call you abusive names and possibly even slug you one because he hasn't a clue as to what he means by lions, or how symbolism works.

Falcons are big in poetic symbolism, and I once got into a row with a poet about a falcon which he had described very poetically, soaring about, being ethereal and all that, some of it lifted from Gerard Manly Hopkins, and I said that there had been a falcon in our garden not long ago. It was small and elegant, a sparrow-hawk (or kestrel) which had just killed a sparrow at our bird-feeder. He pecked away at the poor little corpse for most of the morning, which rather upset me, since those sparrows live in our cedar hedge and I feel responsible for them. Still, that's why sparrow hawks are sparrow hawks, and they have a right to live, too.

But it was not at all ethereal. Neither are lions. They both live on raw meat, which they rip into with unmistakeable relish. The poet got more and more hostile, and it occurred to me that he didn't know nuffink from falcons. He didn't know they are carnivorous. His falcons were fake falcons, like those fake lions in the song. They were symbols with no objective correlative or denotative referent, let's see you beat that for distinguished Snobspeak.

I keep hoping that some day soon there will be a revolution. Poets themselves will reject the slovenly mindlessness of the contemporary style and force themselves into the kind of tough disciplines which produced (for example) Shakespeare's sonnets, Donne's metaphysical imagery, Milton's mighty line, Marvell's exquisite sensory effects. Perhaps the smart ploy for the aspiring Literary Snob would be to start demanding stuff that is manifestly, unmistakeably, NOT PROSE.

Careful, though. If you suggest anything so unorthodox, you may still be written off with that patronizing smile, as a pathetic grocer. A Poemsnob will kindly explain to you that of course *its* poetry isn't anything like Joyce Kilmer's, assuming axiomatically that your idea of great poetry is thinking that you shall never see/A poem lovely as a tree.

The astute Snob will have observed that I am an unsuitable guide for contemporary poetry. You must decide what your position is to be: will you go along with the current opinion that you can write anything you like, as long as it doesn't have any metrical or rhythmic pattern and call it poetry? Or will you insist that if it's poetry, it must SOMEHOW be distinguishable from prose? In this case, you must turn an X-ray eye on everything calling itself poetry, and require evidence that it is not prose. Imagery alone does not make a poem, because good prose often has very elegant imagery. If you detect cases of prose (especially bad prose) masquerading as poetry and getting away with it, you have a duty to stand up and yell, "The Emperor has no clothes on!"

Snobtest: Consider the following, and whether or not it is a poem.

… Because No Man Was Found Worthy

And I wept much, because no man was found worthy to open and read the book, neither to look therein …

in the night iron wheels bruise rails that scream
like a woman in childbirth   stop the pain   the pain
the train calls   lonely   voice of nostalgia and forgotten fears
trailing into darkness

morning stabs the frightened sky   with cruel brightness
and the clouds bleed scarlet tears   as I awake
alone

my body is that unread book

the sun became black as a sackcloth of hair
and the moon became as blood

rest yet, for a little season

where has he gone   my one   my only love   leaving me here
in a cheap hotel on Spadina Avenue
with no money to pay the bill   will he return perhaps   with
breakfast   to share merrily in bed
break … fast   break … heart

to everything there is a season
a time to rend, a time to sew

my wallet is missing

it is time to sew my torn garments   rent by
your ruthless hands' sweetest   avidity
to pierce me   stab with a cruel brightness   like the sun

i shall arise and go now … but innisfree is lost   all lost
hive for the honeybee   empty and overturned

i torn must stumble forth into the mocking street
to patch and mend the rags
and tatters of my life

a plane rises from Pearson mounts screaming like a woman in childbirth
passes that train bruising rails that scream like a woman in childbirth
flies over a hospital where in the maternity wing real women are screaming in childbirth
though they're not very good at it

Answer: I can write this stuff with one hand tied behind my back. It isn't poetry. It's flapdoodle.

Snobnote: Glance back at the opening page of this chapter: Classy (or Bad) Wordsnobs will immediately be tempted to start saying poetaster when they mean poet. They'd better not. A poetaster *is* "a mean or inferior poet." There are a lot of them about.

Another glance: that person who gives you the patronizing smile and explains that poetry doesn't have to rhyme? You will feel a strong inclination to knock his nose sideways. Try not to do this. Smile your own patronizing smile and say kindly, "It is very good of you to explain these things to me. Otherwise I might have confused poetry with doggerel, mightn't I?"

You too can hunt a poetaster down! Just keep patiently asking if a poem should not be distinguishably different from prose. Otherwise, what makes it a poem?

23

Religious Snobbery

I am a millionaire. That is my religion.
— G. B. Shaw, *Major Barbara*.

Oysters are more beautiful than any religion ... There's nothing in Christianity or Buddhism that matches the sympathetic unselfishness of an oyster.
— Saki, *The Chronicles of Clovis*.

Christianity is such a *silly* religion.
— Gore Vidal.

"... soul-butter and hogwash."
— *Huckleberry Finn*.

Faith is believing in something when you know it isn't true.
— schoolboy's definition.

Queen Elizabeth I found religion a serious nuisance, whether she was busy establishing the Church of England or keeping excessive puritanism under control. Her papa, Henry, considered himself a good Catholic, merely repudiating the Roman connection; he attended mass all his life, and hanged a sinful subject for eating meat on Friday. But one suspects that Liz, though she was too smart not to conform to public opinion, probably thought it was all a lot of damn nonsense. She deplored "enthusiasm," which manifested itself too often in the lunatic fringe of the growing Protestant movement. In those days, enthusiasm meant "ill-regulated religious emotion or speculation; rapturous intensity of feeling," etc. Very lower-class stuff, to be snubbed severely.

Today, often described as intense spirituality.

The enthusiasts were producing an enormous variety of what John Milton later called "sects and schisms," among them Quakers, Shakers, Jumpers, Leapers, Rollers, and Quiverers. The agitated behaviour was caused by their custom of working themselves into states of ecstatic trance, in which they shook, quivered, quaked, rolled, jumped, leaped, and in some cases (unsubtantiated by hard evidence) flew. The Holy Rollers were still ecstatically rolling in fairly recent memory, but the Quakers long since gave up quaking for its contrary, quietism, and have been rewarded with a certain mild Snobvalue, although their principles repudiate snobism in all forms.

The all-time flying champion was St. Joseph of Cupertino, who had an unhappy habit of performing involuntary levitations, which he appeared to dislike, for he uttered "shrill birdlike cries" of agitation, and clutched at trees to arrest his trajectory. The Spanish ambassador to the papal court and his wife witnessed one such flight in 1645, in which the saint soared "a dozen paces over the heads of those present," proceeding airborne toward a statue of the Virgin Mary, to which he offered a distracted bow, after which he came down to earth and hurried off to his cell. Several times when poor Joseph took off on a flight, he caught hold of another friar, as if to use him as an anchor, but the Power simply hauled the other friar along with him, and they sailed around together.

In some circles, this was considered highly edifying, and the otherwise undistinguished brother was canonized for his uncomfortable gift. Generally, however, flying was not encouraged by the church, as it seemed a little undignified (as practised by Joseph, at any rate), and was suspect because of its association with witchcraft.

When Margaret Rule of Salem was observed in 1693 by Cotton Mather performing levitations, it was not edifying at all, but evidence of witchcraft. Mr. Mather collected signed statements from six witnesses as to Margaret's affliction, which was also involuntary and hence not her own work; she was bewitched, not practising witchcraft.

In the 19th century, mediums and even clergymen levitated, both in England and America. The skill seems to have been lost, although some disciples of Transcendental Meditation claim to have mastered it through deep meditation. I watched a demonstration on TV, but was unconvinced. They're not levitations, they're jumps. Jumping in the lotus position is a good trick, but it's jumping. Not flying.

Throughout history, nonetheless, in spite of the Socreligsnobs' distaste for its sensational aspects, the "enthusiasts" have been convinced that they are far holier than their more restrained contemporaries, and that the rolling, leaping, flying et al. are evidence of possession by the holy spirit. The phenomenon is by no means confined to Christians; the whirling (and howling) dervishes are their Islamic equivalent. Their lives are dedicated to poverty and austerity, their whirling induces the holy trance state. We thus have two fundamental varieties of Religsnob: the Stately/Sedate and the Undignified Enthusiastic.

Charles II of England, restored to the throne in 1660, pretended all his life to be a moderate Protestant. Everyone wanted to believe this, because they were fed to the teeth with (a) religious wars, and (b) being preached at by Cromwell and his puritan buddies. However, wicked old Charles recanted on his death-bed, admitting that he'd been a damned Papist all the time, because (he told Lauderdale) Presbyterianism was no religion for a gentleman. This is of course a splendid illustration of the workings of Socsnobbery. It also raises the question: did Charles' conversion arise from profound faith, or from snobbery?

He fathered at least fourteen royal bastards, commenting that he "could not think God would make a man miserable for taking a little pleasure out of the way." He also requested on his death-bed that they "let not poor Nellie starve," which was thoughtful, at least. (Orange-seller and actress Nell Gwynne was one of his innumerable mistresses.)

He was a bad lot in other respects, according to religious historians, "sharing the preoccupations of a sceptical, materialist century which gave birth to the Royal Society under his charter." That is, he encouraged science. He allowed greater parliamentary control over revenue and expenditure, and was a patron of the theatre. He had a fine physique, was a brilliant sailor and horseman, but was overly affable and familiar with inferiors, the rotter. John Evelyn mentioned his natural kindness, but deplored the smell of his spaniels which pervaded the court. Weak-minded sentimentalists are unnecessarily tolerant and charitable toward Charles, in spite of his evil penchant for science and democracy, because he was nice to dogs.

He is my all-time favourite Religsnob, though one suspects he was not seriously religious.

Social snobs follow the Liz I and Charles II positions, rejecting enthusiasm and insisting on services suited to gentlefolk, that do not muss the hair or rumple the costume. Thus they are chiefly represented by the Church of England and in the U.S., the Episcopalians. Catholicism is no longer considered a religion for the gentry, because after the time of Charles II, it became associated with the lower orders — ignorant peasants in France and Quebec, policemen and stevedores in Ireland and the U.S., though there is some ambivalence in the latter, because of adherence by the presidential Kennedys. However, as has been noted, the Kennedys are only a short distance (snobwise) from underworld connections, so that no serious Religsnob would invoke them for Socsnobcredit.

The Roman persuasion is also despised by serious environmentalists because of its unenlightened stance on population control, contemporary equivalent among the conscientious with the sin against the Holy Ghost, without of course any credulity about ghosts, holy or otherwise.

Religsocsnobs in the Church of England usually divide themselves into two sub-classes: High Church lay-snobs, who are chiefly old ladies in gloves and antique hats, preferably of blue velvet, who know when Lady Day falls, and why anyone bothers, and what to do about Shrove Tuesday other than eating pancakes. They talk glibly about naves, apses, transepts, and chancels. High Church snobs repudiate the Roman connection, though heavily into genuflecting, crossing themselves and even confession; they have profound contempt for Low Anglicanism (little better than the United Church). Religsocsnobs are a dwindling force in the modern world. When the current crop of old ladies dies, there may be none left.

The other branch of Religsocsnobs is the clerical one. The more extreme among the Ordained, seduced by the joys of the confessional, chanting, incense, and other exciting practices, get so High that they are in constant danger of toppling over into the cesspool of Rome, as Trollope said of the great Dr. Gwynne. Others among the clergy are atheists in private, but believe that religion is probably good for laypeople. They rarely give a damn about holiness, regarding the church as a social institution, but they adore the drama of the ritual, the splendour of the vestments, and the nobility of the language. No revised Prayer Books allowed, and only the King James version of the Bible.

My favourite Canadian lay Religsnob, Conrad Black, has made a heroic effort to be several kinds of Religsnob, successively. A review by Bernard Baskin of our hero's autobiography, *A Life in Progress*, advises as follows:

> Black found God in 1978 when he came to "look upon atheism with intellectual disdain and with fear of the potentialities of the human ego when unleashed from any sense of cosmic proportion and spirituality." He concluded that atheism was barren, unremitting and illogical. Almost a decade later he converted to Roman Catholicism. It was, for him, the preferred religion although unhappily enshrouded in the "haze of human error as in the absurdity of its professed prohibition of birth control, divorce, and socialistic nostrums."
> (*Hamilton Spectator*, Nov. 27, 1993.)

The connoisseur of Religsnob will writhe with pleasure at this, though when Conrad charges atheism with illogicality, one cannot but ponder on pots and kettles. Since his conversion, Conrad has divorced his wife and married none other than adorable, but divorced, journalist Barbara Amiel, which one would think must strike Mother Church as unsuitable. However, accomplished snob that he is, Conrad doesn't let nonsense like facts interfere with his chosen path. Whether he will join Babs in the Jewish faith, we don't yet know; perhaps she will see the error of her ways and convert to the one true faith.

I consulted an atheist for views on Conrad's condemnation, particularly his assertion that atheists are "unleashed" from any sense of cosmic proportion. God knows what Conrad means by cosmic proportion, says the atheist, but most of what he (the atheist) would consider cosmic proportion or cosmic anything else, comes from the study of astronomy which since the time of Galileo has refuted the validity of Biblical cosmology. The church has made only a negative contribution to understanding of cosmic proportion, since for centuries it has done its damndest to stop all research that might contradict the account given in Genesis, which would be a trifle confusing if NASA tried to use it as a guide for space exploration. The last I heard, the Church gave the impression that the dark side of the moon was the Limbo where the souls of unbaptized children were held; such preoccupations would not be useful to moon-landing astronauts.

Still, we can no longer accuse the Church of obscurantism. The Vatican has at last acknowledged that Galileo might have known what he was talking about! That the universe is not geocentric, as The Church has insisted! And it's only four-hundred years late! (Think what else Galileo might have discovered if he hadn't been forced to give up his work, to save his neck.)

And not only that — His Holiness has allowed that evolution is a plausible theory! Is not to be equated with Evil! Holy Smoke! And this only a century late! From its earliest days, the Church has condemned scientific discovery that disagreed with the Bible, fearing that exposure of scriptural fallibility would destroy belief among the humble. Until recently they reinforced their resistance with torture and murder. My atheist claims that most of the scientific work of the last four centuries has involved correcting the errors of the Bible, and the investigators were often handicapped by the danger of being charged with heresy and burned at the stake, like Giordano Bruno, or attacked by bishops, as Darwin was. He also says that the idea of the separateness of body and spirit ("Descartes' error") is cruelly unjust to Descartes, who was no muttonhead, scientifically. But he had the example of Galileo before him, and knew that if he got in trouble with the Church, he too would be prevented from getting any work done.

I asked the atheist about Conrad's disapproval of the unleashing of the human ego from spirituality, but he declined to discuss it without a definition. He claimed to have asked different champions of spirituality several times for such a definition, but had received answers to the effect that it's like, well, uh, sorta like, uh, higher things, like, not materialistic, y'know?

Spirituality is the current buzz word, employed promiscuously in the most improbable contexts; I once heard a native Canadian seriously discussing the spirituality of the game of lacrosse, which I gather establishes some kind of transcendent link between Mother Earth and Father Sky. I've only seen one lacrosse game, and so am not an authority, but in the course of it, play was stopped at least three times by fights. They were very spiritual fights, I've no doubt, but they still involved bloody noses, and one removal on a stretcher.

During the cigarette-smuggling wars, I heard it argued that smoking had great spiritual significance, too, since tobacco had been used ceremonially among the native peoples long before the white men came here. Mmmm, maybe they did, but they weren't smoking store-bought cigarettes, and two packs a day can't be called ceremonial use.

Spirituality is currently the great religious preoccupation, and we'll come back to it shortly.

One would think that the history of the last four or five hundred years would have had a moderating effect on RC Snobbery, what with the Reformation, the burgeoning of Protestantism, the tumescence of fundamentalism, as well as wave on wave of ghastly scandals. Yet only a short time ago I heard a radio discussion in which two theologians (one Protestant, one Catholic) argued the superiority of their creeds. It started off with great politeness and tolerance, but degenerated into a certain degree of asperity. How could the Catholic church make such claims for its exclusive right to expound the rules of human behaviour, hotly demanded the Protestant. I will never forget the sublime confidence with which his opponent replied, "There is only one true church, and it must be conscious of its calling."

If traditional religion is a dwindling force, Enthusiasm is growing by leaps and bounds, as can be established by turning on the TV any hour of the day or night, to be harangued by evangelists, all fundamentalist believers in the literal truth of the Bible, which they hold to have been personally written by God. Their private lives are not good examples (witness the cases of Jim Bakker, Jimmie Swaggart, Peter Popoff et al.) but that doesn't stop them from telling the rest of us how to conduct our affairs, and giving the impression that they have a private line to the Almighty.

The fundamentalists have no monopoly on bad examples: you can't pick up a newspaper without discovering yet another sex scandal among the officially holy. Although his representatives in the field are constantly being exposed in squalid scandals, Pope John Paul II's encyclical *Veritatis Splendor* warns, "Opposition to the teaching of the church's pastors cannot be seen as a legitimate expression either of Christian freedom or of the diversity of the Spirit's gifts. It is prohibited — to everyone and in every case — to violate these precepts ..." Don't do as they do, do as they say.

The Encyclical condemns homosexual acts, although so far the church hasn't had much luck in stamping this out among its pastors. It also forbids contraception, artificial insemination, masturbation, abortion, and euthanasia. The Pope declines to acknowledge the danger of the population explosion, and (as noted earlier) emasculated the Rio conference on the environment by demanding that population be excluded from the agenda. The other participants caved in, perhaps because the habit of belief in the infallibility of the pontiff was too strong for logic. Not surprisingly, the conference failed to achieve anything substantial.

"If people listen to him," grumbled my atheist-cum-environmentalist informant, "the planet will be uninhabitable in another twenty years."

According to the atheist/environmentalist, irresponsible procreation is the worst sin the human race can commit. It's an interesting moral issue. While the RC church and some of the evangelical extremists demand uncontrolled procreation, anxious environmentalists see exploding population (from which all other ecological disasters proceed) as the greatest threat to the future of the planet. Religious snobbery has its roots in an axiomatic assumption that religion = good. The sacred texts of Judaism and Christianity warn that if you don't follow their orders, you're in for an eternity in hell, where they have a lake of eternal fire in which you will writhe in perpetuity.

"Everyone believes in heaven and eternal life in God," a confident cleric wrote in the public prints, and another one observed that disbelief in God constitutes a dangerous form of insanity. However, Atheistsnob Dr. Frank R. Zindler, a professor of biology and geology, and member of many learned societies, suggests that not only does religion cause insanity (with statistics from psychiatrists and mental institutions) but even more interestingly, insanity causes religion. He cites a long list of founders and leaders of various religions who were by medical definition psychotic: Luther, Wesley, Loyola, St. Theresa, Mary Baker Eddy, Joseph Smith, Rev. Jim Jones, Ellen G. White (founder of Seventh Day Adventism) and St. Paul. Several of them suffered from epilepsy, which though not a mental disorder, is often accompanied by auditory and visual hallucinations.

> Religion itself is crazy, and theology has been described as "systematized insanity" … The notion that there is a spirit world which can affect our lives involves delusional thinking and may derive from hallucinatory experiences and illusions. Most religions reinforce obsessional and compulsive behavior (e.g., rosary exercises, frequently scheduled prayers, thinking incessantly about sin, etc.). With their inability to create logically consistent systems of thought and action, and with their often fragmented, inconsistent and reality-ignoring claims about the

> world, most religions appear to be the apotheosis of schizophrenia. Holy books such as Ezekiel and Revelations bear great resemblance to the effusions of schizophrenics. With almost no exceptions, religions inhibit the development of self-reliant, self-assertive behaviour and reinforce infantile, dependent behavior.
> (*American Atheist* , April 1988.)

Atheistsnobs base their arguments on the rational, while Religsnobs have classically based theirs on faith and revelation. However, recently the Religsnobs have decided to appropriate reason and logic as their turf, too, claiming that "the first rational act of any child is to acknowledge the existence of God," citing Thomas Aquinas as their authority. This is a clever ploy, because it leaves argumentative atheists speechless with incredulity and anger at this unethical switching of the ground of argument. However, the atheists have turned the tables by claiming a one-time religious monopoly: *being good*.

"You should go to church, Aunt Annie," a priggish small child advised an elderly relative, "It would make you good."

"I *am* good," snapped the non-church-going elder. She then listed her claims to righteousness. She was kind to animals, having made the lives of many dogs and cats and two horses rich and happy, sometimes to the point of risking bankruptcy from vet bills. She had spent a good part of her life as a non-meat-eater and non-fur-wearer. She paid her debts and taxes promptly, and refrained from molesting little children (or anyone else); didn't steal, didn't get drunk or take drugs or smoke.

"I feed the birds and squirrels all winter, I compost and recycle, I don't litter. I even observe the speed limit. What the hell am I doing wrong, that I need to go to church to make me good?"

"You swear," self-righteously rejoined the brat, and his elderly aunt hit him over the head with a club, cursing hideously as she did so.

She didn't really, but she said it was a near thing.

"Can We Be Good Without God?" ran the headline on a newspaper Religious Page not long ago. According to Aunt Annie and my atheist, yes, we can. Perhaps we should ask whether we can be good *with* God. Many devout church-goers, and a startlingly high percentage of the clergy, are far from good. They're unequivocally bad, in conspicuously nasty ways, which I trust it is unnecessary to describe. If anybody wants evidence, I will be glad to send them photocopies of newspaper stories which now fill several enormous cartons. If I don't stop clipping them, they will fill several rooms, and I'll have to move out of the house and live in the tool-shed.

Even in minor matters, church-going is no guarantee of honesty or generosity. *Psychology Today* reported (December 1989) a study that turned up "no discernible relationship between involvement [in church activities] and charitable acts. In some cases, a negative relationship appears." That is, good church members are stingier than non-church-members in helping the poor. There was "no correlation at all between altruism and attendance at religious services."

In an honours code exam, "atheists were the only group in which a majority did not cheat" and religion was irrelevant to college students' willingness to volunteer time with retarded children. *Religion doesn't make you good*. It does tend to make you smug.

Nevertheless Religsnobs assume their position is axiomatically correct, quoting Aquinas again and claiming that disbelief in God is a sign of abnormality. Belief that God didn't exist was to do violence to the intellect. Of course this argument depends on how strongly you believe in the infallibility of Aquinas. Among non-Catholics it is not much of an argument. I once mentioned Aquinas to a class of college students; the better informed had him confused with Tom Aquino, a pillar of the Conservative Party, and at least one person thought he was a baseball player, I believe a shortstop, though I've forgotten with what team.

A sub-class of Religious Snobbery manifests itself in the press. Journalists are not conspicuously pious, as a rule, but they believe with all their hearts that the simple public is still deeply religious and will cancel its subscriptions unless the publication regularly declares its devout adherence to approved religious positions. These are mostly Christian, but periodically the press makes a patronizing bow in the direction of Buddhism, Islam, and other lesser breeds without the Law. According to my above cited authority on atheism, the press is very snobbish about disbelief, which is by definition evil. The *Toronto Star* once recklessly published a brief article on atheism, but immediately went into a flap of anxiety and had three of its regular religious columnists write refutations of the atheist position, no equal time allowed to the Enemy.

So this concerned atheist helped to organize a humanist group which has tried in vain to make its voice heard, if only to explain its position. (He thought "humanist" would be a less alarming term than "atheist.") The humanists' overtures threw the editors and management into blind panic: many of the members were distinguished professionals whom the Fourth Estate would normally seek to ingratiate rather than snub, so they procrastinated. The humanist pointed out that every week all the big dailies carry a Religion Page, where the conventional religions have regular columns. Even witchcraft sometimes gets a voice, since it claims to be a religion called *wiccecraeft*, a Celtic word meaning "the craft of the wise." If you look it up, you'll find that *Wicce*, which is Old English not Celtic, means simply witch, and is cognate with wicked. The word for "wise" is, pleasingly enough, *wys*. The Christians thought the fertility rites of the aboriginal inhabitants most improper, involving as they did a lot of sex and sympathetic magic; hence the religion was wicked, and its practitioners witches. The word, incidentally, was always used pejoratively until recent times. The aboriginals didn't think they were either witches or wicked; they were practising their religion, poor dears.

After a lot of argument on the above lines, a nervous editor on the *Hamilton Spectator* allowed as how he might run an article on humanism; he would assign a reporter to cover it. He couldn't allow a member of the group to write it, "for obvious reasons."

Not obvious at all, roared the humanists. How can an outsider explain as well as an informed person? Humanists would not give an impartial account, argued the editor; they would be prejudiced.

"You hire Christians to write your Christian columns, and Jews to write on Judaism, and witches to write on witchcraft! Why not humanists to write on humanism?"

He believed it would offend their readers, who would fear their family newspaper had gone over to Satanic atheism. (Unbelief = wicked, and wicked = Satanism.)

"Humanists and atheists don't believe in Satan," moaned the humanist, but it was in vain. They were up against ReligoPressnob, and remain voiceless to this day, except for their own publications which are pathetically underfunded and waste their substance in preaching to the converted, or rather the anti-converted.

Religsnob is an unusual form of snobbery, in that its practitioners don't want to be better than the rest of us. They want to haul everyone up to their own level of holiness. Or so they claim. Actually, there is great competition among Jehovah's Witnesses, Mormons, and other proselytizers as to the number of souls they have saved, or sheep brought back to the fold, as they phrase it in their picturesque language.

Scientific accuracy of the Bible has recently been espoused by the Witnesses, who claim that the Genesis account is a sound description of the origin of the universe.

"You mean that the universe is in fact geocentric?" demanded my atheist friend, following up with a lecture on Galileo. But the Witnesses didn't know from geocentricity and had difficulty identifying Galileo, so that the confrontation ended in general confusion, or failure of communication. It is interesting that the proselytizers so often spend energy on difficult prospects like atheists and humanists; no doubt they offer a challenge.

Now! Let's glance at Spirituality.

As we complained earlier, none of its adherents are willing to provide a definition, claiming that any definition would limit its transcendent beauty. It is not the same as religion, thought it is often associated with religion, but it rejects dogma. It is not to be confused with Spiritualism, though it appears to subscribe to belief in immortality. It is in no sense a system of ethics, and does not demand virtuous behaviour, although virtuous behaviour is often a sort of by-product of Spirituality. As far as I have been able to pin it down, Spirituality seems to be associated with the mystic (oceanic/visionary/ecstatic/religious) experience.

It was once believed that such experiences were the special province of a privileged élite — saints, poets, artists — through their piety and elevated sensibilities. However, during the sixties, experiments with yoga, meditation, and various chemicals made it clear that the experience is biochemical rather than spiritual, and is available to most of us. It can be spontaneous, or induced by meditation or drugs, as reported by Timothy Leary, Richard Alpert and their disciples. It can sometimes induces a reverse mystic experience, where you experience hell instead of heaven. It is also addictive.

ATTENTION: THIS TREATISE DOES NOT ENDORSE NOR RECOMMEND THE DRUG METHOD.

The mystic etc. experience has for most of human history enjoyed great prestige. It was thought to bring spiritual apprehension of truths beyond rational understanding, through union with a non-denominational Deity. These were sometimes revealed through visions or voices, but sometimes they manifested themselves in possession by the Spirit, which in turn manifested itself in trance states. These might be passive and quiescent, OR they might produce wild and uncontrolled behaviour like that mentioned earlier — quaking, shaking, dancing, whirling, howling, leaping, jumping, rolling, quivering, and in a pleasant recent case, laughing: A Toronto church achieved international fame by the eruption of uncontrollable attacks of laughter among its congregations. This was regarded as extremely edifying among the Spiritual, according to whom there have been many cases of miraculous healing associated with the hilarity.

Recent research has cast a new light on mystic experiences, including the near-death experience. It is a complex affair, but I'll keep it brief by over-simplification. The mystic et al. experience is a biochemical, not a spiritual process. It starts with strong emotions, like fear or anger, which trigger what is known as the fight/flight syndrome. The system is flooded with insulin, so that one can run faster, hit harder, whatever, in order to survive attack. Following the fight/flight phase comes a recovery period, in which one must rest and bind up one's wounds. To assist in this, and to control pain, the body produces soothing and healing chemicals called endorphins, which create feelings of peace, happiness, and well-being.

> The word endorphins [is] a contraction of endogenous (meaning internally produced) and morphine. Endorphins are peptides synthesized in the brain ... They seem to act as neuro-transmitters, as neuromodulators (interacting with and affecting the action of various other neurotransmitters) and as hormones ... It has long been known that morphine and heroin produce a state described as the ultimate pleasure by many users, and often sought after to the exclusion of food, sex and every other pleasure. However, what they do to the brain and why they are so highly addictive was a mystery. It was therefore considered a great discovery in the early 1970s when opiate receptors were found in the brain: that is cells that respond specifically to these chemicals. This discovery meant the effects were probably created by the drugs mimicking the naturally pleasurable effects of a chemical made by the brain itself ... It was not long before the chemicals themselves were identified ... as endorphins [which] are now known to be synthesized in the brain and released into the cerebrospinal fluid, which bathes the cells of the brain and spinal cord ... during stress ...
> (Blackmore, 107)

It is in this state that "paranormal" experiences occur: out-of-body experiences, visions and voices, and possibly genuine faculties of the unconscious mind, unavailable in normal consciousness, such as telepathy, clairvoyance and precognition. Mystical experiences sometimes occur during epileptic seizures, in cases affecting the brain structure involved in emotions and memory. Susan Blackmore's book is concerned with its relevance to the "near-death experience." Since all of these phenomena have also been experienced under the influence of drugs, it's hard to deny their chemical/biochemical source.

It's rather sad that so few people are aware of this, since it was clearly explained a century ago by William James in *Varieties of Religious Experience*, still one of the best books on the subject, although he didn't know about endorphins, since the necessary technology hadn't been invented.

Spiritualitysnobs passionately repudiate the chemical/biochemical theories, because these diminish their sublimity. Why is it better if it comes through the gods? Doesn't it reflect great credit on the humble creature that worked its way up from micro-organism to human to sublime?

Between the 18th century and the 1960s, it wasn't done to admit to mystic experiences, because they marked you as weird, if not cuckoo, though the Romantic poets went on about them at length, as did Tennyson. After the sixties, however, they became a vogue, and a rather unedifying competition developed as to the sublimity of one's mystic states, so that it became a new form of Religsnob. There was a most unseemly exchange in a philosophy journal between a couple of clerical gents, a kind of transcendental one-upmanship: "My mystic experiences are more sublime than your mystic experiences, nyaaah." Or words to that effect. Although it is clear that mystic experiences are non-denominational (Buddhists are probably the champs), all combatants in the sublimity competition insist they alone are genuine exponents. In correspondence with one of them, I was told I couldn't have an authentic mystic experience, since I wasn't a Roman Catholic: they have a monopoly.

I ran across an interesting, though rather esoteric, form of Holier-than-thou Snobbery during my researches. Such activities have produced a new variety of Religsnob: levitation snobbery. Levitation, after going underground (bad metaphor) since Victorian times, is back and it's Big! It seems not entirely impossible that in hysterical states, along with quaking, rolling, etc., levitation might be possible, though as mentioned it hasn't got much farther than leaping, in voluntary cases. (Involuntary levitation brings us back to chemical/biochemical.) The big question is whether or not it is edifying: is it a sign of exalted holiness, or of severe illness, perhaps related to epilepsy or some such affliction involving seizures, or even of wickedness, possibly witchcraft or demonic possession? Think before you fly! Among the superstitious, idle-headed eld, such activities were considered evidence of extreme holiness (Holier-than-thou Snobbery) and, as we've seen, by the superior classes as vulgar lack of self-control (Religio-social Snobbery). See Snobnote (*infra*) for current scientific developments.

New Age activities, sometimes identified with spirituality, also attract a good chunk of the lunatic fringe. I heard a New Age expert holding forth on CBC Radio's "Tapestry," and as nuts go, he was a real Brazil. His thesis was something to the effect that, as we all are participants in one another's identities, it doesn't really matter what happens to individuals. The interviewer asked him how he could believe in a benign deity, after such horrors as the massacres in Rwanda and similar nightmares, many of them done in the name of religion. He explained that every so often, humanity got above itself and had to have a really sharp lesson! So the benevolent deity sent a massacre, to make us straighten up. (Said deity obviously related to the Old Testament monster who sent Noah's flood, though the expert didn't admit it.)

What effect will it have on the wealthy and corrupt in other areas to murder a lot of helpless Rwandans? Well, they'll realize that since we all participate in one another's identities, the massacres aren't just happening to the Rwandans, they're happening to all of the rest of us, too. Tell that to the Rwandans who were drowned and starved to death, is all I say. If that's the best the New Age has to say for itself, best it keep its silly mouth shut.

Religion once was the enemy of technology, as of all innovations, but it latched onto communications technology like a zebra mussel to a sewage pipe. Radio and television broadcast religious propaganda from dawn to dark. Now *Time* (Dec. 16, 1996) tells us that if you looked up God on the Web, you'll find 410,000 hits, while Jesus has 146,000. Pornography, I heard somewhere, has several million, so we can see who's winning. Also on the Web is a Vietnamese sect, Cao Daiism, which worships Victor Hugo. Personally, I'm waiting for a scientific cult led (I think) by J. Lovelock, the Gaia man, Briefly Noted on Race and Species Snobbery. He was discussing whether or not life would be destroyed on earth, through war, pollution, a comet crash, whatever. Some forms would be destroyed, he conceded, but the *really important* life-forms would survive, as they survived the dinosaur extinction. Major important surviving life-form? Not the big-brain humans, but BLUE-GREEN ALGAE. We have since then developed a small BGA cult, dedicated to survival. Everyone welcome. Our rituals so far have not gone much beyond a courteous "BGA bless you" when you sneeze, but we look for a big growth spurt once we're on the net.

Religious Snobbery pervades all religions. Even extreme humility demonstrates superiority. Everyone believes its own religion is the only right one, and looks down with snobbish contempt not only on every other religion, but every other member of its own religion. You can't lose.

Relig/Sci Snobnote: The Nijmegen Frog. All religions are concerned with the supernatural, whether it takes the form of deities (malign or benign) or ghosts, angels, demons, poltergeists (literally noisy ghosts), whatever. The Religsnob community naturally cannot deny the existence of the supernatural, but it is often uncomfortable with some of its more bizarre or undignified manifestations.

The scientific community was by necessity required to eliminate the supernatural from its considerations: obviously, you can't understand physical laws if you have to allow for capricious supernatural interventions, such as Someone making the sun and moon stand still over the Vale of Ajalon in order that the Israelites didn't have to fight with the sun in their eyes, said Someone operating on the theory that the sun goes around the earth, and not vice versa. So sometime in the 18th century scientific researchers more or less made a polite bow to Religion, but eliminated it from consideration.

Among matters eliminated were such unlikely phenomena as psychokinesis — the movement of objects by some mysterious, unidentifiable force, usually associated with poltergeists by occultists. When it happens, as it does with some frequency, the scientists attributed it to fraud, hallucination, coincidence, lies, whatever. Because it *can't* happen. (*Eppur si muove*, as Galileo said under his breath, in another context.) What only a few of them seem to have considered was that these phenomena, along with a batch of others like telepathy and precognition, might have natural causes which *could* in fact be studied scientifically.

Every so often we have an outbreak of poltergeistry. Weird things happen. Large pieces of furniture move about inexplicably. Showers of stones have come through roofs. Objects disappear and reappear in improbable places. It did occur to various investigators that the mad phenomena seemed chiefly to be associated with frightened and unhappy little girls (occasionally boys, but not nearly so often), and still more seldom with adults, usually ones with some kind of handicap and severe emotional problems. Why should that make objects move with no apparent source of propulsion?

Obviously, because the place was haunted. Psychics, called in to investigate, pompously announced that they sensed the presence of a disturbed spirit, and performed exorcisms.

So there was a choice: The whole thing was a scam; not a scam, but the delusion of a disturbed mind, accompanied by hallucinations; or we were stuck with ghosts.

Then a Toronto group discovered that they could produce psychokinetic effects deliberately, with no help from spirits, by inducing a certain altered mental/emotional state. The group could send a heavy table rocketing across the room like a demented pony. They filmed and televised it, wrote books describing the experiment, and the scientific community paid no attention whatsoever. Poltergeist phenomena offended their reasoning. Effects with no cause.

Enter the Nijmegen frog. Scientists at the University of Nijmegen levitated a live frog encased in a magnetic cylinder. They did this (according to an Associated Press article) by subjecting the cylinder, frog enclosed, to a powerful electromagnetic field. Does that explain poltergeists?

We know now that extreme emotional stress produces extraordinary chemical and electrical changes. People perform near-impossible feats when intolerably stressed. Remember the story of the little old lady who lifted up the car? (Flat tire, son changing tire, jack slips, car falls on son. Little old lady lifts up car so son can escape.) We still can't measure the energy that goes into poltergeist activity but it has to be powerful. It is unconscious and random — most of its actions are pointless. As A. R. G. Owen pointed out fifty or so years ago (*Can We Explain the Poltergeist?*) the strange activities and noises are a kind of desperate cry for help, from an individual who can't express her terrors and has nowhere to turn for help. Like a little girl being molested by her stepfather. Many poltergeist cases occur in homes where this situation exists, where fear, anger and hatred are repressed for years and eventually erupt, *somehow creating a powerful magnetic field* which causes the phenomena.

Okay, the theory still needs a little work. But we're on the right track. You read it here first.

Snobnote: Psychicsnob. Self-styled psychics are among the world's worst snobs, giving themselves intolerable airs and graces about their special "Powers." Some years ago, Peter Gzowski interviewed Canada's Greatest Psychic, whose name I don't remember; just as well, he'd probably try to sue me. I made careful notes on this case, and kept track of the predictions the psychic made for the following year. I still have those notes, too; somewhere. Buried in the stacks of paper that fill my study, the basement, and my bedroom. However, if I have to find them, I will, given enough time.

The closest I can come to a date is that it was in the period when Gorbachev was in power in Russia. I know this, because one of the psychic's warnings to the world was that Gorby was the Antichrist (so identified by the birthmark on his scalp) and that his peace campaign was the most contemptible of camouflages to cover his real activities, which were to launch a nuclear war, among other evils.

So if he *is* the Antichrist, the poor darling wasn't very successful at the job.

Among other prophecies, our Greatest Psychic said that in the following year, Queen Elizabeth would abdicate, and Prince Andrew take over the crown. He prophesied a lot of other things which I've forgotten, but I kept track as far as I could, and he got *every one of them wrong*.

This is a fairly typical psychic performance.

Actually, a great many people from time to time have so-called psychic experiences, but they are not due to special powers given to them by God, or whomever. They're biochemical events, usually associated with extreme stress, and sometimes with drugs. There are well-attested cases of telepathy and precognition, and they can happen to any of us. Professional psychics, like Canada's Greatest, are almost invariably charlatans.

And Now One Final Snobnote: A peculiarly unattractive form of Religsnob might be labelled Survivorsnob. This is the individual who comes unscathed out of a horrible accident in which hundreds of people are killed or maimed for life, and remarks: "Yessir, the good Lord was certainly looking after me, all right!" The implication is that he has some special virtue that sets him apart as worth saving, while all the other poor wretches were dispensable, and the good Lord couldn't be bothered with them.

Why, one wonders, is the good Lord so inscrutable in his choice of favourites? Thousands of miserable wretches may perish in agony without the least sign of concern from de Lawd, but the Survivorsnob (who rarely shows any special distinction) claims to be singled out for favour. Even if he *thinks* he's God's pet, he could have the decency to keep his mouth shut about it when others just as deserving are groaning in agony from their injuries, or mourning their dead.

24

Sicksnob/Sportsnob

Guys are very vulnerable to sports anguish ...The guy mind does not believe in medical care. Guys will not seek medical treatment, for themselves or others, except in certain clear-cut situations, such as decapitation. Even then ... the prevailing guy attitude is "Let's put his head back on with duct tape and see if he can play a couple more innings."
— Dave Barry, *Complete Guide to Guys*.

Illness and sports seem to belong at opposite ends of the pole, but as we'll see, they are intimately related in snob terms.

Further, you mightn't think that illness is something to feel superior about, but there is a very complicated system of Sicksnobbery, which has changed and evolved interestingly over the ages. Obviously there's no Snobvalue in being seriously ill, or in having something so dangerous or disgraceful that it must be concealed rather than published. The whole point of Snobvalue is that it can be used to indicate superiority, so don't go getting venereal disease or something contagious, in the hope of acquiring Snobpoints, because the effect will be the disastrous opposite of what you want, and besides, it might make you sick.

There used to be certain proverbial male sayings, to the effect that you weren't a man until you'd had a dose, with the suggestion that a bout of gonorrhoea or syphilis demonstrated your virility, but this was more like whistling in the dark than a real snob boast: too many associated horrors, and a dead loss if you mentioned it to your date.

Every epoch in history produces, as well as distinctive fashions in clothes and hair and even body build, its own peculiar brand of popular illnesses. We know from James Laver's researches that fashions do not come about because of arbitrary whims, sly tricks of designers, but reflect the inexorable pressures of social and economic change. Same thing for styles in illness: they are not accidental, but almost inevitable by-products of history, as well as socially useful barometers.

For millennia, the only snob illness of high repute for males was The Wound, whether acquired in war, a duel, or in sport. A maiming or disfiguring wound was rather regrettable, but nonetheless a sign of manliness. Until quite recent times, duelling scars were very big in Germany. Since we know (from Thorstein Veblen, natch) that fighting and hunting are the only vocations of the aristocratic male, then wounds acquired in those pursuits are honourable and admirable. No marks for bruises acquired while running the vacuum cleaner, or cutting yourself while peeling potatoes. These betray you as a domestic serf, doing women's work, incurring snob debits instead of credits. A stab from a manure fork stigmatizes you as rural-prole.

For the first several millennia, as with so many other snob categories, illness snobbery was a male monopoly. Women were expendable, and in any case, since they were illiterate long after men, we naturally only get the masculine point of view.

Non-violent illness did not enjoy any real vogue until around the 16th century, when melancholia became a top-class disability. Hamlet was tagged for posterity as "the melancholy Dane" and Jacques in *As You Like It* boasted that he could "suck melancholy from a song as a weasel sucks eggs." Robert Burton's *Anatomy of Melancholy* was a 17th-century bestseller.

Melancholia was not much fun (one of its symptoms was chronic constipation, for which Burton prescribed appalling purges), but it established you as an intellectual, and set you apart from the common herd. No horny-handed rustics need apply. Silvius in *As You Like It* was miserably pining with love for Phoebe, but he didn't presume to the status of melancholic.

The roots of melancholia were in the despair arising from religious doubt. The discoveries of astronomy had made educated people question Biblical accounts of the origin and nature of the universe; loss of faith led to pervasive depression. "The new Philosophy calls all in doubt," agonized John Donne. A similar phenomenon occurred in the 19th century, after Darwin's theories introduced doubt about the special creation of man.

Melancholia was an okay disease for upper-class males, but women were insufficiently educated to catch it. It remained a masculine monopoly until the late 19th century.

Tuberculosis was frequently associated with distinction in the arts, and had some charm if you could afford a costly spa. (The poor just coughed their lungs up and died.) However, it was too frequently fatal to have real value, and here we must note a significant factor in snob illnesses: they shouldn't make you too ill to enjoy social life, and they definitely shouldn't kill you, to have even rudimentary Snobvalue. Still, a good many poets and artists made quite a good thing out of tuberculosis; much of Keats' poetry has been credited to his TB. It still had Snobvalue in the 20th century, as witness Mann's *The Magic Mountain*. It was also said to increase the sex drive. However, it was always suspect, snobwise, because poor people caught it even more than rich ones.

When a society begins to be ashamed of its humble origins, healthy females tend to lose value. With some leisure time, women discovered the pleasures of hypochondria. Heartiness and independence were regarded as rather coarse. It was ladylike to be a trifle *souffrante*. Fashionable diseases for ladies proliferated. Certain afflictions had high Snobvalue, marking you as belonging to the upper class, because poor women simply couldn't afford them, and would get no sympathy if they tried it on.

An important 18th-century complaint was *the muslin disease*. Ladies wore fewer, and more revealing clothes than they had since fig-leaves went out of style. Under the diaphanous gowns were light muslin petticoats, wrung out in water to attract the eye to the legs, visible for the first time in the history of costume. The wet garments made their wearers susceptible to cold, and the belles of the period suffered everything from a slight cough to pneumonia. No price too high to be in vogue.

Later, in the days of crinolines and tight lacing, the top illness was The Decline. It was non-disfiguring, with the vaguest of symptoms. One day a lady would "find herself poorly" and lie down on her sofa. Her nerves couldn't endure loud noise or extremes of heat or cold. A sofa was indispensable, as were servants to bring tea, calves-foot jelly and hot-house grapes. Rather a nice illness, as you didn't have to eschew society, but could receive guests on your sofa, wearing a loose gown and NO CORSET.

A good many declines occurred when a woman had produced several children and didn't want any more. In the dark days before reliable contraceptives, the decline was sometimes the only birth control method available. Husbands couldn't very well expect a wife in a decline to endure sex, as ladies didn't like sex in those days because it was unladylike. They submitted to the male appetite as a duty, but it was vulgar to show enthusiasm.

Declines were thus a useful illness — they cut down on pregnancies, and were a valid excuse for not wearing a corset. They displayed feminine delicacy and fragility, and were thus clear proof of upper-class status. Still, they must have been a serious bore, and miraculous cures often occurred, reflecting still more credit on the patient, since her recovery might indicate special concern on the part of God. Higher Snobvalue there ain't.

The husband of a lady in a decline was pretty well obliged to take a mistress, or make use of the housemaid; if she got pregnant it didn't matter. She and her shameful bundle could be driven from the door without guilt, because (as we know) the lower classes don't worry about such matters. They aren't sensitive like their betters.

An almost identical ailment, The Vapours, had no such eminence. If a poor relation or aging governess developed the same symptoms, they elicited not pity but sniggers. The Vapours was caused by sexual starvation, attributable to failure to hook a husband. No sofa for the victim, no hot-house grapes brought by solicitous servants, only adjurations to keep busy and not be hysterical.

Elizabeth Barrett declined/reclined on her sofa for years, writing poetry, until Robert Browning came along, when she jumped up, married Robert secretly and in defiance of Papa Barrett, and bounced off to Italy where she had a lively social life, produced a son for Robert, and wrote lots more poetry. Some literary theorists believe her decline was a way of eluding incestuous advances by Father Barrett, but we don't have any reliable information on this. She may simply not have wanted to wear a corset.

"The Inflammation," which was accompanied by agonizing pain, vomiting and other disagreeable symptoms, was usually fatal, and since it struck rich and poor impartially, carried no prestige. When it was identified as appendicitis, curable by expensive surgery, it became high fashion, since you had to be rich to pay for the operation. It left a non-disfiguring scar, and you could monopolize conversations with accounts of what you said to the surgeon and nurses. But now, with universal health insurance, when any lout can afford it, the appendectomy has lost all Snobvalue. In fact, all surgery is Snobnegative. We do not wish to see your scar.

An interesting ladies' affliction was the Victorian practice of swooning, or fainting. It was an important skill in the repertoire of a young lady in search of a husband. When Scarlett O'Hara shamelessly remarked that she had never fainted in her life, she was rebuked by Mammy: "… 'twouldn't do no hahm ef you wuz to faint now an' den … it jes' doan look good de way you doan faint 'bout snakes an' mouses an' sech. Ah doan mean round home but w'en you is out in comp'ny."

A graceful faint, elegantly executed, could be quite visually pleasing, as a delicate creature subsided into the arms of a strategically placed gentleman, who could then bear her in his manly arms to a nice sofa. Fainting was not difficult when a girl was laced into a merciless corset to achieve a tiny waist. Some 19th-century belles actually had ribs removed in order to lace more tightly. No other feature was as important to a Beauty as a slender waist, unless it was a tiny foot, which had a similar value in Mandarin China.

Why should such discomfort and inconvenience be cultivated and admired? Why would any sane man want one of these fainting flowers, with her tiny waist and her tiny feet and her tiny brain, unable to stir without a slave to carry her parasol and her swoon-bottle?

The American South was a slave state; in Europe, domestic servants were cheap and abundant. The uselessness and helplessness of upper-class women was a mark of their distance from the working class. This motivation is still operative: it merely uses different signals.

Since fragile and delicate females are probably not the most stimulating of partners in bed, it was tacitly accepted that men would keep mistresses. Because the fainting flowers were also expected to be dim-wits, and were educated with that in view, men sought intellectual companionship outside of marriage as well, so that the same society produced the salons of the great courtesans. No man who cared for social approval could marry a demi-mondaine lady, but certainly lots of gents lavished money on them, and enjoyed their company more than that of his socially acceptable swooner.

O tempora, O mores.

By the 1920s, the fashion was to be dashing and sophisticated. However, there was still scope for disease snobbery. Mrs. Aldwinckle, in Huxley's *These Barren Leaves* illustrates the prevailing *mores*. She had

> ... three nervous breakdowns, an appendicitis, gout, and various influenzas, pneumonia and the like, but all of them aristocratic and avowable diseases; for Mrs. Aldwinckle sharply distinguished between complaints that are vulgar and complaints of an [upper class] sort. Chronic constipation, hernia, varicose veins ... these obviously were vulgar diseases from which no decent person could suffer, or at any rate, suffering, talk about. Her illnesses had all been extremely refined and correspondingly expensive. (Huxley, 278)

It was dashing for both sexes in the twenties and thirties to have hangovers. This may have had something to do with the forbidden glamour of booze during Prohibition. Hangovers provided a mark of sophistication; their symptoms, and recipes for cures, were the favoured stuff of conversation at parties. Comic accounts of appalling headaches and colossal vomits were infallible laugh-getters.

Generally speaking, any ailment connected with overweight is absolutely non-U: obesity is unmentionable. *Anorexia nervosa* carries a suggestion of chic, although a few deaths among the rich and famous have reduced its Snobvalue. Nevertheless, that skinny Duchess's dictum that "you can't be too rich or too thin" continues to make life a misery for many of us.

Not only fainting has lost its cachet nowadays: there are few socially desirable complaints. Mononucleosis had a certain vogue for a time, and was not dissimilar in its symptoms to the classic decline. But without a servant (slave/sucker) to wait on you, it has few advantages.

The absence of servants also spoils the fun of yuppie flu and chronic fatigue syndrome, which are contemporary versions of the decline. I have suffered from both of these all my life; the symptom which distinguishes them is an overwhelming disinclination to get up in the morning and go to work. Sufferers usually rally on sunny weekends, and vacations. There is no cure, although remarkable recoveries have been noted if the patient inherits, or otherwise acquires, a hefty chunk of cash, allowing it to quit its job. Sometimes even early retirement will have near-miraculous effects.

During the fifties, the highest Snobvalue derived from psychoanalysis. Peter de Vries documented it in *The Tunnel of Love*:

> ... I acquired the sense of lacking caste among subtle and gifted spirits ... All the artists and intellectuals I knew had periods when they couldn't do a tap of work, which they called, as you know, blocks. Then they would have to see their psychiatrists, or blockbusters. They frequently interpreted these blocks as sexual.

This illustrates an important social change. It was no longer enough merely to be rich, and have upper-class diseases. You had also to be creative, to move among the gifted and artistic (the successful gifted and artistic, that is) and suffer as they did.

Being in analysis was great copy, a splendid conversational resource at cocktail parties. Sufferers could learnedly argue the value of the theories of Freud and Jung, impressing the lesser, unanalyzed, guests. Analysis was expensive, and offered a marvellous excuse for bad behaviour: if you got drunk and began breaking up the furniture, or making passes at other people's wives, everyone was sympathetic, making allowances because (they would murmur to one another) "he's in analysis."

Bubonic plague and smallpox may have altered the whole course of history, but they have never had any Snobvalue. High fashion afflictions, although they may be painful and even (ultimately) fatal, always have an element of choice, and this choice is made because the illness has some practical use, most frequently getting out of work.

And now we come full circle, back to The Wound — now no longer a male monopoly.

The only ailments that have any Snobvalue today, for men and women alike, are sports injuries, but they must be associated with approved Snobsports. There is absolutely no point in breaking your leg at ten-pin bowling; you will actually lose Snobpoints for being associated with so plebeian an activity. There is still good Snobvalue in a break resulting from a skiing accident, but make sure that it happens on a difficult run. It is inviting ridicule to break something on the beginners' slope. (In fact, you must never admit to skiing the beginners'.) It should also be executed at a chic resort, not at some dump with a T-bar.

Generally, the Snobvalue of a sport stems from (1) its high cost and (2) its danger. Among Old Money, anything motorized is despised as vulgar, and as not giving you enough exercise. Among Nouveaux, whiplash can have high value if acquired from a collision involving

Porsches and Jags, but remains trite and trivial among Old Money. Nouveaux rejoice in power boats, racing cars, snowmobiles, and the like, and are proud of damage acquired in their operation. Although environmentalists and Old Money are usually ranged in opposite camps, in this case they speak with one voice, for Envirosnobs condemn all motorized sports as polluters, while Old Money despises them as vulgar ... something you can go out and buy, involving no special skills.

Early in the century, any injury arising from motor accidents had tremendous chic, but only as long as cars were the playthings of the rich. Once the *hoi polloi* started driving, the cachet was lost, except as noted above.

Favoured Old Money sports are sailing, polo, and hunting (where they lose environmental support). These are all dangerous or forbiddingly expensive, and generally unavailable to the lower orders. We need hardly say that there is no Snobvalue in "just messing about in boats" Water-Rat style; the only boats that count are sixty-footers requiring a large skilled crew, and which enter races, preferably in salt water.

Sailing can be dangerous, since there's always a good chance of getting drowned, or struck by a boom, or murdered by fellow crew-members, since it engenders bad temper as does no other sport. I know a charming family of pleasant, cultivated people, who once invited me to go sailing with them. I particularly adored the father, who was quite simply a darling, and the courtliest of old gentlemen. On land.

Once we got on the boat, this delightful Dr. Jekyll disappeared and was replaced by a roaring, raging Mr. Hyde, a trigger-tempered old bully who yelled at everyone, terrifying his guests and making little children cry. Not only that, but the same fearsome metamorphosis afflicted all his sons, and the whole family quarrelled among themselves in a way that made me suspect I had the answer to the mystery of the Marie Celeste.

Still, wounds acquired sailing have high Snobvalue and (if you survive) can be exhibited with modest pride. Owning and sailing a large boat involves crippling expense, and has been famously compared to standing in a cold shower tearing up thousand dollar bills.

Figure skating is also good Snobvalue, as it too is expensive and difficult, and adapts well to display and exhibition though this is not necessarily A Good Thing among Old Money. It requires a great deal of leisure time, and much self-sacrifice. With horses and sailing yachts you can leave the hard boring stuff (cleaning stables, hauling boats in and out of the water) to hired help. But with figure skating and skiing, you have to give up your social life, go to bed early, etc.

Figure skating is not as dangerous as downhill skiing, but you can hurt yourself quite badly in falls. In the horsey set, you either hunt or play polo, if you want a genuine Snobrating — just hacking around makes you suspect as a Sunday rider. In both areas, you have to master the trade jargon and talk knowledgeably, but you should, ideally, be able actually to ride or sail; talking a good line is not enough. You should, for Snobcredits, have more than one horse, of creditable ancestry, and should enter shows, if you don't hunt or play polo.

Both polo and hunting can produce nasty but top-class injuries, if you fall or are thrown. This can happen to even the best of riders; notice how often the Royals are photographed flying over their mounts' heads. The Queen broke her wrist in a fall in recent memory. Injuries like the Queen's have important social cachet, and can be profitably imitated.

PLEASE: don't confuse hunting with killing groundhogs or crows (varmints)! And no marks for going out after a deer in your pick-up truck. Snobhunting is fox-huntin', on horseback; Snobshooting is shootin' grouse or pheasant — upper-class birds or beasts. It is considered bad form to shoot, accidentally or on purpose, other hunters. Wounds thus acquired have a proletarian taint, as of the trigger-happy klutz who fires at everything that moves, without bothering to see if it's a deer or a horse or his cousin Jim Bob. No snob should admit to a cousin Jim Bob, to start with.

Downhill skiing is still one of the best ways, in several senses, to acquire a creditable Snobinjury, but you must go abroad to do it; not much Snobcop for schussing the Blue Mountains, unless of course you come from England or Alabama. Equipment is pricey, but once acquired, can be used for years. Can, but may not. New ski accoutrements are invented every year, to make your present outfit obsolete; you must invest continually in the latest new gear, however impractical, and (need I say) in new costumes. Even with high-level snobs setting this good example, skiing is becoming marginalized, Snobcredit-wise. There are far too many teenagers blasting out on rented or hand-me-down skis, while wearing jeans. However, it is also dangerous, and difficult to do well unless you start at the age of two, and so continues to rate fairly high. Cross-country skiing is exercise, not sport.

I constantly hear protests that certain sports are fun, or healthy, and therefore should not be dismissed in this contemptuous fashion. Let me remind my forgetful readers: we are not talking about enjoyment, or health, but about one-upmanship and Snobtechnique. Get that straight or you're doomed to Snobfailure.

Painful though it is, snobwise, perhaps we should pause at cross-country skiing, as it offers such an excellent illustration of how Sportsnob works. Cross-country skiing is hands down, no competition, the best exercise for the whole body. Downhill doesn't compare, because you don't use nearly as many muscles as you slide down, and you ride up in a lift. Doing cross-country gets you out in the fresh air, on lovely woodland trails, where you can see birds and small animals, and come home feeling marvellous, with an appetite like a woof (see Wordsnobbery). You don't even have to ski on trails, but can go across the nearest field or a city park. It is not dangerous, if you exercise the smallest common sense; equipment is inexpensive and will last for years. It is easy to learn, even for people of advanced years. It therefore has no Snobvalue at all.

Neither do long healthy walks in the country, and for the same reason. Efforts have been made to make walking difficult and expensive, by pretending that you have to have special shoes, and trying to make you take lessons ("power-walking") but it simply won't work. It doesn't matter how many miles you walk, or how fit it keeps you, it wins no Snobcredits.

One still hears some talk of joggers' ankle, but no conscientious snob would be caught dead with it. No matter how much you squander on shoes, jogging is a low-cost sport, and I don't see any future for it as a socially satisfactory injury source.

There is, to sum up, little Snobvalue today in any illness except sports injuries. No one wants to hear about your operation, and with socialized medicine, it does not attest to wealth or power. More Snobcredits can be accumulated by staying healthy. Sports injuries, to garner any credit, must be gained at approved sports which are expensive, dangerous, require a great deal of leisure, and are unavailable to the lower classes or the Nouveaux.

Inexperienced snobs are warned particularly against curling, where the presence of brooms is clear evidence of humble origins; against all motorized sports like snowmobiling and drag-racing; and against bicycling, which has from the beginning flourished chiefly among the masses and adolescents. You can do these things if you want, of course, but snobwise they are a waste of time and money.

Other than sports injuries, illness snobbery has no future. The most promising disease of the 1980s was anhedonia, the unhappiness disease, for the man or woman who has everything. Anhedonia attacks you when you have devoted your life to the pursuit of the buck, and have won all the badges. Now you contemplate your indoor swimming pool, your Matisse collection, your villa at Antibes, and despair. Nothing is any fun. It should be a high-prestige illness, unrivalled, in fact — almost as good as a leg broken playing polo with Prince Charles and the Sultan of Brunei.

On inspection, one can see that it is none other than our old friend melancholia, which of course never really left us, but has had different labels over the ages. (Depression, burn-out, etc.) Like most fashionable diseases, it's both genuinely miserable and self-inflicted; it's also within your own power to cure it. Try giving all to the poor, learning the lotus position, un-learning the doctrine of the almighty dollar. But don't give popular lectures about how your soul was saved from Mammon. You might make a lot of money at it, but snobwise it is to elicit the curled lip, the pitying smile.

We must not leave this subject without remembering Samuel Butler's *Erewhon*, where ill health was a crime of which people were ashamed. What we call crime was the ultimate misfortune, eliciting compassion and hospital treatment. If you came down with a minor complaint like a sniffy cold, you excused it sheepishly: "I stole a pair of socks this morning."

"Stealing the socks" was the accepted euphemism for a cold.

Perhaps that's where we're heading now. No illness will have Snobvalue, but if you have criminal tendencies, you'll be given pity and understanding and may even be cured! Though it probably won't get you anywhere in the Snobworld.

Snobnote: Professional team sports. I have been rebuked for not discussing such matters as pro hockey, baseball, basketball, whatever. How about them Blue Jays? Well, I forgot them. Usually I get a little hung up on hockey during the play-offs, but only if a Canadian team is involved. How can anyone get excited about a hockey team from Florida or California?

Well, how about them Blue Jays? My objection to them is that they have nothing to do with Canada, or Toronto, or anything I can identify with. I believe they once had a *bona fide* Canadian on the roster, but he's long gone, and now they all come from Alabama or Cuba or Jamaica … I don't understand how one can feel patriotic about them, as one sometimes does with hockey players.

Supposing one developed a passionate loyalty to I think his name was Joe Carter — if he was the one who so entertainingly leaped about the year they won the Series. What happened to Joe? Someone offered him more money, and he abandoned the Blue Jays without a second thought.

That is, the personnel of the team changes completely every few years, and there's nothing left to be loyal to but the name. How can we work up a passionate devotion to a couple of words with no objective correlative? No denotative identity, except for peanut-loving birds.

One year when the group temporarily known as them Blue Jays was in serious danger of winning the pennant or the Series or whatever it is they win other than a lot of money, I was asked to buy a chance on a pool. I declined, on the grounds that blue jays in my lexicon were feathered creatures who could not wield a bat with their wings, and could not run fast or catch baseballs. This destructive attitude distressed the pool organizer. He told me that I could be doing grave damage to the Blue Jays' chances, which he seemed to think depended on some kind of psychic force generated by supporters.

"You gotta keep the faith," he kept saying, urgently.

"I disapprove of faith," I told him severely. "'There lives more truth in honest doubt/Believe me, than in half the creeds.'"

This was a deliberate misquotation, because the original wording (*faith* instead of *truth* — faith and honest doubt are incompatible) makes no sense. However, Blue Jay fans are seldom good Tennysonians, and he didn't know the difference. But it bears out my thesis: Baseball is not a sport, it's a religion.

Snobnote: It is the worst possible form in any sport to pray that God will help you to win. If both sides are the same religion, and both are praying, it obviously puts God in an embarrassing position. Not only that, but it is unsportsmanlike: you're supposed to be winning through your own skill and strength, whereas if God has a favourite and intervenes on its behalf, the best contender obviously won't necessarily win. You can send in the lousiest incompetent amateur, and if God decides to help it, or its team, the hard-working, talented and dedicated players have wasted their practising. Praying to win is a deplorable practice, and must be discontinued immediately and permanently.

25

Wordsnobbery

"But 'glory' doesn't mean a nice knock-down argument," Alice objected.
"When I use a word," Humpty Dumpty said ... "it means just what I choose it to mean.... Impenetrability."
— Lewis Carroll, *Alice in Wonderland*.

There is one evil which ... should never be passed over in silence, but continually publicly attacked, and that is corruption of the language.
— W. H. Auden.

This is perhaps the chapter in which to reintroduce the concept of Goodsnobbery and Badsnobbery, since these distinctions manifest themselves noticeably in speech and writing habits. Good Wordsnobbery is characterized by steadfast willingness to look up words in a dictionary. It respects — nay, demands — sound language structure, though it has little concern for grammatical quibbles like split infinitives and not using prepositions to defiantly end sentences with.

There is absolutely no Snobvalue in mispronouncing or otherwise misusing words, in spite of which many an aspiring snob has made himself ridiculous by using a fancy expression without taking the trouble to look it up. I have inveighed against this practice at great length in that brilliant work, *In Defence of Plain English*, where it was entertainingly, if laboriously, demonstrated that simple language has it all over fancy language like a tent. In spite of this, I have no hope of any change in the habits of the general public, who will no doubt continue to say unique when they mean unusual, simplistic when they mean simple, and apotheosis when they mean ... God knows what they mean. Snobstudents are advised to get out their dictionaries and look it up RIGHT NOW, so that (a) they will never misuse it themselves, and (b) so they can smile pityingly when other people misuse it, as they do chronically these days, in the effort to sound Classy.

We can now make the equation: Badsnobbery = Talking/Writing Classy. Goodsnobbery = Connoisseurship of Language. In thus recognizing Classyism, I had isolated and identified the *besetting linguistic evil of our time*. I felt like stout Cortez (though of course he was really stout Balboa) or like Archimedes watching the water level rise in his tub ...

"Good God!" I cried. "That's why they're talking about cackaphoney and parameters! *They think it sounds Classy!*" I then set about formulating the Three Essential Rules of Classy.

First rule of Talking Classy (Bad Wordsnobbery): Never use a dictionary.

Second: Never use a simple word if you can find a big pretentious one, no matter how inaccurately or inappropriately.

Third: The more syllables, the better the word. If it's a plain old monosyllable, you have to Classy it up by adding a few syllables which sometimes change its meaning to the exact opposite of what you're trying to communicate. A frequently occurring example is *full*. Everyone knows what full means. It's impossible to mispronounce. Almost everyone can spell it. It is therefore too easy to have any appeal to Classy speakers, and they Classy it up by adding a syllable and making it *fulsome*.

I once heard Barbara Frum, no less, hoping that Mr. Mulroney would provide a more fulsome explanation of something, a terrifying thought. And more recently, Lloyd Axworthy used it in the same way, though happily not of Brian.

For Lloyd's benefit, though really he should look it up, fulsome means "cloying, excessive, disgusting by excess (of flattery, servility, exaggerated affection)." So let's settle for full explanations, and wherever possible avoid fulsome ones, even though they give us that Classy extra syllable. If an established Classy word cannot be found, the Classy speaker invents one: *encaution*, *deploymentation*, *remediate*, *analysations*.

Classyism among the general public is one thing. The media are some things else again. (See what you get into when you carry grammatical correctness too far? But it's fun, like "our old friend causeway.") While I don't expect *anyone* to get that last bit, an inexpensive but valuable prize is nonetheless offered for identification of source. Hint: A Huxley is involved.)

Sorry about that. Okay, the media. They are presumably professionals, and a higher standard of language usage should be damn well mandatory before they're permitted to open their traps on radio or TV, or write a word in a newspaper or magazine. Nevertheless, they're at it all the time — pronouncing *buried* to rhyme with *worried*, instead of as it should be, *berried*. Don't blame me for this. I didn't invent the English language. If I had, I'd have made it a lot more logical.

One frequently hears people speaking in authoritative tones about being *dogmatic*, when they meant *dogged*. They invariably say *litany* (Wow! Classy!) when what they mean is, in Goodsnob, *list*. Do you know what a litany is? You should of course look it up, but just this once I'll tell you, to teach you a lesson in the avoidance of Classy. Listen to the *Concise Oxford:*

> Litany: A series of petitions for use in church services or processions recited by clergy and responded to usu. in recurring formula(s) by people ... [ME f., OF *letanie*, eccl. L. Gk. *litaneia*, prayer (*lit*. supplication).

Obviously, that isn't what you mean when you say there was a whole litany of complaints against Paul Martin/Mike Harris/Alan Eagleson: were any church services or processions with petitions recited by clergy among the complaints?

Since I have already written the afore-mentioned brilliant book on this subject, I will not repeat my full indictment of Classy-speak, because *In Defence of Plain English* is still in print (advertisement).

One morning (Jan. 3, 1997) I was listening to Sheila Rogers interviewing the host of a musical show, and all went swimmingly until the interviewee started to strive for Classiness. First she said *reticent* when she meant *reluctant*, an error of which many others are guilty. Look it up!

When I speak critically of the media, I am usually talking about CBC Radio, but this is not as invidious as it might seem at first glance. I never listen to any other radio stations because the commercials drive me cuckoo, so — as Smee said of the crocodile's pursuit of

Captain Hook — in a way it's a sort of compliment.

The reluctant/reticent confusion is in some measure forgiveable, because only Good Wordsnobs care a whole hell of a lot about the difference, though (smiling slightly) they recognize attempted Classiness in the use of an uptown word like reticent. However, Sheila's guest went on to get *really* classy. She said that a certain singer/pianist found herself on a bed of Prometheus, when she was forced to sing to an unsuitable accompaniment. Now that's Classy at its worst.

Prometheus didn't have a bed, Katie. Prometheus was chained to a rock while an eagle ate his liver, which was renewed every night so that the fun could be indefinitely continued. It was punishment for his having stolen fire from heaven to give to man, when Zeus had denied us its use. Luckily, Hercules came along later, killed the eagle, and freed Prometheus.

Katy was thinking of Procrustes, who invited travellers to spend the night, ushering them to a cosy bed. The hitch was that guests had to fit the bed *exactly*. If they were too long, Procrustes cut off the overhanging bits, whereas if they were too short, he stretched them until they fitted it.

You may hope that references to Prometheus will sound Classy, but to a Good Wordsnob listener, well up on Procrustean beds and Promethean livers, you'll just sound silly.

One reliable rule: it is NEVER ADVISABLE to use language that is genteel, or "refained." It is acceptable in the best circles, however you define them, to use profanity: goddamn, Jesus Christ, etc., but not vulgar euphemism (darn, Jiminy Christmas, and especially not "What the hey") although this will be repudiated by right-wing religious fanatics. But no Good Wordsnobs need concern themselves with the views of religious fanatics.

There are some tempting Snobpronunciations which can be used to good effect with the right audience, if you don't mind sounding a trifle archaic. For example, it is much higher class to pronounce the words tedious and hideous as if they had two syllables (teejus, hijjus) than to give them the more familiar, or colonial, three. Pronouncing girl as "gel" may produce an impression in certain circles; very small, old, circles. It is important not to confuse class, as used *supra* and *infra*, with Classy; class means, roughly, what is more commonly known as U. For upper, remember?

If you are really ambitious, you can proceed to even more outrageous affectations, following the example of Father Chantry-Pigg in Rose Macaulay's *The Towers of Trebizond:*

> Being both old-fashioned and very classy, Father Chantry-Pigg called these animals wooves and woof, for he was apt to omit the l before consonants, and would no more have uttered it in wolf than he would in half, calf, golf, salve, alms, Ralph, Malvern, talk, walk, stalk, fault, elm, calm, resolve, absolve, soldier, or pulverize.
> (Macaulay, 29)

Thus one might say, if one had the nerve, and there was ever an occasion, "Do you see those hijjus wooves stalking the sojers under the em trees on the gof links?"

It is reckless to attempt such feats without preparation, and the aspiring Wordsnob is urged to practise them diligently at home, using a looking-glass (NOT a mirror) before undertaking them in public. The prestige of such language derives from its use by the County, with associated implications of ancestral acres, old money, aristocratic provenance, etc. Some difficulty may arise from the scarcity of wooves and em trees, even of sojers in some parts of the world today, making it frightfully difficult to work them into the conversation. I've had some purely private sport by asking librarians to find me a copy of *Never Cry Woof!* or trying to persuade theatre-goers to see Eugene O'Neill's *Desire Under The Ems*. This is the sport of the fanatic Wordsnob, who doesn't flinch from the labour of manufacturing opportunities to indulge in its obsession.

It was entertaining for the Snobstudent to watch David Frost interviewing Pat Robertson, a Republican of the religious right persuasion, who painstakingly corrected Frost's pronunciation in the approved English style, such as controversy with the accent on the second syllable. Pat required the good Amurrican version (controvurrsy) until Frost was obliged to put a stop to it, suggesting they accept the fact that "you say tomayto, I say tomahto."

Just in passing, I don't accept that tomahto pronunciation. The word has exactly the same structure as potato, but nobody says potahto. The use of the genteel or refained tomahto, instead of the obviously correct tomayto, is a triumph of false Wordsnobbery, to be deplored and condemned.

Aspiring Wordsnobs often study such works as *Noblesse Oblige*, edited and in part written by Nancy Mitford, way back in 1956, frequently mentioned in this study. There were people who seriously tried to follow Nancy's Snobadvice, agonizing over when to use ill and when sick; trying to remember to say lavatory (or loo) paper for toilet paper, and looking-glass for mirror. Then they died of embarrassment when they forgot and said home (genteel) instead of house (U).

Wasted effort. Then as now, most aristocratic British juniors deplore alleged U-usage, and want to sound American, or even Amurrican. Such Wordsnobbery is not for the uninitiate.

Humpty-Dumpty's system is rapidly taking over the language. If one protests against word misuse, there is an immediate and almost invariable response: the protester is a pedantic reactionary, who wants to obstruct the natural change which is essential to the vitality of language.

"Language MUST change, constantly!" cry these liberal thinkers.

And so it must, indeed. One can only ask plaintively why it must always change for the worse? If each of us is free to assign idiosyncratic meanings to words, how can we communicate?

Reverse Classy: The Four Letters (bad words). Andy Rooney, who is said to be an American icon, has condemned the public use of obscenities, particularly what he quaintly calls "the F word." Nothing shocks him, Andy says, but he finds F and the other rude four-letters offensive. He has an ingenious theory that the frequency of their use in films occurs because we watch films in the dark, where our blushes cannot be seen, bless his heart. He believes they don't occur in print media.

Andy can't have read many books lately. The four-letters have taken over literature. In recent fiction, the most frequently used words (barring simple connectives, etc.) are shit, fuck, ass, and asshole. They are used without discrimination, meaninglessly, and incessantly. It gets a bit teejus. "I have to get my ass up to the studio," says a TV broadcaster in a current mystery. In fact, she has to get *all* of herself up to the studio. Why insert that unnecessary ass? "Move your ass," says another, meaning in fact move your body.

Unlike Andy Rooney, in some ways I shock easily, though not at Bad Words. Cruelty shocks me, greed, irresponsibility, hypocrisy … but I can't remember being shocked by a word, though I become melancholy at their abuse and misuse. Yet every time I open my mouth to protest about such abuse and misuse of the four-letters, someone immediately decides that my problem is prudery. In an article in *Books in Canada* I mildly protested against indiscriminate over-use of the Bad Words, and a *Toronto Star* columnist immediately reported gleefully that I was "shocked and appalled." Later a furious feminist ranted against my "purse-mouthed disapproval" of the Big Four Four-letters. She accused me of a lot of other things, too, solemnly warning the world that I was advocating censorship, but in a sneaky crafty non-explicit way instead of coming right out with it.

Give me strength. I believe those wicked words have a legitimate function in language and — appropriately used — should not raise an eyebrow. They will not send people ravening into the streets to rape and murder, or even to defecate in public.

It is the obsessive, silly, inapropos and wearisome OVERUSE of them of which one must plaintively complain, indeed must continually publicly attack, as W. H. Auden recommends. Until comparatively recent times, The Words were *literally* unprintable (George Orwell said it, not me) except in porn. Unlike children, they were heard and not seen. Everyone knew them, although nice girls were expected to faint away with shock if they were uttered in public. They were a male monopoly. However, we've got over all that.

In the literary establishment, unfortunately, there is a lingering belief that (a) those words are shocking and writers "courageous" for using them, and (b) that they constitute Great Literature — the more often they're used, the greater the literature. This is a hangover from the days when writers like Joyce and Lawrence had to fight for the right to use whatever vocabulary was essential for their purposes, and were willing to risk book-banning for that right. Because Joyce and Lawrence were officially Great Writers, and because they were pioneers in print-use of four-letters, some writers and critics immediately made the equation: Dirty Words = Great Literature. As things stand now, you can set up as a Great Writer if you just work in enough four-letters.

In a language as rich as English, it seems perverse to confine one's self to a vocabulary of about ten words, even though they signal Literary Distinction. James Kelman, Booker Prize winner for 1994, gained his crown for a book in which critics counted 4000 of Those Words in 374 pages. In some circles, The Words are considered intrinsically and exquisitely witty; Kelman's book was "riotous." This criterion is passionately subscribed to by stand-up comedians, many of whom know hardly any other words.

"He thinks he's being funny," a teenage female complained of one such, "but he's just being gross."

Sometimes, used perceptively, the Words can be funny. In Barbara Paul's *But He Was Already Dead When I Got There*, a young woman who wants to be dashing and daring keeps repeating "fucking," until her husband corrects her: if she's going to use the word, she must say "fuckin'." The terminal *g* is unidiomatic. She says he's a pedant. "You might as well get it right," he replies patiently.

And even I, who am boycotting the words (except for clinical purposes, like the present), know a very funny joke that necessitates the use of the word, but I only tell it to other old ladies, as it shocks the young on the lips of their elders.

Fuck was once, apart from its nearly forgotten meaning of sexual congress, the ultimate expletive, the desperate cry of a soul too sorely tried. When nothing remained to express absolute disillusionment and despair, it was the final howl of protest against unjust gods. I have on sound authority an anecdote from World War II: an Air Force crew were bailing out of a disabled plane. One crew member, still audible on the intercom, discovered too late that he wasn't wearing his parachute. His last words were, "Well, fuck me."

Before the words lost all value through over-exposure, when someone yelled "Oh, *fuck!*" you knew better than to cross him, or further annoy him. But now it's used more casually than darn or heck, and has just about as much impact. How now to communicate a cry from the last ditch of despair? There simply isn't a word with enough power.

The sexual-scatological monosyllables are considered essential to realistic dialogue, a literary Wordsnobbery for which the useful term "artsy-dirty" was coined by Mimi Kramer, theatre reviewer for *The New Yorker,* who described a play in which the characters "... waxed pseudo-lyrical about sex and pseudo-crude about their bodily functions, spitting and scratching their crotches a lot, in the service of establishing the play's status as Serious Theatre." (May 15, 1991)

A few years ago I sat through a poetry reading which involved much shouting of fuck! shit! asshole! and so on. The poet proclaimed his Elizabethan lust for life, his Rabelaisian enjoyment of vigorous language. Fuck, he said, is a robust Anglo-Saxon word, which we should use with pride. Alas, it is no such thing. It didn't appear in English until the 16th century; neither Chaucer nor Shakespeare used it, and probably never heard of it. Jesse Sheidlower (*The F-word*) traces it to Middle Dutch *fokken,* to thrust, and by extension to copulate. Sheidlower attributes its wide dissemination and subsequent loss of force through over-use by the military, a male enclave where all conversation is conducted in four-letters. If you asked any soldier how many days there were in a year, he would reply "three hundred and sixty-fucking-five."

Even characters in novels are beginning to rebel. Of an assistant whose entire vocabulary consists of sexual and scatological terms, a detective wearily inquires, "Geeze, can't you ever get your head out of your crotch?"

Damon Runyon wrote about underworld characters, and the authenticity of his tough guys is manifest. And yet none of them felt the need for even the mildest profanity, let alone the infamous four-letters. The only Runyon character who used a Bad Word was not a tough guy but the newspaper scribe, Ambrose Hammer, who said on one occasion that he didn't give a D and an A and an M and an N about what happened to a certain tomato.

Remember! When you sprinkle your conversation with the F- and S- words, you risk offending Andy Rooney. Perhaps, under his disapproving eye, the four-letters can be given a well-earned rest, used only when they perform a useful function. They deserve a holiday.

Snobs, and even non-snobs if any exist, should avoid the F-word, the S-word, the P-word, and the A-words, unless they are necessary and relevant.

After which one can only add, IMPENETRABILITY.

Well, no. A word more. Not long ago a new book came out, saying much what I've said above about the four-letters. It was written and published in Britain. I heard it referred to half a dozen times on CBC Radio, everyone endorsing the author's comments, and agreeing it was *about time somebody had the courage to say it*.

This cheered me in one respect, but made me deeply sad in another. I, a humble Canadian author, had said the same thing way back in 1992, and no one applauded or even mentioned it. I couldn't get a word on those CBC shows that praised the Brit author so highly. When *he* said it, it was profound and courageous. When I said it, nobody paid any attention. Because I'm a mere Canadian, of no importance? I said it again in an article in *Books in Canada* and got called a prude and "purse-mouthed."

Classy Wordsnobs are impressed by phoniness and pretentiousness. They illustrate Thackeray's definition of "those who meanly admire mean things." Good Wordsnobs care about their language, and want to keep it precise and clear and simple. They don't use it for showing off, but for communication. Good Wordsnobbery is one of the truly GOOD forms of snobbery. Join the club! Embrace your dictionary!

Conclusion

Post-modern Snobbery must necessarily be quite different from earlier manifestations. The happy 19th-century days of unabashed ostentation are long over. There was a brief Indian Summer during the 1930s, and then the rot set in. After World War II, veterans were allowed — nay! encouraged — to attend university at taxpayers' expense. The universities, jammed with people who could never otherwise afford higher education, ceased to be the private enclaves of the privileged. Many of these newcomers betrayed dangerous pinko-Commie ideas about equality. The whole class system was in jeopardy.

Every day seemed to bring more levelling tendencies, so that it became increasingly difficult to distinguish Uppers from Lowers. Proles and peasants ceased to pull their forelocks or make a leg to the squire. Most of the problems arose from the iniquitous system of taxation that punished people for having worked hard and saved their pennies until they were millionaires. Furious complaints by high income people about the iniquitous rates of taxation which used their money to subsidize layabouts and bums moved Prime Minister John Diefenbaker to appoint a royal commission to reform the tax system. It was called the Carter Commission for its top man, Kenneth Carter.

Linda McQuaig describes, in *Behind Closed Doors*, the fury of the business community over unfair taxation (cf. my dear Old bosses, *supra*) to fund an outrageous welfare system which led to large scale idleness among the lower orders, who did nothing but lie about, drinking beer and watching TV at their betters' expense.

Kenneth Carter seemed a good choice for tax-reformer: a sound establishment man, the right schools, etc. But he soon revealed his treacherous nature. Rather than being overtaxed, he claimed, the rich were grossly *undertaxed*, while low income people carried far more than their share. If average taxpayers ever woke up to what was being done to them, there'd be a revolution! Hitherto dividend income had been taxed far below the level of earned income (earned as in salary and wages, not by clipping coupons); Carter recommended that it be taxed at the same rate as earned income! He wanted to ditch the tax-free status of capital gains. Luckily, alert observers like Harry Jackman warned that such measures would force bright young men to leave the country. The Carter proposals were a dangerous trend toward socialism. "It was that way with Hitler," he reminded us.

In her introduction, Ms. McQuaig comments on the Jackman theory — that high taxes destroy the will to work in high-income executives and professionals, who would be rendered "aimless and despondent" by such disincentives. McQuaig queries why this shouldn't make them work all the harder? She questions why executives are stimulated to work harder if they have large incomes, whereas unemployment insurance benefits completely destroy the Proles' will to work.

Eventually, the good old Wealthsnob forces rose in their wrath and put a stop to the nonsense. When the Carter Report appeared, it was reduced to a pale ghost of itself in a white paper. Even the pallid ghost elicited such outrage that the government was completely intimidated. When Harvard Law School wanted to use the Carter Report in a graduate seminar, they had trouble finding one copy. The Pearson administration found it too expensive to publish. "I've got better things to do with $50,000," the PM told Robert Bryce, the deputy minister of finance.

When the Mulroney government of blessed memory was elected, Michael Wilson reformed the tax system in his own inimitable way. The ten levels of progressively higher taxation were cut down to three by staunchsnob old Michael. According to my income tax man (remember him?) the ten-level had itself been a regressive tax, favouring the very rich. With only three levels, families in the $60,000 – $70,000 range were taxed on the same level as multi-millionaires.

Linda M. claims that those once-higher tax rates on higher

incomes had existed largely on paper; few even of the richest really paid top rates, which remained "largely mythical" because of the many convenient loopholes. If Carter had got his way, everyone would have had to pay the legal rates set down by Parliament. No wonder there was an outcry from suffering Wealthsnobs! To appease them, the revered Lester B. Pearson had estate taxes removed in the early 1970s. But even today they remain unappeased, convinced that taxes (like ignorance, dishonesty, laziness, criminality, malnutrition, disease, and general inferiority) should be confined to the lower orders.

The Globe and Mail reported that in 1982, 239 Canadians earning over $250,000 paid no income tax at all. Don Blenkarn (then in opposition) denounced as "unconscionable" the fact that two Bronfman companies paid no income tax in 1986. Michael Wilson also inveighed against corporate tax evaders, who shifted the burden to the shoulders of the poor. They both saw the light once the Tories were in office.

The redeemed Michael nipped all this dangerous left-wing stuff in the bud, and through his reforms, the lower orders ("the poor") actually began paying a higher percentage of income in tax than the rich! Corporations can defer taxes, apparently indefinitely. "Banks escaped unscathed from Wilson's tax reform moves."

The reformed tax system took $300 annually from people below the poverty line, and donated an extra $706 to the upper incomers, a change of which Ms. McQuaig disapproves. As Barbara Amiel said in another context, could envy have reached such pathological proportions?

Mrs. Thatcher led the world in these enlightened Snobpolicies, and her philosophy was adopted in the U.S., as Reaganomics. Under the guidance of Ole Ron, top level taxes were reduced from 72 to 28 percent, though no one had ever really paid the 72 percent; they hired loophole-specializing lawyers, who saved them from penury.

Thus it can be seen that progress has been made to correct the excesses which so recently threatened to destroy our finest, or at least richest, traditions. (A Canadian capitalist is said to commute by chauffeured Jaguar from his Niagara home to his Buffalo office.) There is still a long way to go in controlling the media and book publishing, which allows such scandalous misrepresentations as the McQuaig books to find publishers, and in re-organizing the education system from top to bottom, though long steps have been taken in this direction in Ontario and Alberta. We're returning to the golden days when only the rich could afford post-secondary education! The taxpayer still stumps up for the major percentage of the cost, but tuition fees are now high enough to bar undesirables.

The Conservative and Reform parties are still urging tax cuts, which will allow investment to increase, so that the economy will become stronger and thus create jobs. But are jobs really good for the economy? In September 1996, the U.S. unemployment rate dropped to a seven-year low of 5.1 percent, which sounds like A Good Thing. But it isn't! The stock markets were alarmed. The markets, said an Associated Press story, had been watching anxiously for "signs of an overly strong economy." Huh? Isn't a strong economy what everyone wants? Nope. It could cause the U.S. central bank to boost interest rates! Inflationary pressures would be bound to develop! If we don't have lots of Unemployed, labour will demand higher wages. Fatal!

An earlier instance of stock market response to danger occurred following Bill Clinton's first official speech as president, Term One. He announced tax increases on corporations and the very rich. Next morning, the Dow Jones index fell by 83 points — a declaration of resistance by big-money interests. How they mourned for the golden days of Reaganomics!

Somehow we have to let our politicians know that Jobsjobsjobs is not a good policy after all, although both Mulroney and Chrétien promised them. If high employment increases interest rates and inflation, investment will drop, the economy will weaken and there won't be any jobs. That is, high employment will increase unemployment. Makes sense?

If only we could return to the climate of the Great Depression of the thirties, when there were no jobs! The jobless would work for next to nothing, rather than see their kids starve. There was no welfare to force taxes up. No unemployment insurance. No health insurance. No pensions. The elderly poor went to the Poor House. Except for a few reckless speculators who jumped out of high windows, the Great Depression was quite profitable for people with comfortable incomes. That utopian state was ruined by the war, which killed off a lot of labour-potential, and wages went sky-high as munitions factories had to be staffed.

We may yet see a return to the happy times of the thirties. Much has been achieved by government measures that allow the rich to get richer while the poor get steadily poorer. One of these is the consumer tax (GST) which hits hard at single parents and the unemployed, and isn't even noticed by the Upper Incomers.

One evolutionary possibility is a *defined* lower class, like the Deltas and Epsilons of *Brave New World*. We'll soon be able to clone them by the scores to become the domestic servants which the Uppers have been missing so gravely. Who knows, we may once again be able to have footmen and parlour maids! Such refractory institutions as unions will cease to exist. To achieve this, we must quickly make changes in the education system: Alberta and Ontario are showing the way by setting tuition fees out of the reach of low earners.

We must model our industrial ethics on the tactics of the Irvings of New Brunswick, as described by Diane Francis in *Controlling Interest:*

> … In 1951, Irving decided to expand an old pulp mill he had bought in 1947. Using his $20 million expansion plans as bait, he extracted a concession from politicians to freeze his taxes for 30 years; he obtained exemption from expropriation, freedom to spill wastes into the St. John River, and immunity from "nuisance cases" in the courts for pollution or other problems. As recently as 1976, Irving was acquitted of polluting the St. John River, even though tests revealed that rainbow trout died in three minutes in the Irving pulp and paper mill's sewers. Atlantic salmon died within 30 minutes.
> (Francis, 22)

That's the recipe. Government and business must work together for tax breaks and immunity from environmental responsibility. The Irvings are an example to all serious snobs.

ON THE OTHER HAND … Lovely though it is to have rich Irvings, some of us would rather have fish. The cod are gone, the salmon and lobsters are going. We would rather have our forests preserved than see lumber companies increase their bank balance. In fact, the Very Rich are destroying the ecology of the planet, and don't care in the least as long as they're making their dishonest bucks.

For a change, perhaps we should stop boot-licking the rich and start demanding ecological responsibility. Environment-abusers and tax-evaders are Badsnobs, even Evil Snobs, who are despoiling our poor planet and lowering the living standards of all its inhabitants except for the thin layer at the top, whose living standards are revoltingly vulgar and ostentatious. As W. H. Auden said of the corruption of language, ecological irresponsibility is an evil which should be continually publicly attacked.

And now, as promised so long ago — HEEEEEERE'S THE SNOB DEFINITION!

It is very difficult to improve on Thackeray's summation: "He who meanly admires mean things is a snob." Difficult but not impossible. It refers only to Badsnobs, with whom this book has been chiefly concerned, but you will recall our suggestion of another category: the Goodsnob. How does one recognize this interesting mutation?

The Goodsnob does not meanly admire mean things. It is unimpressed by vulgar ostentation, such as fur coats, expensive jewellery, fancy parties, expensive cars, power boats — all forms of conspicuous waste. It never tries to sound authoritative in the Classy pattern without doing its homework. It is always willing to learn, and actually takes pleasure in new knowledge. It has no illusions about being infallible, and declines to believe in the infallibility of anyone else. It respects scientific doubt but not religious faith, which it equates with superstition.

It is nevertheless fastidious in such matters as food (won't eat threatened species) and refuses to slavishly follow fads of any kind. It may be a connoisseur in certain fields, but not for the sake of showing off. It is normally peaceful but can be roused to fury by cruelty (especially to animals and small children) and by all forms of racism and speciesism. It is not envious of material possessions, but is profoundly impressed by people of high abilities in such fields as music, organic gardening, non-ostentatious sports and so on. It despises the factitious and pretentious. It doesn't go around blasting loud music in the ears of unwilling listeners.

If it sounds like a self-righteous pain in the neck, it isn't. It doesn't believe in preaching, for reasons that a glance at any TV evangelist should make obvious. It is not interested in such matters as reincarnation or an after-life, since there is too much work needed right here and now on protecting the environment, and getting rid of the population crisis, poverty, injustice, cruelty, greed, and irresponsibility. Many Goodsnobs are scientists, and members of environmental groups. I met a whole bunch recently in the Canadian Organic Growers. Many are health and exercise freaks, without being Sportsnobs. Some famous ones, remembered at random: David Suzuki, Noam Chomsky, J. K. Galbraith (one of the few Goodsnob economists), Maude Barlow, Linda McQuaig, Alexa McDonough ... see what I mean?

Goodsnob Fritjof Capra wrote the only description of "spirituality" that has ever struck me as having any value:

> Deep ecology [as distinguished from superficial environmentalism] is rooted in a perception of reality

that goes beyond the scientific framework to an intuitive awareness of the oneness of all life, the interdependence of its multiple manifestations, and its cycles of change and transformation. When the concept of the human spirit is understood in this sense, as the mode of consciousness in which the individual is connected to the cosmos as a whole, it becomes clear that ecological awareness is truly spiritual.
(Capra, 412)

Bibliography

Amiel, Barbara. "In Defence of the Freedom to Spend," *Maclean's*, 23 October 1989.
"Stop the Petty Sniping at Philanthropists," *Maclean's*, 22 January, 1996.
"The 'Rich Bitch' Answers …," *The Sunday Sun*, 14 November, 1993.

Ashton, Daisy. *The Young Visiters*. New York: Random House, 1986.

Austen, Jane. *Emma*. Boston: Houghton Mifflin, 1957.
Pride and Prejudice. New York: Washington Square Press, 1964.
Sense and Sensibility. New York: Signet, 1961.

Barrie, J. M. *Peter Pan: The Story of Peter and Wendy*. New York: Grosset & Dunlap, 1911.

Barry, Dave: *Complete Guide to Guys*. New York: Random House, 1995.

Beecroft, John (ed.) "My Rival," in *Kipling — A Selection of His Stories and Poems*. New York: Doubleday, 1956.

Blackmore, Susan. *Dying to Live: Near-Death Experiences*. Amherst, NY: Prometheus, 1993

Burridge, Christina (ed.) *Autobiographies*. Vancouver: William Hoffer/Tanks, 1987.

Butts, R. Freeman. *A Cultural History of Western Education*. Toronto: McGraw-Hill, 1955.

Cannadine, David. *The Decline and Fall of the British Aristocracy*. New Haven: Yale University Press, 1990.

Capra, Fritjof. *The Turning Point*. Toronto: Bantam Books, 1988.

Coleridge, S.T. "Kubla Khan," in *Selected Poetry and Prose of Coleridge*. New York: Random House, 1951.

Crisp, Quentin. *The Naked Civil Servant*. London: Fontana Books, 1978.

Fenster, Bob. *The Last Page*. Menlo Park: Perseverance Press, 1989.

Forster, E. M. A *Passage to India*. London: Penguin, 1950.
A *Room with a View*. London: Penguin, 1958.

Francis, Diane. *Controlling Interest*. Toronto: Macmillan, 1986.

Fussell, Paul. *Class*. New York: Ballantine Books, 1983.

Gibbons, Stella. *Cold Comfort Farm*. London: Penguin, 1948.

Hastings, Selina. *Nancy Mitford*. London: Hamilton, 1985.

Hughes, Pennethorne. *Witchcraft*. London: Penguin, 1973.

Hunter, Alfred A. *Class Tells*. Toronto: Butterworth. 1986.

Huxley, Aldous. *Those Barren Leaves*. London: Penguin, 1955.

Macaulay, Rose. *The Towers of Trebizond*. London: Futura, 1983.

McQuaig, Linda. *Behind Closed Doors*. Toronto: Penguin, 1990.

Mitford, Nancy (ed.) *Noblesse Oblige*. London: Penguin, 1959.
Love in a Cold Climate. London: Penguin, 1954.

Nabokov, Vladimir. *Pnin*. New York: Atheneum, 1965.
Lolita. New York: Crest, 1961.

Rieu, E. V. (ed. and tr.) *Homer: The Iliad*. London: Penguin, 1951.
Homer: The Odyssey. London, Penguin. 1952.

Shaw, G. B. *Man and Superman*. New York: Bantam Books, 1959.

Smart, Elizabeth. *By Grand Central Station I Sat Down and Wept*. Ottawa: Deneau, 1981.
In the Meantime. Ottawa: Deneau, 1986.
The Assumption of the Rogues and Rascals. London: Cape, 1978.

Spark, Muriel. *The Takeover*. London: Penguin, 1978.

Sullivan, Rosemary. *By Heart*. Toronto: Penguin, 1991.

Thackeray, William Makepeace. *The Book of Snobs*. New York: Worthington Co., (n.d.).
Vanity Fair. New York: Worthington Co., 1848.

Veblen, Thorstein. *Theory of the Leisure Class*. New York: Modern Library, 1948.

Weldon, Fay. *Letters to Alice*. London: Coronet, 1985.

Victoria Branden herewith presents her sixth book. Earlier lunacies: *Mrs. Job* and *Flitterin' Judas*, novels; *In Defence of Plain English*, non-fiction; and two books (*Understanding Ghosts* and *Give Up the Ghost*) enunciating a non-occultist theory of the paranormal. Her articles and short stories have appeared in *The Atlantic Monthly*, *Chatelaine*, *Saturday Night*, *Canadian Forum*, *New Horizons*, *Homemaker's*, and many others. For years she wrote short stories and plays for the CBC which have won a variety of awards and honours. Ms. Branden attended the Universities of Alberta and Toronto and has studied a wide range of organizations investigating the paranormal. She has worked in publishing, journalism, academia, lifeguarding, and strawberry-picking. She lives in Waterdown, Ontario, with her dog and several drop-in cats.

ACKNOWLEDGMENTS

Snobs has leaned very heavily on illustrious predecessors William Makepeace Thackeray and Thorstein Veblen, to whom we will never be able adequately to express our gratitude. We have also borrowed outrageously from the ideas of our brilliant younger contemporary, Linda McQuaig, to whose penetrating intellect all of Canada is indebted. We can only hope that our use of their work will send some readers to study the originals.

We must also thankfully acknowledge permission to publish as follows:

From *Dying to Live: Near-Death Experiences*, by Susan Blackmore (Amherst, NY: Prometheus Books) Copyright 1993. Reprinted by permission of the publisher.

Dave Barry's Complete Guide to Guys, by Dave Barry. (New York: Crown Publishing) Copyright, 1995.

A Concise History of Costume, by James Laver. (London: Thames and Hudson International Ltd.) Copyright, 1969.

Class, by Paul Fussell. (New York: Ballantyne Books.) Copyright 1983. By permission of the author.

The Last Page, by Bob Fenster. (Menlo Park, Cal., Perseverance Press) Copyright 1989.

Cold Comfort Farm, copyright Stella Gibbons 1932, by permission of Curtis Brown, London.

TheTurning Point, by Fritjof Capra. New York: Simon & Schuster. Copyright, 1982.

The Tunnel of Love, by Peter de Vries. New York: Little Brown & Co., 1952